'At last, an accessible evidence-based book that cuts through the media panic about young people and technology. Cat Page Jeffery writes with wit, insight and empathy to produce a book that every parent should read and every child wishes they would.'

Catharine Lumby, Professor of Media and Communications, University of Sydney

PARENTING IN A DIGITAL WORLD

This book focuses on the challenges of parenting in the digital age, providing a counter-narrative to, and critique of, risk and cyber safety narratives, as well as some suggestions for a way forward.

Drawing on qualitative research with Australian families, this book explores the knowledges, practices, anxieties and lived experiences of families themselves. It demonstrates that the realities of family life in the digital age are more complex than the headlines and cyber safety advice would have us believe, as parents grapple with balancing their own anxieties and social expectations about what it means to be a 'good' parent, with the practices, desires, and rights of their child. It addresses key questions including: How much attention should we pay to media headlines about the dangers of contemporary media? What is actually worrying Australian parents and how do they address these concerns? Why do young people love media so much? How capable are young people of actually managing online risk? What is the right way to parent in the digital age to ensure young people's safety and wellbeing while minimising family conflict?

Aimed at media studies scholars and students, as well as parents and policy makers seeking a more comprehensive understanding of the broader academic research surrounding young people, media and parenting, this book argues that parent and child knowledges, practices and experiences must be better accounted for within the online safety ecosystem as well as in policy development, and that families need encouragement and guidance to help them adopt more democratic approaches to parenting in the digital age.

Catherine Page Jeffery is a Lecturer in Media and Communications at the University of Sydney, Australia. She is currently on the board of Children and Media Australia and previously worked in internet content regulation and online safety for the Australian Government.

PARENTING IN A DIGITAL WORLD

Beyond Media Panics Towards a New Theory of Parental Mediation

Catherine Page Jeffery

Routledge
Taylor & Francis Group

LONDON AND NEW YORK

Designed cover image: @Getty

First published 2025
by Routledge
4 Park Square, Milton Park, Abingdon, Oxon OX14 4RN

and by Routledge
605 Third Avenue, New York, NY 10158

Routledge is an imprint of the Taylor & Francis Group, an informa business

British Library Cataloguing-in-Publication Data
A catalogue record for this book is available from the British Library

ISBN: 978-1-032-38774-1 (hbk)
ISBN: 978-1-032-38773-4 (pbk)
ISBN: 978-1-003-34670-8 (ebk)

DOI: 10.4324/9781003346708

Typeset in Galliard
by SPi Technologies India Pvt Ltd (Straive)

For Eve and Harriet

CONTENTS

TABLES

ACKNOWLEDGEMENTS

There are many people who contributed to this book.

First I'd like to thank my colleagues at the University of Canberra, but particularly Glen Fuller for his feedback, support and encouragement over many years. I'd also like to thank Kerry McCallum for her mentorship during the Safe Online Together project, as well as Deborah Lupton and Caroline Fisher for their feedback on early drafts.

There were many people who made the family workshops that form such an important part of this book a success. I'd like to thank our community services partners Community Services #1 and Capital Region Community Services who provided essential input into the project – especially Romney Kelly who was a pleasure to work throughout the entirety of the project, and Amalia Fawcett for her initial input. I'd also like to thank Caitlin Graham and all the other students who contributed to the workshops. Very special thanks go to Sue Atkinson who expertly co-facilitated the family workshops, and whose skills and knowledge were invaluable.

I'd also like to thank my current University of Sydney colleagues, including all those in MECO for providing such a stimulating and supportive work environment. I'd like to especially thank Justine Humphry and Jo Gray for providing feedback on parts of the manuscript; Jonathon Hutchinson for his ongoing support as Discipline Chair, and Catharine Lumby for her continued mentorship.

I also wish to thank all the parents and young people who contributed to this research. The candid accounts and experiences so generously shared by parents—some of which were deeply personal—provided the foundations for a rich and nuanced exploration of an issue routinely framed one dimensionally in public and media discussion. The involvement of young people in the family workshops provided some welcome counter-narratives to parental accounts, adding greater depth and insight. I hope that this work provides some comfort to parents that they are not alone in addressing the challenges of parenting in the digital age. I hope it lets young people know that their views and opinions matter.

To my family, huge thanks go to my dad, Phil Page for proof-reading and stepping up to provide last-minute suggestions and edits and to Helen Page for her assistance finalising the manuscript. To the rest of my family, my mum Anna, and brother Andy thanks for your ongoing interest, love, and support.

To my husband, David Jeffery, you are hands down the best partner ever. Thank you for your calm and level-headed approach to parenting and life in general. Finally, to my two daughters, Eve and Harriet, you have both grown considerably during the years I have been undertaking this research. When I started, your screen time consisted of Peppa Pig and Play School. Now you have your own devices and social media and I am living out many of the parenting struggles documented throughout the pages that follow. But I hope and trust that what I have learned in the process of writing this book will make me a better, and less anxious, parent now and into the future.

This research was undertaken with the assistance of the Australian Government through a Research Training Program Scholarship, as well as through the Online Safety Grants Program.

INTRODUCTION

Managing adolescent use of digital technologies has become one of the most difficult aspects of contemporary parenting (Lim, 2019; Livingstone & Blum-Ross, 2020). Digital media technologies such as the internet, mobile phones, tablets, computers, and gaming consoles have become part of the critical infrastructure of contemporary Australian life. Australian families are highly connected, with 99 per cent of Australian homes with a child aged 2–17 connected to the internet (eSafety Commissioner, 2021). Valued by parents and children alike, we have come to rely on networked technologies for an increasing range of daily activities, including connection, entertainment, work, and schooling. At no other time did this become more apparent than during lengthy COVID-19 lockdowns throughout the country during 2020 and 2021, where Australians came to depend on networked technologies to maintain some continuity with their pre-pandemic lives. In many ways we have reached a state of near constant connection – we have become 'digital by default' – which on a micro level has reshaped family dynamics, reconfigured parent/child power relations, and for some parents, increased the parenting burden; and at the macro level led to media panics, knee-jerk political responses, increased pressure on platforms to act more responsibly, and expectations that governments hold big tech to account.

Concerns about digital media use and constant connectivity have, for the most part, focused on youth, and amplified perennial concerns about access to inappropriate content, 'dumbing down', stranger danger, social media and mental health, cyberbullying and displacement of more 'worthwhile' activities. Contemporary media discourses frequently invoke a nostalgic rhetoric about what childhood was like before mobile phones, Instagram, TikTok and online gaming, lamenting a loss of childhood innocence as children stare into screens. Yet despite contemporary media panics presenting the problem as urgent, and the likes of which we have not previously seen, these concerns are hardly new. As numerous scholars have pointed out (Rooney, 2011; Drotner, 1992; Leick, 2018), many of these concerns have been raised time and again over the generations, with each generation raising the alarm about movies, radio, comics, television and video games. Kirsten Drotner (1999) refers to this tendency to forget earlier concerns about media once a new form of media captures our attention as 'historical amnesia'.

DOI: 10.4324/9781003346708-1

A paradigm of risk and harm has long framed media discourse, education and policies related to young people's use of digital media technologies (S. Livingstone & Third, 2017; Mavoa et al., 2017; Third et al., 2019). Recurrent media panics about online risks have dominated Australian media and policy debate since the late 1990s (Lumby, 1997; Potter & Potter, 2001). While the paradigm of risk and harm is not unique to Australia, we have for many years adopted a paternalistic and protectionist approach that is oriented towards harm reduction, with Australia being the first country to introduce comprehensive online safety legislation which established the world-first Office of the eSafety Commissioner. Within this regulatory and discursive context, young people have become 'sites of cultural anxiety requiring containment and control' (Third et al., 2019, p. 2), and parents have borne the brunt of most of this anxiety and carried the burden for protecting their children from the purported litany of online harms that threaten their wellbeing.

Concerns about young people's media use are, if sometimes exaggerated, not unfounded, particularly in an era of networked media. There is no denying that the affordances of contemporary media give rise to a number of risks, some of which pose significant threats to the wellbeing of not only children and young people, but also adults. Government, schools and parents all play an important role in helping young people safely navigate online spaces. But, as I argue throughout this book, the dominant discourses of risk and harm are at odds with the reality of most adolescents' digital experiences. For young people, digital media have become an integral part of their lives as adolescents use them in a myriad of ways to advance their own interests, goals, needs and desires. The lived experiences of young people thus exist in tension with the dominant conceptualisation of the child at risk and in need of protection.

There are very real consequences for both parents and children when concerns about risk, harm and online danger dominate the public discourse the way that it does in Australia (and elsewhere). Adolescents and their parents have been known to reproduce mainstream narratives about digital technologies, focusing on adult-centric safety concerns. This limits adolescents' and their parents' ability to conceptualise and realise the benefits afforded by digital media (Third et al., 2019). Relatedly, for adolescents a protectionist approach curtails their rights to autonomy and engagement in the digital world (Simpson, 2020). This compromises their ability to develop resilience and skills for effectively managing online risks (Livingstone et al., 2015; Third et al., 2019). For parents, the failure to live up to discursively constructed parenting expectations undermines their confidence, leading to feelings of anxiety, powerlessness and a culture of parental blame when harm reduction strategies are challenged or fail (Livingstone & Blum-Ross, 2020; Page Jeffery, 2020, 2022). For families as a whole, the focus on risk and harm at the expense of more mundane quotidian challenges faced by families navigating digital media, limits the utility of much of the online safety resources and advice, which often fail to resonate with their intended audience.

This book focuses on the challenges of parenting in the digital age, providing a counter-narrative to, and critique of, risk and cyber safety narratives, as well as some suggestions for a way forward. A central argument is that parent and child knowledges, practices and experiences must be better accounted for within the online safety ecosystem as well as in policy development, and that families need encouragement and guidance to help them adopt more democratic approaches to digital parenting with their adolescents. The problem is not a lack of information or resources for families: a plethora of cyber safety resources and programs has been developed with the aim of helping parents mediate their children's media use to minimise risk. However, most of these resources adopt a deficit model of communication, which assumes that parents (and children) are unaware of the risks and simply need to be educated, or provided with the right tools, to mitigate them. Far from being 'digital immigrants' who are relatively clueless when it comes to digital technologies compared to their 'digital native' children, most parents are risk-aware and adept at using digital technologies. The problem instead lies in the difficulties of negotiating day-to-day media use in the home, as parents struggle to reconcile the broader expectations about what good parenting looks like with their children's media practices and preferences and growing desire for autonomy, independence and privacy. Despite their best efforts at good parenting, parents report feeling left-behind by their children's digital skills, exasperated by failed attempts at mediation, and worn down by the ensuing parent-child conflict that results.

This book proposes a new direction forward in approaches to online safety. This approach, while acknowledging potential online harms, does not foreground risk as the primary locus of concern. It acknowledges that families do seek knowledge and information, but accounts for their existing knowledge and practices, and does not operate from an assumed deficit. It recognises that young people may be more vulnerable to harm and online influence, but does not adopt a one-size-fits all approach, and recognises young people's growing agency. It acknowledges that digital media are an essential and highly valued part of contemporary life, providing numerous benefits to young people. It argues that the distinction between the online and offline worlds is neither clear nor terribly useful. It recognises that parent/child relationships are not equal, but that approaches to managing digital media are best negotiated democratically as a family. It seeks to move beyond the risk-harm/opportunity-benefit dichotomy which has dominated contemporary scholarly research. It supports child agency and young people's right to participate in the digital world.

Research overview

The chapters that follow draw on qualitative research with parents and some of their children from two research projects.[1] The first project consisted of focus groups and interviews with 40 Australian parents of teenagers aged 12–16 over a one-year period in 2016 and 2017. In this project, parents were asked to talk about their teens' digital media practices, their concerns and what shaped them, and how they addressed their anxieties about their children's digital media use through mediation. This project took place before the COVID-19 pandemic which resulted in prolonged lockdowns throughout Australia and a concomitant shift in how families used digital technologies. The second project utilised a participatory action research approach (Hearn et al., 2009) consisting of a series of family workshops aimed at facilitating mutual understanding between parents and their children about media use to reduce family digital conflict. Thirteen workshops were held in 2021 with 225 participants (115 and 110 children), and workshops averaged 15–20 participants. Most of the children were aged between 10 and 16. The workshops consisted of several activities aimed at facilitating understanding between parents and their children about media to reduce conflict. During the workshops, young people had the opportunity to talk about their digital practices and what they valued about digital media; as well as demonstrate their approaches to mitigating online risk. Parents shared their anxieties and concerns about their children and digital media, as well as how they managed their children's media use. Both parents and young people talked about the main sources of digital conflict, and we workshopped ways to reduce it. Importantly, both parents and their children were given the opportunity to share what they wish the other knew.[2]

About this book

In the chapters that follow, I explore a range of parental concerns, insights, experiences and strategies related to their children's media use, and the extent to which these are addressed by current educational and legislative interventions. I identify the key issues and challenges for families in the digital age, going beyond the most publicised and most serious (but usually most unlikely) risks to explore the quotidian issues related to negotiating digital media that are typically glossed over in public conversations, but which affect family harmony, cohesion and wellbeing. I demonstrate that young people have a range of strategies for mitigating online risk, and make a case that young people need to be involved in decisions which affect them, both at the level of the household as well as at the national policy level. I conclude with a 'wish list' outlining what I believe needs to happen in order to address young people's online safety, and help young people thrive in a digital world. These wishes encompass recommendations both at the governmental/policy level, as well as at the family level, to help families to realise safe, beneficial and appropriate media use while minimising family conflict and maintaining family cohesion. I don't provide all the answers – all families are different and there is no one-size-fits-all approach – however I aim to provide empirically informed recommendations that recognise adolescent agency, boost parental confidence, and provide contemporary families with the tools and guidance to thrive in a digital world.

The research presented throughout spans both pre-COVID and COVID times. The COVID-19 global pandemic necessitated a fundamental shift in digital media use within families around the world, as digital devices became critical for facilitating schooling, work, and connection. Children's media ownership and use increased dramatically as a result (McCArthur et al., 2021; McClain, 2022; Qustodio, 2021; Revealing Reality, 2020 cited in Willett & Zhao, 2024). This shift – scholars argue – removed any discretionary choice from families in relation to digital media. As Sefton-Green argues, our shift to 'digital by default' 'removes the concept of choice, and it removes the illusion that parents and their preferred mode of parenting can stand between these assumed [media] effects and their children' (Sefton-Green, 2024, p. xiii).

There is little doubt that the COVID-19 lockdowns were significant in terms of the ways in which media shaped family dynamics and practices. Yet, the data presented in this book does not reveal fundamental differences in knowledges and concerns amongst parents before the pandemic compared to during and immediately after lockdowns. The parental concerns remained fundamentally the same – screen time was one of the most prevalent concerns amongst parents both before the pandemic and after. Regarding parental control, parents before the pandemic indicated that they already felt as though their control over their children's media use was undermined by schools due to the requirement that their children acquire a device and complete an increasing array of school tasks on them (Page Jeffery, 2022). Any rules or restrictions that parents had previously managed to maintain, especially rules around screen time, were thrown out the window during the pandemic (Willett & Zhao, 2024). This book, however, does not, nor is it intended to, provide a detailed comparison of media use before, during and after the pandemic – first because the timing of the project does not allow it,[3] and second because there is now an emerging body of research explicitly exploring media, parenting and the pandemic, including the purported 'lasting' effects (see for example, Willett & Zhao, 2024). What we can tentatively conclude from the accounts described in the chapters that follow, however, is that rather than producing a fundamental change in parental concerns about their children's media use, the pandemic served to intensify existing anxieties and further diminish real or perceived parental control of their children's media use while fuelling media panics about young people's declining mental health and the purported association with media use.

The pandemic may, however, have led to some more positive outcomes in terms of parents' understanding of their children's digital practices. First, it may have highlighted the increasing redundancy of the broad term 'screen time', as young people engaged in a diverse range of online activities each with different perceived value and utility. The limitations of this term has been highlighted by scholars for years, as they acknowledge that it is a weak and inadequate concept for representing the diversity of young people's screen-based activities (Livingstone, 2021; Sefton-Green, 2024). Any movement away from this concept as a way of conceptualising and making sense of young people's media use is welcome. Further, the lockdowns may have led to increased involvement by parents in their children's digital practices, increasing parental knowledge of their children's online activities. Such knowledge is, as I argue in Chapter 6, a necessary condition for inter-generational understanding about digital media use.

The empirical findings presented throughout this book are derived from research with Australian families, most of whom were middle-class. Yet, the findings and recommendations that follow have a much broader applicability beyond Australia. Extensive research has shown similar digital risks, opportunities, and challenges across the developed West, including in the UK, USA and Europe, all highly connected countries with high digital adoption.[4] There are, however, several features which are unique to the Australian context. Australia was the first country to establish an eSafety Commissioner, who is granted comprehensive legislative powers to take action in relation to illegal content, as well as cyber-bullying and image-related abuse. Several scholars have also suggested that the Australian discourse framing young people's use of media is particularly focused on risks and harms, particularly compared to several European jurisdictions (Mavoa et al., 2017; Third et al., 2019; Zaman et al., 2020). Yet this risk focused approach exists within an environment where information communication technologies (ICT) are strongly promoted by Australian schools for their educational capabilities, and as such are heavily incorporated into the Australian school curriculum, creating a tension between discourses of risk/harm and opportunity/benefit which create further challenges for Australian families (Page Jeffery, 2022).

Chapter 1 documents the dominant discourses surrounding young people's use of digital media technologies. This chapter draws on theories around moral and media panics to describe the discourses of risk and harm that have dominated in Australia, with this discourse, however, are techno-utopian discourses of opportunity and benefit which highlight the educational affordances of ICTs, and envision a future in which the ubiquity and dominance of ICTs in work, school and play is inevitable. Such a discourse frames digital skills as essential to young people's future success. These contradictory framings have led to scholars and public policy conceptualising young people's use of digital media in terms of a risk/harm vs opportunity/benefit binary (Livingstone et al., 2015; Livingstone & Haddon, 2009; Third et al., 2019; Vickery, 2017). The dominance of discourses of harm has also led to parental anxiety and young people's digital media use being curtailed.

Chapter 2 provides an account of the Australian online safety environment, documenting the creation of legislation in 2015 which established the Office of the eSafety Commissioner, and which was updated in 2022 to further strengthen the Commissioner's powers, as well as a range of other interventions. An extensive range of cyber safety resources and programs has been developed by the Government as well as a suite of independent providers, to educate young people and parents about online risk. I argue that too many programs and resources adopt a deficit approach which does not adequately account for the existing knowledges, experiences and practices of children and their parents, thereby limiting their utility. Resources for parents, in tandem with the dominant discourses outlined in Chapter 1, discursively construct the figure of the 'good' parent, as one who monitors and restricts their children's media use.

A deeper exploration of the figure of the 'good' parent in contemporary Australia, and what this means for contemporary parents, is the focus of Chapter 3. The subject of parenting has generated a huge amount of popular and scholarly material, resulting in contradictory discourses of 'good' parenting. In this chapter I outline the broader cultural shifts in parenting over the decades, from earlier notions of child rearing which involved providing and caring for children, to the more recent notion of 'parenting'. I argue, in line with other scholars in this area, that contemporary constructions of 'good' parenting have expanded the expectations placed upon parents so that they are tasked with not only protecting their children from harm, but increasingly with ensuring that they reach their full potential. This sets up a contradictory, and particularly challenging, set of expectations in relation to parenting in the digital age, as parents are expected to simultaneously protect their children from online harm while ensuring that they use media to reach their full potential.

Chapter 4 explores the ways in which parents make judgements about the 'appropriateness' of their children's digital practices, drawing on discourses of development. It examines the ways in which parents negotiate the tension between technological development and the various benefits that technology affords their children, and the perceived risks and harms that these technological developments may pose to their children's 'natural' development. This chapter highlights that parents distinguish between media use that is considered to enhance their children's development and uses which have the potential to disrupt it, by categorising various activities as appropriate and inappropriate. These findings are important because they highlight the limitations of the risk vs benefit dichotomy which has long framed discussions of young people's digital media use.

An exploration of digital media as a source of family conflict, drawing on data from a series of participatory family workshops involving parents and their children, is the focus of Chapter 5. While acknowledging that adolescence is known as a period of 'storm and stress' in which young people seek increasing autonomy, privacy and independence from their parents, digital media technologies present additional challenges and complexities for families. This chapter identifies the main sources of parent/child digital conflict: screen time and time displacement/balance, 'inappropriate content'; behavioural effects, and sibling influence and conflict. It argues that digital conflict between parents and their children is symptomatic of a lack of shared understanding between parents and their children.

Parental attempts to understand their children's digital practices, including what they value and the things that they like to do online, as well as acknowledgement of young people's existing knowledge and skills for identifying and managing online risks are a necessary first step towards mutual understanding, increased parent/child trust, and reduced conflict.

Chapter 6 challenges the assumed deficit in young people's online knowledge and skills by building on data from a 'story completion' activity which sought to gain insights into young people's and their parents' ability to identify and respond to a series of online risks. Through a series of story stems, each of which outline a scenario introducing a potential online risk, young people were asked to complete the story – providing details about what they would do in that situation, and how they would feel. Adolescents demonstrated empathy and compassion for the hypothetical protagonists, and also demonstrated a range of practical, technical and discursive/communicative strategies for addressing risk. Interestingly, most participants – but especially the children – demonstrated a pragmatic approach that drew on a range of practical skills and knowledges, eschewing sensational-ised accounts documenting worst-case scenarios. The data presented in this chapter shows that young people are able to recognise and, in theory at least, mitigate online risks.

In Chapter 7 I argue that parents and children often conceptualise and talk about online risks and practices using different terminology, which presents a barrier to open dialogue and discussion between parents and their children about online risks. The chapter draws on data from the family workshops where parents and their children each shared key mes-sages that they wanted the other to know. A number of common themes emerged from both parents and young people. Parents wanted to emphasise to their children that tech-nology is only good if it is used in a balanced way; that technology is 'just a tool' that should be used 'wisely'; that there's 'more to life than technology'; to be critical and safe online, and that technology is distinct from, and no substitute for, the real world. Conversely, young people wanted to share with their parents all the ways they value tech-nology and how it enhances their lives; that they shouldn't worry because it's 'not all bad', and that they have more knowledge and competence than they are given credit for. The findings point to the need for ongoing dialogue between parents and their children to understand and value each others' perspectives.

Chapter 8 sums up the key arguments made throughout the book, and concludes with several recommendations, or a wish list. It acknowledges that there have been some encouraging developments since the first data was collected, including better educational materials and resources for parents and children, social media platforms taking some action to embed more safety features into their platforms, and greater recognition of young peo-ple's rights. Yet, media panics remain a familiar feature within the Australian news cycle, and young people remain, for the most part, excluded from decision making. Collective concern about young people's media use appears to have reached fever pitch, with politi-cians, media personalities and other high profile commentators calling for outright bans to exclude young people accessing social media all together. The book concludes by arguing that we need to move away from the risk vs benefit binary that has characterised both scholarly and mainstream approaches to online safety. We also need to move beyond paren-tal mediation theories which focus primarily on parents, and instead move towards more democratic modes of parenting. Importantly, resources and policies aimed at helping young people thrive online must account for both adolescent and parental knowledges and perspectives, and should be geared towards facilitating ongoing parent/child discussion.

Notes

1 More detail about the research methods can be found in Appendix A.
2 For a more detailed account of how the workshops were conducted, see Page Jeffery et al. (2022).
3 While the second project took place during lock-downs, there is not enough data to draw detailed conclusions about the after-effects of the pandemic.
4 See for example the UK Kids Online Study, and its Australian equivalent AU Kids Online.

References

Drotner, K. (1992). Modernity and media panics. In M. Skovman & K. C. Schroder (Eds.), *Media cultures reappraising transnational media* (pp. 42–62). New York, London: Routledge.

Drotner, K. (1999). Dangerous media? Panic discourses and dilemmas of modernity. *Paedagogica Historica, 35*(3), 593–619.

eSafety Commissioner (2021). Digital families: Connected homes and technology use. https://www.esafety.gov.au/research/digital-parenting/digital-families. Accessed 4 December 2024.

Hearn, G., Tacchi, J. A., Foth, M., & Lennie, J. (2009). *Action research and new media: Concepts, methods and cases.* Cresskill, NJ: Hampton Press.

Leick, K. (2018). *Parents, media and panic through the years: Kids those days.* Basel, Switzerland: Palgrave.

Lim, S. S. (2019). *Transcendent parenting: Raising children in the digital age.* New York: Oxford University Press.

Livingstone, S. (2021). The rise and fall of screen time. In V. C. Strasburger (Ed.), *Masters of media: Controversies and solutions* (pp. 89–104), Rowman & Littlefield.

Livingstone, S., & Blum-Ross, A. (2020). *Parenting for a digital future: How hopes and fears about technology shape children's lives.* USA: Oxford University Press.

Livingstone, S., & Haddon, L. (2009). *Kids online: Opportunities and risks for children.* Bristol, UK: Policy Press.

Livingstone, S., Mascheroni, G., & Staksrud, E. (2015). *Developing a framework for researching children's online risks and opportunities in Europe.* EU Kids Online. https://eprints.lse.ac.uk/64470/1/__lse.ac.uk_storage_LIBRARY_Secondary_libfile_shared_repository_Content_EU%20Kids%20Online_EU%20Kids%20Online_Developing%20framework%20for%20researching_2015.pdf

Livingstone, S., & Third, A. (2017). *Children and young people's rights in the digital age: An emerging agenda.* UK: London, England: Sage Publications.

Lumby, C. (1997). Panic attacks: Old fears in a new media era. *Media International Australia, 85*(1), 40–46.

Mavoa, J., Gibbs, M., & Carter, M. (2017). Constructing the young child media user in Australia: A discourse analysis of Facebook comments. *Journal of Children and Media, 11*(3), 330–346.

Page Jeffery, C. (2020). "It's really difficult. We've only got each other to talk to." Monitoring, mediation and good parenting in Australia in the digital age. *Journal of Children and Media, 15*, 1–16.

Page Jeffery, C. (2022). It's just another nightmare to manage: 'Australian parents' perspectives on BYOD and 'ed-tech' at school and at home. *Learning, Media and Technology, 47*(4), 471–484. doi:10.1080/17439884.2021.2022691

Page Jeffery, C., Atkinson, S., & McCallum, K. (2022). The safe online together project: A participatory approach to resolving inter-generational technology conflict in families. *Communication Research and Practice, 8*(2), 136–151. doi:10.1080/22041451.2022.2056426

Potter, R. H., & Potter, L. A. (2001). The internet, cyberporn, and sexual exploitation of children: Media moral panics and urban myths for middle-class parents? *Sexuality and Culture, 5*(3), 31–48.

Rooney, G. (2011). Women and children first: Technology and moral panic. *The Wall Street Journal.* 11 July. Accessed at https://www.wsj.com/articles/BL-TEB-2814

Sefton-Green, J. (2024). Preface. In R. Willett & X. Zhao (Eds.), *Children, media and pandemic parenting* (pp. xii–xvi). United Kingdom: Routledge.

Simpson, B. (2020). Law, digital media, and the discomfort of children's rights. In L. Green, D. Holloway, K. Stevenson, T. Leaver, & L. Haddon (Eds.), *The Routledge companion to digital media and children* (pp. 308–317). New York and London: Routledge.

Third, A., Collin, P., Walsh, L., & Black, R. (2019). *Young people in digital society: Control shift*. London, UK: Palgrave Macmillan Nature.

Vickery, J. R. (2017). *Worried about the wrong things: Youth, risk, and opportunity in the digital world*. Cambridge, Massachusetts: The MIT Press.

Willett, R., & Zhao, X. (2024). *Children, media, and pandemic parenting: Family life in uncertain times*. London: Taylor & Francis.

Zaman, B., Holloway, D., Green, L., Jaunzems, K., & Vanwynsberghe, H. (2020). Opposing narratives about children's digital media use: A critical discourse analysis of online public advice given to parents in Australia and Belgium. *Media International Australia*, *176*(1), 120–137.

1

MEDIA PANICS AND NARRATIVES OF RISK

Parenting teens in anxious times

There is a long history of concerns, anxieties and moral panics about children's use of media (Buckingham & Strandgaard Jensen, 2012; Drotner, 1999; Drotner & Livingstone, 2008; Wartella & Jennings, 2000), and these panics have served as catalysts for bringing children's media use into the public eye (Drotner & Livingstone, 2008), and illuminating the potential social effects of media. The construction of children as a 'protected species' – 'innocent', corruptible and 'at risk' – renders them especially vulnerable to the supposedly pernicious effects of new media and technologies, and parents are tasked with governing their children's activities and behaviours so as to mediate potential social effects. Collective anxieties about children's relationship with media and technology have been expressed in numerous ways over the decades: through 'media panics' (Drotner, 1992b, 1999) that typically play out within the mass media; popular discourse (for example, popular books and public commentary); and government attention to particular issues which usually takes the form of policy initiatives or regulatory responses that seek to address these concerns. Examining previous panics about children and media is important for understanding contemporary collective concerns about young people's use of digital media, as moral panics leave a discursive legacy which establish the terms in which issues are debated (Cohen, 2002, p. 12).

The concept of the moral panic was originally a sociological framework developed by Stanley Cohen in the 1970s primarily concerned with social deviance, delinquency, and youth subcultures. Cohen's (2002) work on 'moral panics' has been so influential that the term has now become part of the standard repertoire of public debate, providing our mass-mediated world with a way of repudiating the forces of hyperbole and hysteria (Garland, 2008). For Cohen, a 'moral panic' describes the way in which the mass media employs particular media templates to overstate or exaggerate the threat posed by a particular deviant, 'folk devil' group to the general social order (in Cohen's case, he was referring to the Mods and Rockers of the 1960s). Kirsten Drotner (1992b) argued that such panics are an inherent quality of modernity. She expanded the application of the concept to new media (at the time) such as comics, video, and film, arguing that 'the introduction of a new mass medium causes strong public reactions whose repetitiveness is as predictable as the fervour with which they are brought forward' (Drotner, 1992b, p. 43).

DOI: 10.4324/9781003346708-2

There is a distinct pattern to the way moral panics have followed every major technological or media development in modernity. Media panics are not confined to new technologies, with literary texts (including comics) and film also generating their own panics
(Drotner, 1992b; Springhall, 1998). Yet despite variations in the specific types of media
eliciting panic, there remain 'repetitions and continuities over many generations in the
anxieties induced by fears of new technology interacting with revised forms of popular
culture' (Springhall, 1998, p. 136). The persistence and repetition of media panics over
the years have generated a 'diffuse feeling of anxiety' (Cohen, 2002, p. 7) about children
and media, thus laying the foundations for future panics. Yet despite these repetitions,
continuities, and similarities, contemporary media panics typically reappear as a new and
urgent problem – as if it were the first time such issues have been publicly debated – that
we must take immediate action to address, highlighting an 'intrinsic historical amnesia'
(Drotner, 1992b, p. 610).

This diffuse feeling of anxiety (Cohen, 2002) about children has never really disappeared. Contemporary discussions about children and media often take the form of a
continuous yet multi-dimensional risk commentary about children's various digital practices, where the specific locus of concern changes over time – rising and then receding in
response to various criteria of newsworthiness – but the underlying anxiety is sustained.
Newsworthy events that elicit concern about a particular issue might include the occur-
rence of a tragic event – such as a suicide allegedly the result of cyberbullying[1] – or the
emergence of a new technological fad which purportedly poses some kind of threat to
children. Some examples include the online game, Fortnite, eliciting concern about gaming addiction when it first emerged[2]; Omegle and other platforms, raising concerns about
online platforms being 'weaponised to abuse young children' (Shepherd, 2023); and social
media platform TikTok which rapidly rose to become one of the most popular social media
sites amongst teens (eSafety Commissioner, 2021; Pew Research Centre, 2022), raising a
plethora of concerns ranging from online predators, privacy breaches, algorithmic curation
of content, and exposure to self-harm and suicide content.[3]

Alice Marwick (2008) has used the term 'technopanics' to describe panics about new
technologies. The concept of the 'technopanic' attempts to 'contextualise the moral panic
as a response to fear of modernity as represented by new technologies' (Marwick, 2008,
para 22). Marwick identifies three characteristics of technopanics. First, they focus on new
media forms, which currently take the form of computer mediated technologies. Second,
technopanics generally pathologise young people's use of this media (she cites as examples
hacking, file sharing or playing violent video games, but more recent examples of behaviours that are pathologised might include 'excessive' use, mimicking behaviours depicted
in social media content, and sexualised practices of self-representation). And third, she
notes that this cultural anxiety manifests itself in an attempt to modify or regulate young
people's behaviours by controlling young people's use of technologies, or the creators of
media products (Marwick, 2008).

There is a link between the ways in which technology, and in particular, technologies of
communication, underpin the reproduction of social norms. Moral panics have historically
played out in relation to the bodies of children, and also women (Rooney, 2011; Drotner,
1992b; Valentine & Holloway, 2001). In most contexts, media panics are underpinned by
at least two overarching and related key concerns. First, the role of and potential for media
technologies to disrupt these social norms; and second, the positioning of media

technologies in opposition to 'high culture', thereby constructing a hierarchy of values (Drotner, 1992b). The former assumes agency on the part of the media user, and represents concerns primarily (although not exclusively) about their *behaviours* or *activities* and the competencies that children develop through media use which pose threats to the established power relations (Drotner, 1992b). Drotner (1992b, p. 56) also argues that media content emphasises 'emotional investment and bodily expressiveness and experimentations' which are 'sharply opposed to the norms governing employment and school relations' (Drotner, 1992b). The latter – placing media in opposition to high culture – primarily represents concerns related to the 'debased' status of new media and its potential *effects* on the user which may subsequently lead to a transgression of social norms.

One example relates to earlier panics that followed the invention of the telephone and telegraph. At the time, these new communications technologies evoked concern that young women might make use of these new technologies to make contact with 'inappropriate' romantic partners and dangerous strangers. Thus the telephone and telegraph were perceived as disrupting the social norms related to the proper behaviours and place of women in society. The telephone in particular raised concern as it not only provided:

> unprecedented opportunities for courting and infidelity, but for romancing unacceptable persons outside one's own class and even one's own race in circumstances that went unobserved by the regular community.… The potential for illicit sexual behaviour had obvious and disquieting power to undermine accustomed centers of oral authority and social order. (Marvin, 1988, cited in Cassell and Cramer, 2008 p. 61).

Much later, the mobile phone similarly became the subject of panics. Goggin and Crawford (2011) document a range of anxieties about young people's use of mobiles and the perceived role that they play in strengthening or eroding community bonds. Panics about young people's use of mobile phones ranged from concerns about excessive connectivity to social isolation, thus signifying a disruption of social norms related to social conduct and community. Young people, they argue, are reportedly using 'SMS to avoid face-to-face confrontations and avoiding the responsibility of full contact with their friends and family' (Florez, 2003 cited in Goggin & Crawford, 2011, p. 250). With the advent of social media, these concerns are arguably even more prevalent today.

The potential for media to reconfigure established power relations thus remains at the heart of concerns about disruptions to established social norms, and media panics more broadly. Those deemed to occupy more subordinate positions in society, such as women and children, are afforded greater agency through their use of communications technologies. New communications technologies enable young people to venture into the outside world privately and secretly while in the 'safety' of their own home, and to move beyond the 'sphere of adult control' (Cassell & Cramer, 2008, p. 70). At the same time, the newfound agency of young people results in a diminution of parental (and societal) control. Thus, panics come to represent power struggles between distinct groups, namely adults and young people – as adults attempting to 'protect' (or control) young people's activities, and young people attempting to exercise their own independence and agency online. Digital devices and platforms have thus become a key site of intergenerational contestation.

Anxiety about media effects

The introduction of comics, video, film, and television triggered media panics (Drotner, 1992a; Lumby & Fine, 2006; Springhall, 1998) that mobilised an apparently new set of anxieties about *exposure* to potentially damaging, 'immoral' or 'unsavoury' content. The arrival of cinema raised questions about its possible harmful effects on children, leading to studies on the effects of movie viewing on children and youth in the late 1920s (Paik, 2001). But it was the arrival of television into millions of homes in the 1950s which led to considerable debate about its potentially harmful effects within popular discourse, the mass media, as well as academia. Ever since Hilde Himmelweit and her colleagues' early pioneering research on children and television (Himmelweit et al., 1958), researchers have been asking questions about the potential effects that this almost omnipresent medium of entertainment and information might have on the cognitive, emotional, social and behavioural responses of children (Singer & Singer, 2012). Concerns about the potential risks of exposure to media content, often promulgated via media panics, generated an extensive body of research that is now commonly referred to as the 'media effects' research tradition. Livingstone (1996) previously noted that the 'research effects tradition' focused predominantly but not exclusively on the effects of television rather than other media and on child audiences in particular. Consequently, a significant body of research examining the possible harms of television emerged with an urgency that derived from these public concerns rather than an academic agenda (Livingstone, 1996). These concerns led to a series of studies, reports, and inquiries from the 1950s to the 1970s (Paik, 2001). The purported harms to children exposed to certain television content were many and varied, leading to numerous studies investigating the potential effects of television exposure to: violence (Bushman & Huesmann, 2001; Groebel, 2001); sexual content (Donnerstein & Smith, 2001; Malamuth & Impett, 2001); frightening and potentially traumatizing material (Cantor, 2001); and advertising and commercial culture, including junk food advertising (Horgan et al., 2001; Kunkel, 2001). Over time, greater attention was given to the link between television viewing and obesity (see for example Dietz & Gortmaker, 1985; Gortmaker et al., 1996; Olds et al., 2006; Robinson, 2001; Salmon et al., 2006) as well as various other problematic outcomes from television viewing (Ferguson, 2017).

Exposure to other forms of media, including 'deviant' music such as rap and heavy metal has also elicited media panics since the 1980s due to its purported damaging effects on youth, in particular, the belief in its ability to incite youth suicide, often via subliminal messages (Wright, 2000). Rap and heavy metal were considered to 'foster social pathologies amongst its listeners ranging from occultism and satanism, through sexism and racism, to murderous and suicidal tendencies' (Wright, 2000, p. 370). Tipper Gore's (1987) *Raising PG Kids in an X-Rated Society* is a particularly notable example of extreme anxiety about the effects of 'explicit' content, 'evil' and 'satanism' contained in popular music and other forms of popular media. As Grossberg (1992) notes, Gore is concerned with 're-asserting some control over the cultural environment in which our children are raised' (Gore, 1987, p. 13, cited in Grossberg, 1992, p. 193), and thus 'the regulation of youth and the regulation of cultural consumption collapse into a project of rescuing the moral fabric of the nation' (Grossberg, 1992, pp. 193–194). Concerns about 'deviant' genres of music appeared to focus not only on satanic or suicidal subliminal messages, but also on music as a possible gateway to 'dangerous' sub-cultures. More recently, rap and hip-hop have been perceived as a threat to social order and public safety, leading to surveillance and censorship of well-known artists such as Rage Against the Machine, Snoop Dogg, Eminem and Akon (Lee et al., 2023). 'Drill rap', a globally popular sub-genre of hip-hop that deals with issues such as violent crime and street life, has been the subject of media panics amid (unfounded) concerns that the music incites violence and helps to recruit gang members (Lee et al., 2023).

From exposure and *effects* to engagement and *context*

Despite some consensus amongst mainstream psychologists about some of the purported negative effects of media, cultural studies theorists, and humanities and media scholars have argued that a focus on media effects is insufficient in a contemporary media context. Notwithstanding criticism that the media effects research tradition is a simplistic response to a complex problem which fails to adequately address the agency and interpretative capacities of audiences, Buckingham (2008) argues that laboratory experiments designed to test media effects are an unreliable guide to real life behaviour, and Livingstone (1996) has long argued that focusing only on 'effects' does not sufficiently account for a range of other relevant contextual and cultural factors. Importantly, studies purporting to measure media effects typically only show an association between a form of media and a particular effect, rather than causation – despite frequent unsupported claims of the latter (McKee et al., 2022). Nonetheless, it is clear that there has been a profound shift away – in relation to both practices and accompanying anxieties – from mere *exposure* to content, towards *interaction* and *engagement*. Indeed, contemporary media culture is characterised by *active participation* in media, rather than *passive consumption* of television and other screen-based content that characterised earlier concerns. The affordances of contemporary media technologies such as social networking, online gaming, and other networked platforms, are enabling young people to *interact* with digital media through creating and sharing their own content and connecting with others.

Many scholars have documented this broader shift, characterised in part by the dissolution of firm boundaries between both media companies and 'consumers', as well as different, previously distinct forms of media. Yochai Benkler refers to a 'hybrid media ecology' to describe how various commercial, amateur, government, non-profit, educational, activist and other players interact with each other in more complex ways (Jenkins & Deuze, 2008). Henry Jenkins (2006) coined the term 'convergence culture' to describe a more 'participatory' media culture in which old and new media collide, and grassroots and corporate media, as well as media producer and consumers intersect and interact. And Axel Bruns coined the term 'prosumer' to reflect the merging of the previously distinct processes and correlative subject positions of producer and consumer (Bruns, 2009).

Public debate and collective concerns about children's use of digital media have followed this shift and given rise to a rearticulation of anxieties about children's use of digital media. 'Technopanics' about children's purported 'addiction' to their mobile phones appear to have replaced moral panics from the 1950s that focused on television, and later, videos (Livingstone, 1996). Advice and guidelines, such as those from the American Association of Paediatrics (AAP), now account for the interactive affordances of digital media, and the additional challenges they present. Contemporary popular parenting books about managing children's media consumption are now predominantly concerned with digital and interactive media, suggesting that concerns about digital media have eclipsed earlier concerns about television (see for example, Gold, 2014; Heitner, 2016; Janis-Norton, 2017; Kamenetz, 2018). Public policy has shifted in part away from primarily focusing on children's exposure to potentially harmful material on screen such as violence, to concerns about the more general physiological effects of 'excessive' screen engagement, such as obesity, disrupted sleep, and attention disorders.[4,5] Whole organisations have been established to provide advice and information about managing children's use of digital technologies. While more optimistic voices suggest that new media 'enable young people to participate more actively in interpreting, personalising, reshaping and creating media content' (Ito, 2008, p. 397), the changing nature of children's engagement with media, away from passive consumption towards active participation, has given rise to a new set of anxieties (Ito, 2008). That's not to say that concerns about the potential *effects* of exposure to certain content (such as pornography and extreme violence) have disappeared. Indeed, recent public debate about the problem of gendered violence in Australia has singled out the prevalence and nature of online pornography as a contributing factor (see, for example, Marin & Rutledge, 2024; Roberts, 2024). Scholars agree, however, that we should not abandon the question of media effects entirely (Livingstone & Das, 2010). However, the shift in the nature of media consumption demonstrates the limitations of the media effects research tradition. Indeed, the television centred concerns that characterised early debates about screen time would likely elicit some bemusement amongst contemporary parents who decry that television is the least of their worries. It is evident, however, that there has been a rearticulation of collective concerns about children's use of digital media away (although not entirely) from what might be 'done to' children by media, towards anxieties about what children might do as a result of engaging with digital media.

Increasingly anxious: From TV and cinema to the internet and smartphone

Not surprisingly, concerns about television, cinema and music have been overshadowed by the internet and related digital technologies such as mobile phones which have become a site where these broad but familiar anxieties coalesce. Indeed, the introduction of a new media fad, and the preoccupation with the threats which it is said to pose, 'immediately relegates older media to the shadows of acceptance' (Cohen, 2002, p. xvii). However, as I discuss further below, the internet and other forms of digital media become sites where concerns about media effects due to exposure to certain forms of content converge with concerns about the ways in which digital media disrupt social norms by shaping certain behaviours and encouraging certain activities. Importantly, the ubiquity of screens further compounds these anxieties. Screens have remained a central component within the changing media landscape (Blum-Ross & Livingstone, 2016; Goggin, 2009; Livingstone, 1998) and now pervade almost all aspects of children's (and indeed adults') daily lives. A key overarching concern has emerged regarding young people's screen time. I engage with this issue more substantively in later chapters.

In addition to the multiplication of screens across various contexts and the combination of concerns about both effects as well as engagement, the shifting location and proximity of screens raises additional challenges for parents. Television and cinema screens were characterised by a fixed location which was typically 'public', and media consumption or exposure often occurred in the company, or under the scrutiny, of others (usually parents).

This can be contrasted with the 'mobile' screens of contemporary digital media, which are geared towards individual, private consumption which more easily evades scrutiny and surveillance of adults and other authority figures (although, as I argue later, some parents have utilised various other surveillance techniques as a way of mediating their children's digital media use).

Internet and digital media-related concerns have typically been categorised as either 'contact', 'content', or 'conduct' related risks (boyd & Hargittai, 2013; Ponte & Simões, 2009). Early collective concerns about media effects, both in relation to television, music, cinema and the internet, clearly reflect concerns about content. However, while many of the *issues* that have traditionally elicited concern remain broadly static (for example, sexualised or violent content), I suggest that there has been a partial shift away from 'content' being the primary locus of concern, towards conduct related concerns, as a result of the interactive affordances of digital media. While concerns about media effects have always encompassed some kind of behaviourally related concern (for example, that exposure to violent content increases aggression), conduct related concerns are no longer wholly premised upon a 'cause and effect' view of media effects, and instead encompass a broader range of social (or anti-social as the case may be) behaviours. Further, in addition to content and conduct, contemporary concerns also encompass the notion of 'displacement' due to screens – that screen time is displacing other activities deemed more worthwhile, raising questions about what might be being lost in contemporary childhood.

For the remainder of this chapter, I explore these points further by documenting some contemporary media panics about children and digital media: the 'dumbing down' of culture; pornography and the sexualisation of culture; sexting; internet predators; and cyberbullying. Across all of these discourses children are framed as vulnerable, 'at risk' and lacking the skills and maturity to safely navigate online spaces (Coulter, 2020). While this list is hardly exhaustive, panics about these issues serve an important diagnostic purpose, in that they highlight a range of potential social effects that parents are required to negotiate and mediate in relation to their own children.

Moral panics and media effects

Media commentary and public discourse, including moral panics, invoke the notion of childhood in crisis (Kehily, 2010), as well as a sense of nostalgia that things used to be safer, contributing to a general, unfocused fear that pervades discussions about children, and thus the notion that danger and risk have become a central feature of everyday life (Altheide, 2002). Lee et al. (2014) argue that the concept of risk in recent years has expanded to resonate with parenting culture, and describe the various feelings and responses of parents in terms of 'risk consciousness', which is marked by a preoccupation with unwanted or dangerous outcomes that *might* happen, rather than what is *likely* to happen.

Thus fear and anxiety have become standard ingredients in contemporary parenting culture in which parents feel that they have less control over their own lives as well as their children's (Clark, 2013). Parents are said to be increasingly uncertain, overanxious (Nelson, 2010) fearful and paranoid (Furedi, 2002), as they attempt to simultaneously ameliorate risk while embracing change and opportunity. Amongst these discourses of risk and danger, and discursively constructed ideals around 'good parenting', it is not surprising that parental anxiety emerges as parents struggle to avoid feelings of guilt, worry, failure and shame (Faircloth & Murray, 2015).

Dumbing down

Anxieties about new media being the trigger for 'dumbing down' culture have shifted from a critical scholarly and popular concern for the critical capacity of audiences based on *exposure* to commercialised cultural forms through various iterations to being concerned with new media encouraging a kind of *active* stupidity. In the 1940s, Theodor Adorno and Max Horkheimer (2002) presented a scathing critique of what they termed the culture industries, which encompassed media ranging from Hollywood films, soap operas, radio to jazz music. Adorno and Horkheimer argued that the culture industries mass-produced a standardised commodity designed primarily to serve capitalist interests, for an audience which was unthinking, passive and had become mere objects of manipulation. While Adorno and Horkheimer's theory of 'enlightenment as mass deception' (Horkheimer et al., 2002) has attracted significant scholarly critique, concerns about the dumbing down of audiences have never really gone out of fashion.

Neil Postman (1985), in *Amusing Ourselves to Death: Public Discourse in the Age of Showbusiness*, suggested that the merging of information and entertainment was in effect, dumbing down public discourse. Ivo Mosley (2000, p. 5), in *Dumbing Down: culture, politics and the mass media*, lamented the 'dumbing down' of culture 'in all walks of life' including the media, which seeks the widest audience, creating the 'lowest common denominator' effect. Jane Healy (1991), in *Endangered Minds: Why Children Don't Think, and What We Can Do About it*, examined how television, video games, and other components of popular culture are distracting our children and jeopardising their ability to process information.

While the purported dumbing down of culture is, according to these authors, bad for us all, for children and young people the stakes are, as always, significantly higher. Media panics about the 'dumbing down' effects of 'new' media are premised upon a dichotomy between high and low culture (sometimes framed in terms of art vs entertainment). It is a dichotomy, or 'hierarchy of value' which Drotner (1992b) argues underpins all media panics. According to Drotner (1992b), media panics assume that children are being exposed to 'low culture' through new media and this is compromising their very psychological development. In acknowledging that children and young people are continually defined as victims in media panics, she asserts that according to this assumption:

> Cultural development and human development are aspects of one and the same process. Children's cultural edification is part of, indeed proof of their social elevation. Therefore, their cultural fare must be guarded, watched over and protected, because its composition is vital for their mental growth. Following this logic, if we as adults watch soap operas every afternoon, then our humaneness is gradually undermined. But if children watch soap operas every afternoon, then they never even get a chance to develop this humaneness... Cultural and mental development, according to this belief, are two sides of the same coin. This coin is called 'enlightenment.'
>
> *(Drotner, 1992b, p. 54)*

The advent of the internet and other digital media has brought about a shift in the character of these concerns, away from a form of *passive* stupidity whereby dumbing down is 'done to' audiences via *exposure* to commercial cultural forms and 'debased' public discourse, towards concern about a more *active* form of stupidity whereby the internet and digital media are thought to encourage an active or wilful displacement of intellectual endeavour. According to popular narratives, young people these days have come to depend on the instant answers and intellectual short-cuts provided by the internet. Thinking has, so to speak, been outsourced, or delegated to a device. This alleged intellectual abandonment is said to be eroding our deep-thinking skills and ability to concentrate. Anxiety about the potential stunting of our mental capacities, the shortening of attention spans, and the possible effects on critical thinking skills have thus been revived in a digital age said to be characterised by quick rewards, shallow thinking and instant gratification.

Popular books frame these concerns in subtly different ways. Nicholas Carr (2010), in his best-selling book *The Shallows: What the internet is doing to our brains*, suggests that the internet is rewiring our brains and affecting our ability to read and think deeply. Maggie Jackson (2008), in *Distracted: The Erosion of Attention and the Coming of the Dark Age*, argues that new technologies are 'eroding our capacity for deep, sustained, perceptive attention – the building block of intimacy, wisdom and cultural progress' (p. 13). Susan Greenfield, a UK neuroscientist, argues that new technologies, including social networking sites, can damage people's brains (2009, 2015). Jean Twenge explores 'Why Today's Super-Connected kids are Growing Up Less Rebellious, More Tolerant, Less Happy – and Completely Unprepared for Adulthood' in her 2017 book *iGen*. As well as impaired thinking and concentration skills, the implicit effect of this active form of stupidity, panic discourses suggest, is diminished emotional intelligence. Collective anxiety about the potential effects of media and technology on our social relationships, which are increasingly mediated via digital technologies and resulting in us being 'alone, together' (Turkle, 2011) have been mobilised. More recently, Jonathon Haidt's bestselling book '*The Anxious Generation: How the Great Rewiring of Childhood is Causing an Epidemic of Mental Illness*' (Haidt, 2024) which argues that 'addiction' to smartphones and a decline in unsupervised play have 'rewired' a generation, leading an 'epidemic' of anxiety and depression internationally, has reignited fierce debate about the issue. Concerns about the potential dumbing down, distracting, and disconnecting effects of media are typically amplified when applied to children, who not only are considered especially impressionable and vulnerable because their brains are still growing and developing (Healy, 1991), but are also seen to be the most enthusiastic adopters and consumers of digital media. Still, even claims about the alleged vulnerability of young people are contested, with some scholars claiming that youth are no more vulnerable to media effects than adults (Schiffer, 2024).

These arguments have attracted legitimate criticism. Many claims about media effects are, and have long been, premised on a correlation rather than causation which is notoriously difficult to determine (Livingstone, 1996). Haidt's recent book has generated fierce debate about the validity of his claims, with many highly credible scholars pointing out that there is an absence of evidence for screen media causing mental health problems amongst youth (Ferguson et al., 2022; Odgers, 2024).[6] Yet, these arguments have clearly struck a chord with parents who have long been primed to believe that media may compromise their children's development (Odgers, 2024), who struggle with their children's media use and increasingly their children's mental health, and who are looking for easy answers to the problem. But, as many have argued, blaming everything on the phone and social media is simplistic, reductive, and diverts attention from some of the real challenges facing young people, and parents, today (Odgers, 2024).

Pornography and the sexualisation of culture

There have been notable shifts in the nature and locus of concern about pornography and other forms of sexualised or sexually explicit content over the decades. Earlier concerns about *exposure* to sexually explicit material through magazines (typically sexualised female nudity) have been superseded by concerns about exposure to internet pornography, which more often comprises depictions of actual sexual activity including depictions that are considered to transgress acceptable sexual norms. Concerns about children's exposure to pornography intensified with the widespread adoption of the internet throughout Australian homes in the 1990s (Potter & Potter, 2001). The mid-2000s saw a rearticulation of these concerns, whereby the focus apparently shifted from mere exposure to sexually explicit content to encompass concerns about the potentially damaging 'effects' of sexualised representations across media more generally. The sexualisation of children moral debate which took place in Australia and throughout the Anglophone West in the late 2000s claimed that sexualised representations in turn 'sexualised' children (almost always girls), by fostering a desire among children to emulate what they see. According to the moral entrepreneurs in the debate, this was said to lead to a raft of potentially damaging consequences, including low-self-esteem, precociousness, and self-destructive behaviour, amongst other things (Egan & Hawkes, 2010).

Contemporary panics about internet pornography thus appear to stem from the perceived disruption to social norms related to sexual behaviour (or indeed, 'lack' of sexual behaviour and expression, which is the accepted norm in relation to children and young people) rather than from concerns about exposure alone. For example, popular discourse frames the impact of porn on the sexual expectations of young males in particular, and draws links between risky behaviours and the consumption of internet pornography, as young people are assumed to enact sexual practices that they see online and be incapable of distinguishing fantasy from reality. Young people are positioned as especially vulnerable to porn's effects amid claims that young people are learning about sex primarily through internet pornography, which is skewing their perception of what is 'normal' sexual relations. (Of course, as Byron et al. (2021) have demonstrated, perceptions of 'normal' or 'acceptable' sexual behaviour typically consist of heteronormative sex between a monogamous couple in a loving relationship, despite these representations not representing young people's sexual preferences). Discussions about consent laws in Australia have called for greater government regulation of pornography, citing how damaging online pornography is as cultural education, especially for young boys and men in particular. A reported increase in the practice of 'choking' (also known as 'breath play') has similarly been attributed to the prevalence of online pornography (Marin & Rutledge, 2024). All of this is despite recent research which demonstrates the nuanced ways in which young people perceive online pornography, and how these differ from dominant risk discourses. Far from reproducing the 'risk talk' which highlights the purported damaging effects of pornography, young people have expressed a desire for agency, pleasure, entertainment, education and exploration. Importantly, they expressed the desire to determine when and how they experienced online pornography, as well as the right to avoid it altogether if so desired (eSafety Commissioner, 2023).

Sexting

'Sexting' is the practice of sending sexual photos, messages, or videos to another person, typically via a mobile telephone. It is a practice enabled by the communicative and photographic affordances of smartphones and thus became the subject of recurring media panics shortly after the widespread adoption of smartphones in 2008. Like panics around pornography, sexting panics similarly mobilised anxieties about the role of digital media in the shifting sexual norms and expectations of young people. Panics about sexting present the agentic self-representation practices of girls as a serious problem that demands attention (Ringrose & Harvey, 2015), and are thus indicative of deeper anxieties about the sexual self-expression of young people (almost always girls), which are seen to be a transgression of childhood norms.

By the end of 2010, sexting as a serious problem threatening the innocence and well-being of children appeared firmly rooted in the Australian cultural consciousness. Sexting education, strategies and tips for parents and children alike started to emerge around this time. Schools across the country began running anti-sexting workshops and other cyber safety educational programs. Statistics and research findings began to emerge which reported apparently alarming findings. In a report that attracted media attention, Walker (2012) raised the concern that adolescents were facing pressure to conform to gendered stereotypes and that girls in particular were feeling pressured into sending images. Panics about sexting practices appeared to peak around this time (Page Jeffery, 2017). These panics frequently invoked other risk narratives around young people and technology as a rhetorical strategy to escalate and amplify the alleged threat posed by the issue. For example, in what could be viewed as an attempt to resuscitate earlier anxieties about predators on social networking sites, police invoked the spectre of the paedophile, warning that sexually explicit images that are sent as sexts were ending up in the hands of paedophiles (see, for example, O'Connell, 2010).[7] Similarly, as Ringrose and Harvey (2015) point out, the news media frequently dramatises extreme incidents of sexting 'gone wrong' so that sexting becomes synonymous with cyberbullying. The conflation of these issues represents what Hall et al. (2013) refer to as convergence – the act of linking two or more activities in the process of signification so as to draw parallels between them. The convergence of sexting – a practice which is frequently carried out consensually by young people in relationships without any negative consequences – with other issues which do have the potential to harm young people, making otherwise relatively innocent practices of sexualised self-expression difficult to ignore. Inflated media claims about the prevalence and dangers of sexting, however, do not appear to be supported empirically. While the statistics vary, incidences of sexting have recently been shown to be less common than previously thought and the majority of sexting incidences are in fact consensual and do not result in any negative consequences (Lavoipierre, 2017; What's Up In Your World Survey, 2018). Importantly, these debates do not match the language that is used by young people in making sense of the practices, with Albury (2015, p. 1734) noting that young people reject the term 'sexting' and instead used a typology of 'pictures' that included private selfies, public selfies, and inoffensive sexual pictures. Albury notes that the young people 'called attention to the ways that the term 'sexting' was misapplied to young people's digital practices' (Albury, 2015, p. 1738). This highlights a disjuncture between the ways in which young people talk about some of their digital practices, and the ways that these are conceptualised and talked about by adults and other people in positions of authority. This will be explored more in later chapters.

Internet predators/paedophiles

Early concerns about the social and interactive affordances of the internet coalesced around the figure of the paedophile. Indeed, the danger of paedophiles and the form of entrapment known as grooming emerged as a principal discursive articulation of new media technologies and parental control. Fears about online predators have long been the focus of moral panics throughout the Anglophone west (Cavanagh, 2007; Critcher, 2002, 2008; Marsh & Melville, 2011). The advent and rapid uptake of popular social networking platforms – especially during the mid to late 2000s – resuscitated these anxieties with numerous media reports portraying online spaces as teeming with creepy middle-aged men lurking in the shadows of cyberspace and grooming unsuspecting young boys and girls. Predator panics appeared to peak in the mid-2000s throughout several developed countries. Social networking site Myspace (now passe and largely defunct) gave rise to a panic around this time in the UK about potential online predators targeting its users (the majority of whom were children and teenagers) due to the anonymity afforded by the internet (Marwick, 2008). More recently, the rapid rise of social media sites such as TikTok and Omegle have once again focused collective attention on the spectre of the online predator, with TikTok and Omegle variously referred to as havens or 'hunting grounds' for predators. An Australian documentary hosted by popular Australian television personality Todd Sampson titled *Mirror Mirror* in 2022 drew particular attention to Omegle as a platform used by predatory men with immoral motives.

The uptake of smartphones and other portable devices in the late 2000s elicited a new range of anxieties and risk narratives in relation to children and technology and online predators. In Australia, the media seized on the tragic murder of a 15-year-old girl, Carly Ryan, in 2006 by a 50-year-old paedophile posing as a teenage boy online. This incident led to the introduction of Carly's Law in 2016, which grants authorities new powers to act against would-be predators who lie about their age online (Yaxley, 2017). Panic re-emerged in early 2017 fuelling fears with multiple news reports about paedophiles posing as Justin Bieber online, grooming - and in some cases abusing - young girls (ABC News, 2017). Parents and teenagers alike were warned that images parents post of their kids on Facebook could end up in the hands of paedophiles (Lattouf, 2016; Richards, 2015), and that 'brazen perverts are using your seemingly innocuous family photos to pool their resources and identify where you live and who you are' (Scarr, 2017). While the risk of online grooming is no longer the primary focus of cyber safety resources, it nonetheless remains a perennial risk reported by the mass media and other popular discourse. As is characteristic of media panics, the anxiety about the issue of online predators is not commensurate with the rate such incidents are said to occur. Children are still most at risk of abuse by people directly known to them (YWCA, 2023).

Cyberbullying

The dark side of the networked and mediated sociality that has been part of the attraction of older community-of-interest-based online forums and newer social media platforms is described as 'cyberbullying' in much of the existing literature. While some scholars have noted the ambiguity of the term and what it encompasses (boyd, 2014; Görzig & Frumkin, 2013; Livingstone et al., 2016), the Office of the eSafety Commissioner adopts a broad definition, stating that 'cyberbullying is when someone uses the internet to be mean to a child or young person so that they feel bad or upset.' (eSafety Commissioner, 2024). Kowalski et al. (2012) define cyberbullying as aggression that is intentionally and repeatedly carried out in an electronic context.

Cyberbullying has been the subject of a sustained panic since the early days of the internet. Earlier reports indicated that the issue had 'exploded on to schools' radar', having reached a critical point where it was said to be 'a bigger issue than doing drugs' (Gleeson & Fife-Yeomans, 2016). Media momentum in relation to this issue appears to have been sustained by tragic suicides that were reported to be bullying related.[8] In early 2023 Julie Inman Grant, the eSafety Commissioner, reported a 'post-pandemic surge' in online bullying complaints which were said to have reached 'concerning' levels (Butler, 2023). The perceived severity and scale of the cyberbullying risk is demonstrated in part by the enactment of federal legislation to address the issue. The *Enhancing Online Safety Act 2015*, and the strengthening of these powers in 2021, grant the eSafety Commissioner a wide range of functions and powers to investigate cyberbullying complaints and enhance online safety for Australian children (eSafety Commissioner, n.d.).

A number of non-government, not-for-profit, and charity organisations have either been established to address cyberbullying, or are turning their focus to the issue.[9] In 2015, Apple released a new emoji to call out cyberbullying (ABC, 2015). Like with other panics, however, the dangers or cyberbullying may be overblown and young people themselves often distance themselves from claims about cyberbullying, preferring instead to refer to negative peer online interactions as 'drama' (Marwick & boyd, 2014). Further, several studies show that that bullying, as a form of peer-related aggression, showed higher incidences offline than online (Campbell, 2005; Livingstone et al., 2016) and incidences of bullying were once reported to be in decline (Finkelhor, 2014). Scholars have argued that cyberbullying should not be considered a separate entity brought about entirely as a result of digital media, but instead should be considered within the broader context of bullying more generally, an issue which has been affecting children for generations (Livingstone et al., 2016)

Screen time, social media and mental health

Where some panics about distinct risk issues have, for the time being at least, lost some of their momentum, collective anxieties about content, conduct and contact such as those identified above frequently coalesce around the overarching issues of screen time and social media use. In an extraordinary move that was reported globally, in May 2023 the US Surgeon General Dr Vivek Murthy issued an advisory warning that social media use by children and teenagers can pose a 'profound risk of harm' to their mental health and wellbeing. Advisories 'are reserved for significant public health challenges that require the nation's immediate awareness and action' (US Surgeon General, 2023). The advisory, while noting some of the benefits of social media, went on to list a litany of potential harms including double the risk of depression and anxiety symptoms with use that exceeds three hours per day; and notes the *correlation*[10] between social media use and harm in adolescent girls in particular, due to, among other things, poor body image, disordered eating, social comparison, low self-esteem, and higher depressive symptom scores (US Surgeon General, 2023: 8). It should be noted at this point that concerns about the effects of unrealistic and unachievable depictions of women's bodies in the media are hardly new, and that if anything social media have spurned numerous body positivity accounts and facilitated exposure to a more diverse range of bodies.

Murthy's advisory is demonstrative of the tendency to conflate the issues of screen time and social media. Adolescents are widely cited as enthusiastic social media users, spending increasing time on a range of platforms including TikTok and Instagram which – as popular discourse goes – not only exposes them to potentially harmful content, contact and conduct, but may also disrupt sleep, lead to compulsive online behaviours or addiction, cause ADHD, and lead to feelings of exclusion (US Surgeon General, 2023, pp. 9–10). Building on the Surgeon General's Advisory, the Biden Administration announced the formation of an interagency Task Force on Kids Online Health and Safety 'to advance the health, safety and privacy of minors online with particular attention to preventing and mitigating the adverse health effects of online platforms on minors' (The White House, 2023). In 2023, the Chinese Government imposed time restrictions on under 18s' use of smartphones (Makortoff, 2023). At the time of writing in mid-2024, proposals to ban or limit access to social media to children have been debated and trialled in the EU, and discussions to ban social media for children under 16 have gained bipartisan support in Australia (for more about this, see Chapter 2).

Media narratives frequently highlight the purported negative effects of excessive screen time, with coverage veering at times towards panic. In a particularly bizarre manifestation of this concern, in 2019 headlines in leading publications such as the Washington Post and NBC News claimed that excessive smartphone use was causing young people to grow horns in their skulls (Charles, 2019; Stanley-Becker, 2019), a claim that was subsequently debunked. A quick media search using the Factiva News database revealed a range of Australian stories with familiar headlines, including 'Excessive screen time hurts' (The Hobart Mercury, 22 August 2023), 'Screen-time problems' (Herald Sun 22 August), both of which link screen time and developmental delay; and 'Tik Tok brain kids' attention down the Tube' (Julie Jargon, The Australian 15 August) claiming that short videos on TikTok lead to 'tiktok brain' (a term invented by the journalist), 'hurt kids' attention spans and makes it harder for them to participate in activities that don't offer instant gratification'.

The current panic

At the time of writing (July 2024), Australia was in the midst of another media panic focusing on the potential harms of social media for young people leading to a proposed ban on the 'scourge' of social media for young people under 16 and receiving bipartisan support (Manfield, 2024; Middleton, 2024). Calls for the ban by both the Prime Minister Anthony Albanese and opposition leader Peter Dutton were precipitated by an announcement by South Australian Premier Peter Malinauskas that he would engage a former Chief Justice to investigate legal avenues for imposing a ban on social media for children, a move which was subsequently 'applauded' by the Prime Minister (SBS News, 2024), who stated that he wants "people to spend more time on the footy field or the netball court than they're spending on their phones" (Middleton, 2024). In June opposition leader Peter

Dutton announced that he would ban people under 16 from accessing social media in the first 100 days of a coalition government. He stated

> we wouldn't in the real world allow our kids to go into a park or into a shopping centre just to hang out with any adult that came by, would read anything put in front of them, without us knowing what it was

invoking concerns that were most common in the early days of the internet – that is, pornography and predators.

But we are no longer in the earlier days of the internet, and young people's use of networked technologies and social media is complex, dynamic, and varies tremendously. While online predators remain a legitimate concern, blanket claims about the evils of online pornography and the damaging mental health effects of social media on young people proliferate despite an absence of compelling evidence. Indeed, contrasting evidence exists which demonstrates the various benefits that young people derive from social media. A brief database search of the media coverage about the social media ban in June 2024 highlights a notable absence of evidence of the purported harms of social media to justify such a ban, with politicians and several other advocates for the ban taking social media harms as well established and axiomatic. Vague claims on both sides referred to the 'negative impact on young people's mental health and on anxiety', and there being "no doubt" that social media was damaging Australian children" (Armstrong, 2024b) and the importance of 'protecting kids'. Social media appears to have become a lightning rod for everything that is allegedly wrong with young people today.

The demonising of 'social media' as an implicitly distinct entity is also problematic for several reasons. First, many of the alleged harms of social media, such as potentially harmful content and algorithms and recommender systems function across the internet more broadly, not just social media. Still, opposition leader Peter Dutton himself said 'nobody's saying ban the internet or any of that sort of nonsense' (Armstrong, 2024a). Further, what exactly is meant by 'social media' in these debates is similarly vague, with moral entrepreneurs using the term as an apparent proxy for young people's online practices more generally. As researchers from QUT's Digital Media Research Centre rightfully pointed out in their submission to the Joint Parliamentary Inquiry into Social Media and Australian Society, it is 'not clear' what the term social media encompasses in these debates:

> Is the Committee concerned about a select few apps and vendors, or all forms of digitally mediated social life? To what degree do popular (but perhaps more peripheral) apps such as Bluesky, Linked-In, Slack, Twitch, Zoom and Discord fall under the scope of this inquiry? Popular but non-English apps such as WeChat, VK, Line, KakaoTalk, and Zalo, which are used by Chinese, Russian, Japanese, Thai, Korean and Vietnamese communities? What about the clandestine uses of Gumtree, Telegram and Signal? Online games and the buying and selling of virtual goods via voice chats or in-game markets? Distributed or blockchain-based social networks? Anonymous bulletin-style messaging via 4Chan, Reddit? Online dating? Social betting? Liking or leaving a comment? Having a personal site or blog? AI? Are Australian children to be 'protected' from all of these?

(QUT Digital Media Research Centre, 2024, p. 9)

Parallel movements and petitions calling for a ban on social media also gained momentum. A petition started by News Corp calling for an increase in the age limit for social media access to 16 entitled Let Them Be Kids[11] claimed that "a generation of children is being lost to the billion-dollar social media giants". The petition claims 'skyrocketing' rates of youth suicide, mental health problems, eating disorders, loneliness, sleep deprivation and reduced social skills, all purportedly due to social media. (Although, as Bernard Keane from Crikey noted, News Corp does not, nor has it ever, cared about children, and argues that the cited connection between youth suicide and social media use simply doesn't stack up, Keane, 2024).

The reality is that young people derive many benefits from online networked technologies including social and community connections, (something that is particularly important for Indigenous and marginalised youth), civic engagement and political activism, educational benefits and learning opportunities, and entertainment and pleasure. Banning mainstream social media platforms will likely drive young people to other, more clandestine spaces which have less regulation and oversight. Further, as I argue in Chapter 4 the distinction between risks and benefits is no longer clear, which has important implications for parents. The public discourse about young people's media use, and parents' role in mediating this, is now and has long been reductive, polarised and protectionist, assuming to know what is best for children without accounting for young people's actual experiences, preferences and practices, nor their existing knowledges and skills in managing online risk.

Conclusion: Where are we at now?

The headlines and risk examples identified above present a small snapshot of contemporary debates and collective anxieties about young people's use of digital media. I present them here not to wholly dismiss them – social and digital media do pose some risks to children and also adults. Rather I document them here to illustrate the ways in which perceptions of risk and harm have typically dominated discussions about young people's media use in Australia, and which in turn establish the discursive coordinates for how we talk about, think about, and respond to young people's media use.

There have been shifts over the years in how collectively we perceive and talk about young people and technology. Most recently, there are encouraging signs that there has been a partial shift away – within online safety discourse if not the mass media – from a primary focus on online harm and worst-case scenarios. There still appears, however, to be a long way to go before the risk/harm and deficit model of online safety education is abandoned altogether. This is significant, because there are real, often unintended consequences when the risk and harm paradigm dominates the public narrative in the way that it does in Australia and in other developed nations such as the US and UK. First, it limits children and their parents' ability to fully exploit the benefits and opportunities of digital media technologies (Holmes, 2009). Some studies have shown that children and their parents reproduce public scripts and mainstream narratives about digital technologies, focusing on the adult-centric concerns of online safety initiatives (Third et al., 2017). This is especially the case with high profile risks such as online predators and cyberbullying, where young people distance themselves from their own positive online experiences to reproduce sensationalist media panics (Mascheroni et al., 2014). This not only constrains children's and their parents' perceptions of digital media, thus limiting online opportunities (Third et al., 2017), but also results in parents adopting more restrictive forms of mediation in response to their concerns about online risk (Livingstone & Helsper, 2008). Second, a risk-focused protectionist approach often leads to policy and legislation that curtails young people's participation rights, diminishes their perspectives and undermines their agency, compromising their ability to develop resilience and skills for effectively managing risks (Livingstone et al., 2015; Livingstone & Third, 2017; Vickery, 2017). Such an approach also jeopardises their rights to autonomy and active engagement in the digital world (Simpson, 2020). Current debates about a ban on social media for young people exemplify the ways in which this harm-focused approach may significantly curtail young people's digital rights. Third, as I discuss in Chapter 3, for parents the failure to live up to 'good' parenting expectations in terms of protecting their children often results in them feeling anxious and powerless when restrictive harm reduction strategies are challenged or fail. Parents – who are ultimately responsibilised for protecting their children from harm – typically adopt more restrictive approaches to parental mediation in response to discourses of risk and what 'good parenting' looks like within this context. While reducing online risk, this approach also reduces online opportunity (Duerager & Livingstone, 2012; Haddon, 2020), and increases family conflict. Further, when the dominant discourse is one of risk and panic, society prefers to criticise parents for their digital practices rather than enable or support them (Livingstone & Blum-Ross, 2020).

Panics and collective concern, particularly concerning young people, historically bring about some kind of remedial response to address the problem, or to 'restore equilibrium'. The discussion about social media bans is one – quite extreme – example. Australia has a history of interventions, including educational programs, policy and legislative initiatives aimed at addressing the 'problem' of young people's use of media technologies. These will be explored in the next chapter.

Notes

1 The tragic suicide of 14 year-old girl Amy 'Dolly' Everett in January 2018 allegedly as a result of cyberbullying is one example of a tragic event that served to resuscitate anxieties about cyberbullying. See, for example, Roe (2018).
2 Media commentary about the popular online game warned of the game's 'obsessive' and 'addictive' tendencies said to be 'sending kids to rehab' (Barbour, 2018; Swan, 2018), and warns of its potential for bullying or abuse (Zhou, 2018).
3 See for example (Magennis, 2022).
4 For example, the Australian Department of Health screen time guidelines, as well as a number of state and territory guidelines, frame the screen time issue with reference to sedentary behaviours and inactivity and the potential effects on childhood weight and obesity, rather than in relation to exposure to content. See for example, the South Australian screen time guidelines privilege active play over screen time http://www.sahealth.sa.gov.au/wps/wcm/connect/bf5f3e0045d0b6eda24fae9f9859b7b1/OPALscreenfactsheet-sss-20110217.pdf?MOD=AJPERES&CACHEID=bf5f3e0045d0b6eda24fae9f9859b7b1; The federal Department of Health factsheets also focus on the association between sedentary behaviours, inactivity and screen time https://www.health.gov.au/topics/physical-activity-and-exercise/physical-activity-and-exercise-guidelines-for-all-australians/for-children-and-young-people-5-to-17-years; the West Australian Government focuses on the association between screen time and sedentary behaviour http://healthywa.wa.gov.au/Articles/S_T/Screen-time.
5 It's worth noting however, that concerns about excessive screen time leading to inactivity and possible obesity in relation to television are not new. In Australia, the 'Life. Be in it' campaign of

the late 1970s urged people to engage in more physical activity, and less sedentary behaviours. More recently the locus of these concerns has shifted away from adults and more towards children in response to widespread concern about increasing childhood obesity.

6 Indeed, some studies even show an association between positive mental health outcomes and screen-based media. (Grieve & Watkinson, 2016; Utz, 2015).

7 There were parallel warnings in the US, with former district attorney George Skumanick arguing in 2009 that criminal charges for sexting are necessary because 'sexting provides the gateway for child predators to our children (Donohue & Hailstone, 2009, p. 11 cited in Hasinoff). A former prosecutor made a similar argument for punishing consensual sexters, stating that "adults in the real child pornography business will hunt you down and take advantage if they find these pictures, and they will' (Donohue & Hailstone 2009, cited in Hasinoff, 2013).

8 See for example the tragic case of Dolly Everett (ABC News Breakfast, 2019; Roe, 2018).

9 See, for example. Bully Zero http://bzaf.org.au/about-us, and the Alannah and Madeline Foundation https://www.amf.org.au/who-we-are/about-us/.

10 I responded with a critique which can be found here https://theconversation.com/is-13-too-young-to-have-a-tiktok-or-instagram-account-199097.

11 The 'let them be kids' refrain is a familiar one, variations of which have been used for decades to promote outrage about children and young people behaving in ways which are seen to transgress acceptable norms. See, for example, concerns in the early 2000s about the alleged sexualisation of children. For more information, see Page Jeffery, 2017).

References

ABC. (2015). #IAmAWitness: Apple releases new emoji in partnership with anti-bullying campaign. *ABC News*, 23 October.

ABC News. (2017, 9 March). Justin Bieber impersonator charged with over 900 child sex offences. Retrieved from https://www.abc.net.au/news/2017-03-09/justin-bieber-queensland-man-impersonate-singer-child-sex-charge/8338730

ABC News Breakfast. (2019, 19 September). Dolly Everett's suicide leads teen to create 'powerful and relevant' cyberbullying ad. *ABC News*. Retrieved from https://www.abc.net.au/news/2019-09-19/teen-suicide-of-dolly-everett-sparks-new-ad-on-cyberbullying/11523028

Albury, K. (2015). Selfies, sexts and sneaky hats: Young people's understandings of the gendered practices of self-representation. *International Journal of Communication*, 9, 1734–1745.

Altheide, D. L. (2002). Children and the discourse of fear. *Symbolic Interaction*, 25(2), 229–250.

Armstrong, C. (2024a). Dutton backs raising the age. *Cairns Post*. Retrieved from https://www.cairnspost.com.au/subscribe/news/1/?sourceCode=CPWEB_WRE170_a_GGL&dest=https%3A%2F%2Fwww.cairnspost.com.au%2Fnews%2Fnsw%2Fdutton-backs-raising-social-media-age-to-16%2Fvideo%2F7ce9aeaf8fae968e7a36fc43a6f12ff1&memtype=anonymous&mode=premium#

Armstrong, C. (2024b). We'll enforce online ban. *The Advertiser*.

Barbour, M. (2018). Girl, 9, in rehab for Fortnite addiction after becoming so hooked she WET HERSELF to keep playing; Her horrified parents told how the primary school child is in intensive therapy after getting hooked on the apocalyptic game. *Irish Mirror*. Retrieved from Lexis Uni. https://www.mirror.co.uk/news/uk-news/girl-9-rehab-after-becoming-12673590

Blum-Ross, A., & Livingstone, S. (2016). *Families and screen time: Current advice and emerging research*. Retrieved from http://eprints.lse.ac.uk/66927/1/Policy%20Brief%2017-%20Families%20%20Screen%20Time.pdf

boyd, d. (2014). *It's complicated: The social lives of networked teens*. London, New York: Yale University Press.

boyd, d., & Hargittai, E. (2013). Connected and concerned: Variation in parents' online safety concerns. *Policy & Internet*, 5(3), 245–269.

Bruns, A. (2009). From prosumer to produser: Understanding user-led content creation. Paper presented at the *Transforming Audiences Conference 2009*, 3–4 September, London.

Buckingham, D. (2008). Children and media: A cultural studies approach. In K. Drotner, & S. Livingstone (Eds.), *The international handbook of children, media and culture* (pp. 219–236). London: SAGE Publications Ltd. doi:10.4135/9781848608436

Buckingham, D., & Strandgaard Jensen, H. (2012). Beyond "media panics": Reconceptualising public debates about children and media. *Journal of Children and Media*, 6(4), 413–429.

Bushman, B. J., & Huesmann, L. R. (2001). Effects of televised violence on aggression. In D. G. Singer & J. L. Singer (Eds.), *Handbook of children and the media* (pp. 223–254). Thousand Oaks, California: Sage.

Butler, J. (2023, 23 January). Child cyberbullying at 'concerning levels', Australia's eSafety commissioner says Retrieved from https://www.theguardian.com/australia-news/2023/jan/23/child-cyberbullying-at-concerning-levels-australias-esafety-commissioner-says

Byron, P., McKee, A., Watson, A., Litsou, K., & Ingham, R. (2021). Reading for realness: Porn literacies, digital media, and young people. *Sexuality & Culture*, 25, 786–805.

Campbell, M. A. (2005). Cyber bullying: An old problem in a new guise? *Journal of Psychologists and Counsellors in Schools*, 15(1), 68–76.

Cantor, J. (2001). The media and children's fears, anxieties, and perceptions of danger. In D. G. Singer & J. L. Singer (Eds.), *Handbook of children and the media* (pp. 207–221). Thousand Oaks, California: Sage.

Carr, N. (2010). *The shallows: How the internet is changing the way we think, read and remember*. New York: Atlantic Books Ltd.

Cassell, J., & Cramer, M. (2008). High tech or high risk: Moral panics about girls online. In Tara McPherson (Ed.), *Digital youth, innovation, and the unexpected*. The John D. and Catherine T. MacArthur Foundation Series on Digital Media and Learning (pp. 53–76). Cambridge, MA: The MIT Press.

Cavanagh, A. (2007). Taxonomies of anxiety: Risks, panics, paedophilia and the Internet. *Electronic Journal of Sociology, 1198*, 3655.

Charles, S. (2019, 21 June). Tech disorder? Smartphones linked to bizarre horn-like skull bumbps. *NBC News*. Retrieved from https://www.nbcnews.com/health/health-news/tech-disorder-smartphones-linked-bizarre-horn-skull-bumps-n1019736

Clark, L. S. (2013). *The parent app: Understanding families in the digital age*. New York: Oxford University Press.

Cohen, S. (2002). *Folk devils and moral panics: The creation of the mods and rockers* (3rd ed.). New York: Routledge.

Coulter, N. (2020). Child studies meets digital media: Rethinking the paradigms. In *The Routledge companion to digital media and children* (pp. 19–27). New York and London: Routledge.

Critcher, C. (2002). Media, government and moral panic: The politics of paedophilia in Britain 2000-1. *Journalism Studies*. 3(4) 521–535.

Critcher, C. (2008). Moral panic analysis: Past, present and future. *Sociology Compass*. 2(4) 1127–1144.

Dietz, W. H., & Gortmaker, S. L. (1985). Do we fatten our children at the television set? Obesity and television viewing in children and adolescents. *Pediatrics*, 75(5), 807–812.

Donnerstein, E., & Smith, S. (2001). Sex in the media: Theory, influences, and solutions. In D. G. Singer & J. L. Singer (Eds.), *Handbook of children and the media* (pp. 289–307). Thousand Oaks, California: Sage.

Donohue, M. J., & Hailstone, E. A. J. (2009). Reply brief of appellant, George Skumanick, JR. *Miller et al. v. Skumanick: Legal Documents*.

Drotner, K. (1992a). Modernity and media panics. In M. Skovmand & K. C. Schroder (Eds.), *Media cultures reappraising transnational media*. London: Routledge.

Drotner, K. (1992b). Modernity and media panics. In M. Skovman & K. C. Schroder (Eds.), *Media cultures reappraising transnational media* (pp. 42–62). New York, London: Routledge.

Drotner, K. (1999). Dangerous media? Panic discourses and dilemmas of modernity. *Paedagogica Historica*, 35(3), 593–619.

Drotner, K., & Livingstone, S. (2008). Editors' Introduction. In K. Drotner & S. Livingstone (Eds.), *International handbook of children, media and culture*. London: Sage.

Duerager, A., & Livingstone, S. (2012). How can parents support children's internet safety? EU Kids Online. *LSE Research Online*. Retrieved from http://eprints.lse.ac.uk/42872/1/How%20can%20parents%20support%20children%E2%80%99s%20internet%20safety%28lsero%29.pdf

Egan, R., & Hawkes, G. (2010). *Theorizing the sexual child in modernity*. New York: Palgrave Macmillan.

eSafety Commissioner. (2021, February). Retrieved from https://www.esafety.gov.au/sites/default/files/2021-02/The%20digital%20lives%20of%20Aussie%20teens.pdf

eSafety Commissioner. (2023). *Accidental, unsolicited and in your face. Young people's encounters with online pornography: A matter of platform responsibility, education and choice.* Retrieved from Canberra: Australian Government.

eSafety Commissioner. (2024, 23 May). Cyberbullying. Retrieved from https://www.esafety.gov.au/key-topics/cyberbullying#what-is-cyberbullying

eSafety Commissioner. (n.d.). Our legislative functions. Retrieved from https://www.esafety.gov.au/about-us/who-we-are/our-legislative-functions

Faircloth, C., & Murray, M. (2015). Parenting: Kinship, expertise, and anxiety. *Journal of Family Issues, 36*(9), 1115–1129.

Ferguson, C. J. (2017). Everything in moderation: Moderate use of screens unassociated with child behavior problems. *Psychiatric Quarterly.* doi:10.1007/s11126-016-9486-3

Ferguson, C. J., Kaye, L. K., Branley-Bell, D., Markey, P., Ivory, J. D., Klisanin, D., … McDonnell, D. (2022). Like this meta-analysis: Screen media and mental health. *Professional Psychology: Research and Practice, 53*(2), 205.

Finkelhor, D. (2014). *Trends in bullying and peer victimization.* Durham, NH: Crimes against Children Research Center. Updated August, 2014.

Furedi, F. (2002). *Paranoid parenting: Why ignoring the experts mahaidty be best for your child.* Chicago: Chicago Review Press.

Garland, D. (2008). On the concept of moral panic. *Crime, Media, Culture, 4*(1), 9–30.

Gleeson, J., & Fife-Yeomans, A. (2016). Cyber-bully crisis. *The Daily Telegraph.* 9 November.

Goggin, G. (2009). Assembling media culture: The case of mobiles. *Journal of Cultural Economy, 2*(1–2), 151–167.

Goggin, G., & Crawford, K. (2011). Generation disconnections: Youth culture and mobile communication. In R. Ling & S. W. Camp (Eds.), *Mobile communication: Bringing us together or tearing us apart* (pp. 249–270). New Brunswick (USA) and London (UK): Transaction Publishers.

Gold, J. (2014). *Screen-Smart parenting: How to find balance and benefit in your child's use of social media, apps, and digital devices.* New York: Guilford Publications.

Gore, T. (1987). *Raising PG kids in an X-rated society.* Nashville: Abingdon Press.

Gortmaker, S. L., Must, A., Sobol, A. M., Peterson, K., Colditz, G. A., & Dietz, W. H. (1996). Television viewing as a cause of increasing obesity among children in the United States, 1986–1990. *Archives of pediatrics & adolescent medicine, 150*(4), 356–362.

Görzig, A., & Frumkin, L. A. (2013). Cyberbullying experiences on-the-go: When social media can become distressing. *Cyberpsychology, 7*(1), 4.

Greenfield, S. (2009). *ID: The quest for meaning in the 21st century.* Great Britain: Sceptre.

Greenfield, S. (2015). *Mind change: How digital technologies are leaving their mark on our brains.* London: Rider – Trade.

Grieve, R., & Watkinson, J. (2016). The psychological benefits of being authentic on Facebook. *Cyberpsychology, Behavior, and Social Networking, 19*(7), 420–425. doi:10.1089/cyber.2016.0010

Groebel, J. (2001). Media violence in cross-cultural perspective: A global study on children's media behavior and some educational implications. In D. G. Singer & J. L. Singer (Eds.), *Handbook of children and the media* (pp. 255–268). Thousand Oaks, California: Sage.

Grossberg, L. (1992). *We gotta get out of this place.* Great Britain: Routledge.

Haddon, L. (2020). The domestication of touchscreen technologies in families with young children. In L. Green, D. Holloway, K. Stevenson, T. Leaver, & L. Haddon (Eds.), *The Routledge companion to digital media and children* (pp. 87–95). New York and London: Routledge.

Haidt, J. (2024). *The anxious generation: How the great rewiring of childhood is causing an epidemic of mental illness.* New York: Penguin Random House.

Hall, S., Critcher, C., Jefferson, T., Clarke, J., & Roberts, B. (2013). *Policing the crisis: Mugging, the state and law and order.* England, UK: Palgrave Macmillan.

Hasinoff, A. A. (2013). Sexting as media production: Rethinking social media and sexuality. *New Media & Society, 15*(4), 449–465. doi:10.1177/1461444812459171

Healy, J. (1991). *Endangered minds: Why children don't think and what we can do about it.* New York: Simon and Schuster.

Heitner, D. (2016). *Screenwise: Helping kids thrive (and survive) in their digital world.* Brookline, United States: Taylor & Francis Inc.

Himmelweit, H., Oppenheim, A., & Vince, P. (1958). *Television and the child; an empirical study of the effect of television on the young.* London: Oxford University Press.

Holmes, J. (2009). Myths and missed opportunities: Young people's not so risky use of online communication. *Information, Communication & Society, 12*(8), 1174–1196.

Horgan, K., Choate, M., & Brownell, K. D. (2001). Television food advertising. In D. G. Singer & J. L. Singer (Eds.), *Handbook of children and media* (pp. 447–461). Thousand Oaks, California: Sage.

Horkheimer, M., Adorno, T. W., & Noeri, G. (2002). *Dialectic of enlightenment.* Stanford: Stanford University Press.

Ito, M. (2008). Mobilizing the imagination in everyday play: The case of Japanese media mixes. In S. Livingstone & K. Drotner (Eds.), *International handbook of children, media and culture* (pp. 397–412). Los Angeles: Sage.

Jackson, M. (2008). *Distracted: The erosion of attention and the coming of the dark age.* New York: Amherst.

Janis-Norton, N. (2017). *Calmer easier happier screen time.* London, United Kingdom: Hodder & Stoughton General Division.

Jenkins, H. (2006). *Convergence culture: Where old and new media collide.* New York and London: NYU Press.

Jenkins, H., & Deuze, M. (2008). Convergence Culture. *Convergence, 14*(1).

Kamenetz, A. (2018). *The art of screen time: How your family can balance digital media and real life.* New York: Ingram Publisher Services US.

Keane, B. (2024). News Corp's 'Let them Be Kids' campaign is a mix of stupidity and hypocrisy. Retrieved from https://www.crikey.com.au/2024/05/21/news-corp-let-them-be-kids-social-media-age-verification/

Kehily, M. J. (2010). Childhood in crisis? Tracing the contours of 'crisis' and its impact upon contemporary parenting practices. *Media, Culture & Society, 32*(2), 171–185.

Kowalski, R. M., Limber, S. P., Limber, S., & Agatston, P. W. (2012). *Cyberbullying: Bullying in the digital age.* West Sussex: John Wiley & Sons.

Kunkel, D. (2001). Children and television advertising. In D. G. Singer & J. L. Singer (Eds.), *Handbook of children and the media* (pp. 375–393). Thousand Oaks, California: Sage.

Lattouf, A. (2016). Dancewear company Frilled Neck Fashion accused of sexualising pre-teen models. *ABC News*, 18 July.

Lavoipierre, A. (2017, 7 November). Sexting: Not as rife as you think! *ABC: The World Today.* Retrieved from https://www.abc.net.au/radio/programs/worldtoday/sexting-not-as-rife-as-you-think/9125976

Lee, E., Faircloth, C., Macvarish, J., & Bristow, J. (2014). *Parenting culture studies.* Basingstoke and New York: Palgrave Macmillan.

Lee, M., Ravulo, J., & Martin, T. (2023, 10 May). No, music doesn't cause crime – not even 'drill rap'. *The Conversation.* Retrieved from https://theconversation.com/no-music-doesnt-cause-crime-not-even-drill-rap-203912

Livingstone, S. (1996). On the continuing problems of media effects research. In J. Curran & M. Gurevitch (Eds.), *Mass media and society* (2nd ed.). London: Edward Arnold.

Livingstone, S. (1998). Mediated childhoods: A comparative approach to young people's changing media environment in Europe. *European Journal of Communication, 13*(4), 435–456.

Livingstone, S., & Blum-Ross, A. (2020). *Parenting for a digital future: How hopes and fears about technology shape children's lives.* USA: Oxford University Press.

Livingstone, S., & Das, R. (2010). POLIS media and family report. POLIS, London School of Economics and Political Science, London, UK.

Livingstone, S., & Helsper, E. J. (2008). Parental mediation of children's internet use. *Journal of Broadcasting & Electronic Media, 52*(4), 581–599.

Livingstone, S., Mascheroni, G., & Staksrud, E. (2015). *Developing a framework for researching children's online risks and opportunities in Europe.* EU Kids Online. https://eprints.lse.ac.uk/64470/1/__lse.ac.uk_storage_LIBRARY_Secondary_libfile_shared_repository_Content_EU%20Kids%20Online_EU%20Kids%20Online_Developing%20framework%20for%20researching_2015.pdf

Livingstone, S., Stoilova, M., & Kelly, A. (2016). Cyberbullying: Incidence, trends and consequences. *LSE Research Online*. Retrieved from http://eprints.lse.ac.uk/68079/

Livingstone, S., & Third, A. (2017). *Children and young people's rights in the digital age: An emerging agenda*. UK: London, England: Sage Publications Sage.

Lumby, C., & Fine, D. (2006). *Why TV is good for kids: Raising 21st century children*. Australia: Pan Macmillan.

Magennis, M. (2022, 15 December). The 'deeply disturbing' TikTok videos Aussie teens are shown every 39 seconds. Retrieved from https://7news.com.au/technology/tiktok/the-deeply-disturbing-tiktok-videos-aussie-teens-see-every-39-seconds--c-9171686

Makortoff, K. (2023). Chinese plans to limit smartphone use for children hit tech shares. *The Guardian*. Retrieved from https://www.theguardian.com/business/2023/aug/03/chinese-plans-to-limit-smartphone-use-for-children-hit-tech-shares

Malamuth, N., & Impett, E. A. (2001). Research on sex in the media. In D. G. Singer & J. L. Singer (Eds.), *Handbook of children and the media* (pp. 269–287). Thousand Oaks, California: Sage.

Manfield, E. (2024). Social media age limits might be popular with politicians and parents, but experts warn they aren't simple. *ABC News*. Retrieved from https://www.abc.net.au/news/2024-06-14/social-media-age-limits-experts-warn-they-aren-t-simple/103975740

Marin, S., & Rutledge, D. (2024). Degrading behaviour towards women is part of 'mainstream' pornography. What are the risks of this? *ABC News Online*. Retrieved from https://www.abc.net.au/news/2024-05-25/degrading-behaviour-women-pornography-risks-australian-teenagers/103827668

Marsh, I., & Melville, G. (2011). Moral panics and the British media–a look at some contemporary 'folk devils'. *Internet Journal of Criminology*, *1*(1), 1–21.

Marvin, C. (1988). *When old technologies were new*. Oxford: Oxford University Press.

Marwick, A., & boyd, d. (2014). 'It's just drama': Teen perspectives on conflict and aggression in a networked era. *Journal of Youth Studies*, *17*(9), 1187–1204.

Marwick, A. E. (2008). To catch a predator? The MySpace moral panic. *First Monday*, *13*(6). doi:10.5210/fm.v13i6.2152

Mascheroni, G., Jorge, A., & Farrugia, L. (2014). Media representations and children's discourses on online risks: Findings from qualitative research in nine European countries. *Cyberpsychology: Journal of Psychosocial Research on Cyberspace*, *8*(2), 2.

McKee, A., Litsou, K., Byron, P., & Ingham, R. (2022). *What Do We Know about the Effects of Pornography After Fifty Years of Academic Research?* Abingdon and New York: Taylor & Francis.

Middleton, K. (2024). Albanese follows Durtton's lead with toucher position on children's social media ban. *The Guardian*. Retrieved from https://www.theguardian.com/media/article/2024/jun/13/anthony-albanese-peter-dutton-social-media-ban-age-16

Mosley, I. (2000). *Dumbing down: Culture, politics and the mass media*. Thorverton UK: Imprint Academic.

Nelson, M. K. (2010). *Parenting out of control: Anxious parents in uncertain times*. New York and London: NYU Press.

O'Connell, R. (2010). Police warn of sexting danger. *The West Australian*. 8 February.

Odgers, C. (2024). Book review: The great rewiring: Is social media really behind an epidemic of teenage mental illness? *Nature*. Retrieved from https://www.nature.com/articles/d41586-024-00902-2?ref=platformer.news

Olds, T., Ridley, K., & Dollman, J. (2006). Screenieboppers and extreme screenies: The place of screen time in the time budgets of 10–13 year-old Australian children. *Australian and New Zealand Journal of Public Health*, *30*(2), 137–142.

Page Jeffery, C. (2017). Too sexy too soon, or just another moral panic? Sexualisation, children, and 'technopanics' in the Australian Media 2004–2015. *Feminist Media Studies*. doi:10.1080/14680777.2017.1367699

Paik, H. (2001). The history of children's use of electronic media. In D. G. Singer & J. L. Singer (Eds.), *Handbook of children and the media* (pp. 7–27). Thousand Oaks, California: Sage.

Pew Research Centre. (2022, 10 August). *Teens, Social Media and Technology 2022*. Retrieved from https://www.pewresearch.org/internet/2022/08/10/teens-social-media-and-technology-2022/

Ponte, C., & Simões, J. A. (2009). Asking parents about children's internet use: Comparing findings about parental mediation in Portugal and other European countries. *Paper presented at the EU Kids Online-Final Conference*. London.

Postman, N. (1985). *Amusing ourselves to death: Public discourse in the age of show business*. United States: Viking Penguin.

Potter, R. H., & Potter, L. A. (2001). The internet, cyberporn, and sexual exploitation of children: Media moral panics and urban myths for middle-class parents? *Sexuality and Culture, 5*(3), 31–48.

QUT Digital Media Research Centre. (2024). *QUT DMRC Submission to the Joint Select Committee on Social Media and Australian Society*. Retrieved from https://www.aph.gov.au/Parliamentary_Business/Committees/Joint/Social_Media/SocialMedia/Submissions

Richards, V. (2015). Paedophile websites steal half their photos from social media sites like Facebook. *The Independent*. 30 September.

Ringrose, J., & Harvey, L. (2015). Boobs, back-off, six packs and bits: Mediated body parts, gendered reward, and sexual shame in teens' sexting images. *Continuum, 29*(2), 205–217.

Roberts, G. (2024). Nearly $1bn funding announced to support victim-survivors leaving violence, combat online misogyny and AI porn. *ABC News Online*. Retrieved from https://www.abc.net.au/news/2024-05-01/national-cabinet-meets-to-address-violence-against-women/103789304

Robinson, T. N. (2001). Television viewing and childhood obesity. *Pediatric Clinics of North America, 48*(4), 1017–1025.

Roe, I. (2018). Dolly Everett: 'Heartbroken' Malcolm Turnbull joins bullying debate in wake of 14-year-old-girl's suicide. *ABC Premium News (Australia)*. Retrieved from Nexis Uni. https://www.abc.net.au/news/2018-01-11/online-bullying-suicide-sparks-national-discussion/9321226

Rooney, G. (2011). Women and children first: Technology and Moral Panic. Interview by Ben Rooney, ed., *Wall Street Journal*. 11 July. https://www.wsj.com/articles/BL-TEB-2814

Salmon, J., Campbell, K. J., & Crawford, D. A. (2006). Television viewing habits associated with obesity risk factors: A survey of Melbourne schoolchildren. *The Medical Journal of Australia, 184*(2), 64–67.

SBS News. (2024). Prime Minister 'applauds' South Australian move to ban children from social media. Retrieved from https://www.sbs.com.au/news/article/prime-minister-applauds-south-australian-move-to-ban-children-from-social-media/5jlubxyaa

Scarr, L. (2017). Perverts' playground – Special investigation. *The Daily Telegraph*. 25 February.

Schiffer, Z. (2024). Inside the debate over The Anxious Generation. *Platformer*. Retrieved from https://www.platformer.news/anxious-generation-jonathan-haidt-debate-critique/

Shepherd, T. (2023, 2 July). Online roulette: The popular chat sites that are drawing in children and horrifying parents. *The Guardian*. https://www.theguardian.com/australia-news/2023/jul/02/online-roulette-children-cybersafety-omegle-roblox-video-chat-popular-websites

Simpson, B. (2020). Law, digital media, and the discomfort of children's rights. In L. Green, D. Holloway, K. Stevenson, T. Leaver, & L. Haddon (Eds.), *The Routledge companion to digital media and children* (pp. 308–317). New York and London: Routledge.

Singer, D. G., & Singer, J. L. (2012). *Handbook of children and the media*. Thousand Oaks, California: Sage.

Springhall, J. (1998). Censoring Hollywood: Youth, moral panic and crime/gangster movies of the 1930s. *The Journal of Popular Culture, 32*(3), 135–154.

Stanley-Becker, I. (2019, 25 June). 'Horns' are growing on young people's skulls. Phone use is to blame, research suggests. *The Washington Post*. Retrieved from https://www.washingtonpost.com/nation/2019/06/20/horns-are-growing-young-peoples-skulls-phone-use-is-blame-research-suggests/

Swan, D. (2018). Hooked, online and sinking deep into Fortnite. *The Australian*, (30 June). Retrieved from Nexis Uni. https://www.theaustralian.com.au/business/technology/kids-hooked-online-and-sinking-deep-into-fortnite/news-story/8e9f5d6640503bf68364082553e7b970

The White House. (2023). *Fact Sheet: Biden-Harris administration announces actions to protect youth mental health, safety and privacy online*. 23 May. https://www.whitehouse.gov/briefing-room/statements-releases/2023/05/23/fact-sheet-biden-harris-administration-announces-actions-to-protect-youth-mental-health-safety-privacy-online/

Third, A., Bellerose, D., De Oliveira, J. D., Lala, G., & Theakstone, G. (2017). Young and online: Children's perspectives on life in the digital age. The State of the World's Children 2017 Companion Report). https://apo.org.au/sites/default/files/resource-files/2017-12/apo-nid139346.pdf

Turkle, S. (2011). *Alone together: Why we expect more from technology and less from each other*. New York: Basic Books.

US Surgeon General. (2023). Social media and youth mental health: The US surgeon general's advisory. Retrieved from https://www.hhs.gov/sites/default/files/sg-youth-mental-health-social-media-advisory.pdf

Utz, S. (2015). The function of self-disclosure on social network sites: Not only intimate, but also positive and entertaining self-disclosures increase the feeling of connection. *Computers in Human Behavior, 45*, 1–10. doi:https://doi.org/10.1016/j.chb.2014.11.076

Valentine, G., & Holloway, S. (2001). On-line dangers?: Geographies of parents' fears for children's safety in cyberspace. *The Professional Geographer, 53*(1), 71–83.

Vickery, J. R. (2017). *Worried about the wrong things: Youth, risk, and opportunity in the digital world*. Cambridge, Massachusetts: The MIT Press.

Walker, S. (2012). *Sexting and young people: A qualitative study*. (Master of Primary Health Care Masters). University of Melbourne, Retrieved from https://minerva-access.unimelb.edu.au/bitstream/handle/11343/37683/287493_SJW%20thesis%207-11-12.pdf?sequence=1

Wartella, E. A., & Jennings, N. (2000). Children and computers: New technology. Old concerns. *The Future of Children, 10*(2), 31–43.

What's Up In Your World Survey. (2018). *ABC Trip J Hack*. Retrieved from https://www.abc.net.au/triplej/programs/hack/whats-up-in-your-world-the-census-for-young-people/10051266

Wright, R. (2000). 'I'd sell you suicide': Pop music and moral panic in the age of Marilyn Manson. *Popular Music, 19*(3), 365–385.

Yaxley, L. (2017, 16 June). Carly's Law: Parliament passes bill to protect minors from online predators. *ABC News*. Retrieved from https://www.abc.net.au/news/2017-06-15/carlys-law-passes-federal-parliament/8621292

YWCA. (2023). Bravehearts: Child sex offenders. Retrieved from https://bravehearts.org.au/research-lobbying/stats-facts/child-sex-offenders/

Zhou, N. (2018). Fortnite: Schools warn parents of 'negative effects' of video game on students; Several Australian schools have issued advice to parents about potential for bullying or abuse. *The Guardian* (20 June). Retrieved from Nexis Uni. https://www.theguardian.com/games/2018/jun/20/fortnite-schools-warn-parents-of-negative-effects-of-video-game-on-students

2

LEGISLATIVE, POLICY AND EDUCATIONAL RESPONSES TO ONLINE RISKS

Media panics typically lead to some kind of corrective response to attempt to diffuse panic and restore equilibrium. In this chapter I chart a short history of online content regulation in Australia, highlighting ways in which regulatory responses have often followed distinct media panics. Australia was the first country to introduce an eSafety Commissioner who is granted a wide range of powers in relation to online regulation and safety. While concerns about young people's use of digital media are hardly unique to Australia, Australian scholars have noted a tradition of adopting a child protection and harm reduction perspective in media discourse, education, and policies related to children and young people (Albury & Crawford, 2012; Mavoa et al., 2017; Page Jeffery, 2021; Third et al., 2019; Zaman et al., 2020). Within this broader regulatory and discursive context, young people have become objects of concern and regulation, whose preferences, perspectives and growing agency have for a long time been largely overlooked.

The Australian response to online risks has been quite comprehensive, however there were regulatory limitations is the early days of internet regulation, and regulatory policy has arguably been one step behind technological innovations. The Office of the eSafety Commissioner was established and tasked with investigating complaints about online content and 'empowering all Australians to have safer, more positive online experiences' (eSafety Commissioner, 2024). The Office has secured tens of millions of dollars in Government funding in recent years. There is also a growing number of providers – both not-for-profit and commercial – offering online safety educational programs and resources. Indeed, some scholars have argued that online safety campaigns within Australia have well and truly surpassed 'saturation point' (Third & Idriss, 2013).

Legislative responses

Internet regulation in Australia precedes the establishment of the Office of the eSafety Commissioner. Initially, internet content regulation in Australia was exercised under the *Broadcasting Services Act (BSA) (1992)* and administered by the Australian Broadcasting Authority (ABA) and its successor, the Australian Communications and Media Authority

DOI: 10.4324/9781003346708-3

(ACMA). Governing legislation has undergone various changes in the last 20 or so years in an attempt to keep pace with technological change. Government responses have included the introduction of legislation in relation to some extreme forms of harmful online content (including types of pornography, child abuse material, and detailed instruction in crime and violence) (*Broadcasting Services Act, 1992*), and more recently, with respect to cyberbullying and image - based abuse (*Enhancing Online Safety Act, 2015; Online Safety Act, 2021*).

Early days of online content regulation – Schedules 5 & 7 of the Broadcasting Services Act 1992

Part of the Australian Government's approach to internet regulation has been to regulate content through Schedule 5 to the *Broadcasting Services Amendment (Online Services) Act 1999*, and later through the *Online Safety Act (2021)*. Schedule 5 extended the co-regulatory system for broadcasting to cover online content as well as a complaints-based scheme for assessment of internet content (Australian Law Reform Commission, n.d.). Under Schedule 5 to the Act, the Australian Broadcasting Authority, and later the Australian Communications and Media Authority[1] was empowered to investigate complaints from the public about online content that may be considered prohibited or 'potentially prohibited'. Prohibited content is content that has been classified by the Australian Classification Board[2] as X18+ or RC (refused classification), or Australian hosted R18+ content not subjected to age verification systems, whereas potentially prohibited content is content that has not been classified by the Classification Board but that that would likely be classified X18+ or RC if it were to be.[3] Content is classified according to the National Classification Code and Guidelines. X18+ content is material depicting actual sexual activity, and RC (refused classification) content is material that contains depictions that would 'offend against the standards of morality, decency and propriety generally accepted by reasonable adults' (Australian Law Reform Commission, 2012). RC content encompasses child abuse material, sexual violence, revolting or abhorrent phenomena, sexual fetishes, detailed instruction in crime or violence, among other things. Under the scheme, the action undertaken would depend on where the potentially prohibited content was hosted and whether the content was deemed 'sufficiently serious' (e.g. child abuse material). Under the Act, Australian-hosted potentially prohibited content would be subject to take-down notices administered to content hosts (usually internet service providers). Potentially prohibited content hosted offshore (the vast majority) would be referred to Australian Internet Service Providers so that they could add it to their filters, which were provided to their customers. Sufficiently serious content was referred to law enforcement agencies for investigation.

The Act also sets out a co-regulatory framework which mandates the development of Industry Codes of Practice, covering such issues as complaint handling processes by industry and promoting awareness of online safety issues, including 'giving parents and responsible adults information about how to supervise and control children's access to content provided by commercial content services or live content services' (Federal Register of Legislation).

Schedule 5 to the BSA also set out an online safety community education function. The key educational messages at this time reflected two key concerns about young people and the internet – inappropriate and harmful content (i.e. pornography, extreme violence), and inappropriate contact (i.e. online predators). The legislation tasked the ABA/ACMA with advising parents in relation to the supervision and control of children's access to internet content, and to conduct and co-ordinate community education programs (Schedule 5, Part 11). Activities during the mid-2000s included providing cyber safety pamphlets to schools and community organisations, and running the Cybersmart Detectives (CSD) activity. The aim of the CSD activity was to teach children key internet safety messages in a school environment (Dooley et al., 2011), bringing together a variety of agencies with an interest in promoting online safety, including state and federal police, schools, and government (Dooley et al., 2011). The game involved a fictional scenario played out in real time online in which a year seven girl goes to meet a boy that she met on social media. The 'friend' turns out to be a 37-year-old man. The activity aims to educate children about the potential dangers of online predators and reinforces key safety messages around remaining anonymous online. During the period 2004–2011 the game had been played by over 28,000 students in Australia (Dooley et al., 2011).

An infamous incident in 2006 involving the broadcasting of a sexual assault on the reality TV program Big Brother led to the introduction of legislation to regulate online content not previously captured under existing legislation. The Big Brother 'turkey slap' incident occurred during filming of the reality television program and involved two male contestants rubbing their penises in the face of a female contestant (Cunningham, 2020). The offending content fell between the regulatory cracks so to speak – it was not broadcast on television so was not covered by the broadcasting codes of practice, but rather was streamed live at 4:17 am via the internet. It was not, however, captured under Schedule Five which governs stored website content (at the time content needed to be able to be accessed via a URL in order to be investigated). Schedule 7 to the Broadcasting Services Act was introduced in 2007 to address the loophole.

Big Brother had not been without controversy up to this point. The turkey slap incident followed a previous incident the year before in which a male contest was filmed putting his penis on a female contestant during a massage. The turkey slap attracted widespread media attention, outraging politicians including the Australian Prime Minister at the time – John Howard – who called for the program to be axed, and triggering a debate about the adequacy of content regulation in Australia. Schedule 7 of the Broadcasting Services Act was subsequently introduced to capture live and ephemeral online content. Specifically, it broadened the category of prohibited content to include MA15+ content that is provided on a commercial basis (i.e. for a fee) unless it is subject to a restricted access system (Department of Infrastructure, ND).

The turkey slap incident highlights how regulation is often one step behind technological innovation. Internet regulation in Australia up to this point was concerned primarily with content – namely, banning altogether potentially prohibited online content, or restricting user (in particular, children's) exposure to certain forms of inappropriate online content, and even then, these regulatory powers were fairly limited. Indeed, under Schedule Five to the Broadcasting Services Act, the regulator could only take concrete action against illegal or prohibited content hosted in Australia through the issuing of a take-down notice to the internet service provider responsible. The vast majority of prohibited and illegal content was hosted offshore, in which case it was referred to relevant offshore bodies, as well as Australian filter providers so that it could be blocked to users of those filters. Community education was provided to address the issues that regulation could not. The community education programs at the time focused on protecting young people from inappropriate online content and contact.

The early days of the internet were accompanied by a celebratory rhetoric of the internet as a technology of freedom that should not be regulated in the same way that broadcast media had been. As Terry Flew points out, there was a strong consensus that the internet's development should be driven by a market-led model and that the role of the Government should be minimised (Flew, 2021, p. 9). An early proponent of this view was Ithiel de Sola Pool, who argued that the new electronic networks of communication required a 'policy of freedom' and 'freedom from government' (Flew, 2021, p. 15). While certain types of online content were restricted via filters, including pornographic material, hate speech, and promotion of terrorism, attempts at online regulation were met with significant resistance. This included attempts to introduce mandatory ISP-level filtering in the mid-2000s, which were successfully blocked by a range of industry and civil society organisations (Flew, 2021).

Yet, as Flew argues, there has been a significant shift during the 2010s in public attitudes towards internet regulation. The growing support for online regulation has been precipitated in part by 'platformisation' which highlights the 'changing political economy of the internet, particularly around the rise of platform monopolies and oligopolies' and a concomitant shift in 'debates around governance from whether the internet is or should be governed to how it is governed and who makes the relevant decisions' (Flew, 2021, p. 22). Other factors have also contributed to growing pressure for greater online regulation. These include a number of 'public shocks' – that is online public events that 'suddenly highlight a platform's infrastructural qualities and call it to account for its public implications'[4] (Annany & Gillespie, 2017, p. 2, cited in Flew, 2021, p. 20); growing concerns about the potential harms posed by networked platforms including privacy breaches' mis- and disinformation, and the rise of artificial intelligence.

Establishment of the Office of the eSafety Commissioner

The Enhancing Online Safety Act (2015) came into effect in 2015, creating a separate entity – the Office of the Children's eSafety Commissioner – tasked with regulating online content and protecting young Australians from online harms. The establishment of the Office signalled a notable expansion in the Australian Government's regulatory powers. While the Office was still tasked with regulating illegal or restricted online content and engaging in online safety education activities, its powers were extended to encompass various online behaviours, including cyberbullying and imaged-based abuse. In 2017, the role of the office expanded to all Australians, not just children, and the Office was renamed the Office of the eSafety Commissioner. The Australian Government claims that Australia is a 'world leader in online safety' (Australian Government Department of Infrastructure, April 2024).

In 2021 new legislation further strengthened the Office's regulatory powers. The *Online Safety Act (2021)* saw the creation of a 'world-first Adult Cyber Abuse Scheme'. It also broadened the cyberbullying scheme to capture harms that occur on services other than social media and updated the image-based abuse scheme to address the sharing and threatened sharing of intimate images without consent. Thus, the Office is empowered to investigate and take action in relation to cyberbullying, image-based abuse, adult cyber abuse, and harmful online content. Its enforcement powers include working with online services providers and end-users to resolve problems and issuing service provider notification and removal notices. Where a provision of the Act has been breached, the Office can issue infringement notices, pursue a court-ordered injunction, and seek court ordered civil penalties.

The *Online Safety Act (2021)* places obligations on platforms to implement Basic Online Safety Expectations (BOSE). These expectations include that the service provider will take reasonable steps to ensure that users can access the service in a safe manner, minimise harm, ensure that the best interests of the child are taken into account, minimise potentially harmful material (and provide complaints mechanisms in relation to such material), and ensure that they have terms of use, policies and procedures for dealing with complaints.

The act also sets out the development of industry codes and standards in relation to certain types of prohibited and potentially prohibited online material. This material, now known as Class 1 and Class 2 material, is content which is, or would be likely to be, classified as 'RC' or 'X' under the Classification Act. Class 1A and 1B online materials includes harmful materials such as child sexual exploitation material, pro-terror materials and extreme violence. Class 1C and Class 2 materials include online pornography that is deemed inappropriate for children. Under the Act, service providers are required to proactively deal with this sort of material at a systemic level. According to the Office, there are currently six industry codes in operation to help protect users from illegal and restricted online content (eSafety Commissioner, 2024).

There are, however, limits to the powers of the eSafety Commissioner. Nowhere were these limits more publicly on display than in 2024 when the eSafety Commissioner sought but failed to have graphic content of a church stabbing in Sydney permanently removed from the social media platform X (formerly Twitter), resulting in a public stoush between the eSafety Commissioner, Julie Inman Grant, and X owner, Elon Musk. Ensuring the safety of young people online is therefore seen as a shared responsibility with important roles for Government, parents, young people, and platforms and online providers. Recently, there has been increasing pressure on platforms to do more to ensure the safety of their users.

The Safety by Design framework encourages industry to anticipate and mitigate potential harms through the design, development and deployment of a product or service. The framework recognises that the burden of safety should not fall solely upon end users or parents and caregivers (eSafety Commissioner, 2019). The approach seeks to minimise existing and emerging risks and harms that may occur, rather than retrospectively addressing harms after they occur (eSafety Commissioner, 2024). As such, it is a move towards more *proactive* responses to online risk. The Safety by Design initiative is, however, voluntary. As acknowledged by eSafety, designing platforms in such a way so as to ensure that the safety of users is the primary concern requires major cultural change in the tech industry (eSafety Commissioner, 2024). As many have noted, major online proprietary platform companies generate profits from the ongoing attention and engagement of their users. As such, they are unlikely to prioritise the safety and wellbeing of their users if it does not contribute to their profits – unless required by law to do so.

International regulation

In recent years, there has been a growing focus on online safety and regulation globally. As Gray et al. (2024) note, this was demonstrated at the G7 summit in 2021, where the governments of the UK, France, Italy, Japan, Canada, Germany, US and the European Union all signed a ministerial declaration setting out a number of principles designed to guide member states in improving online safety. In October 2023, the UK Government passed the *Online Safety Act (2023)*, which goes further than Australia's Online Safety Act in terms of mandating platforms' obligations to ensure safety on their platforms (Gray et al., 2024). The Act aims to make social media companies and search services more responsible for end-user safety by requiring platforms to implement measures to reduce the risks posed by their services. This includes a requirement that services take 'robust' action against illegal content and activity, and implement systems for removing illegal content and reducing the risk that users encounter illegal content via their services. Additionally, the Act requires that services and platforms implement age-assurance mechanisms for sites and apps that publish or display pornographic content to ensure that children are not able to access such material (Ofcom, 2023). To help services comply with the new online safety laws, Ofcom – the UK regulator responsible for enforcing the Act – released guidelines in 2023 on 'highly effective age checks to stop children accessing online porn services'. Such methods include 'ID matching, facial age estimation and credit card checks' (Ofcom, 2023). The guidelines also outline strict criteria which age checks must meet to be considered highly effective (Ofcom, 2023). Additionally, the Act aims to make services and platforms more transparent about the kinds of potentially harmful content they allow, and ensures that platforms and services provide parents and children with clear and accessible mechanisms for reporting problems online (Department for Science, 2024). The Act also introduces a range of criminal offences ranging from cyberflashing to threatening communications and encouraging serious self-harm. Platforms and services providers who fail to meet their new obligations under the Act can be fined up to £18 million or ten per cent of their revenue, whichever is greater, and senior managers face criminal prosecution (Department for Science, 2024). We might reasonably expect that the UK legislation will provide a powerful precedent for jurisdictions around the world seeking to require platforms to do more to protect their users' safety (Gray et al., 2024).

Debate about restricting the age of social media users with a view to ensuring their protection is also gathering momentum in Europe and the US. In the European Union the Digital Services Act aims to 'create a safer digital space where the fundamental rights of users are protected' (European Commission, 2024), and also contains a number of measures to protect children and young people online. These include parental controls, age verification and reporting systems in relation to prohibited online content and cyberbullying. France recently implemented a law restricting access to social media for children under 15, and has been exploring various age-verification options (Telefonica, 2024).

It is evident from these international examples that determining young people's age through age assurance and age verification systems – known as age-gating – is one of the key regulatory initiatives proposed by regulators to ensure that content is suitable for young people online (Humphry et al., 2023). In March 2023, the Office of the eSafety Commissioner was tasked with developing a roadmap for introducing mandatory Age Verification in Australia, with a focus on preventing access to online pornography by children (eSafety Commissioner, 2023).[5] Notwithstanding the noted difficulties in implementing age-verification systems, scholars have noted that age-gating mechanisms fail to take into account the diversity of young people's online experiences and their maturity and capacity, and may infringe on the privacy rights of young people (Humphry et al., 2023; Nash, 2021).

Current developments (2023–2024)

In February 2024 the Australian Government announced a statutory review of the *Online Safety Act, (2021)*, to ensure its 'effectiveness and ensure they can address new and emerging harms' (Rowland, 2024). The Australian Government in 2024 also announced a Joint Parliamentary Enquiry into Social Media and Australian Society. Collectively, these public debates and ongoing regulatory and policy changes highlight a collective concern about digital platforms in Australia that spans not only online safety issues, but platform power and accountability more broadly. But while there appears to be encouraging momentum for greater platform regulation to keep users – particularly children – safe online, responsibility for recognising and navigating online risks is still to a large extent devolved to families, especially parents. Indeed, the Office of the eSafety Commissioner states that its primary goal is to prevent online harms from happening in the first place through research, education and training programs that 'aim to build the capacity of Australians to interact safely online' and identifies 'parents and carers as the first lines of defence' in online safety (eSafety Commissioner, 2024, p. 3). eSafety also highlights the role of industry in educating its users to prevent online harms, which includes 'equipping parents, carers and other adult supporters – as well as children and young people themselves – with the information and tools they need to stay safe online' (eSafety Commissioner, 2024).

However, despite the significant resources that have been directed towards helping Australian families navigate the digital world safely – including the $42 million annual funding for the Office of the eSafety Commissioner – research reveals that only 2 per cent of respondents would turn to the Office for help with online safety (Rowland, 2022), suggesting that online safety initiatives and resources are either not reaching or resonating with Australian families. This is despite the fact that young people and parents have expressed a desire for more information about online safety and potential harms to enable them to deal with these independently and help others (Humphry et al., 2023).

Online safety education

There is currently a growing number of organisations within Australia that play a role in online safety education, including for young people, schools and educators, and parents and guardians. The Office of the eSafety Commissioner – under its 'prevention' pillar – has a wide range of educational resources aimed at providing families with the skills and knowledge to stay safe online.

The government-supported *Raising Children Network*, a partnership of organisations which covers a range of general parenting topics, claims to provide evidence-based information on a diverse range of parenting issues, including media and technology (cyber safety research and advice however is not its primary mandate).[6] Additionally, the Australian Federal Police (AFP) runs a flagship online safety program for parents called *ThinkUKnow* (which a number of participants in my research reported attending). Provided nationally via schools, the program is said to

> provide information on the technologies young people use, the challenges they may face, and importantly, how they can be overcome… The presentation covers topics such as social media reputation management, cyberbullying, 'sexting', online grooming, online

gaming, inappropriate content, privacy management identity theft, how to protect your devices, and how to report matters when things go wrong' (Think U Know, 2019).[7]

The title alone implies an assumed deficit in knowledge on the part of the intended audience (children and their parents).

Additionally, numerous community and not-for-profit organisations, and a growing number of independent commercial providers, offer resources, training and advice to young people and their parents to help them minimise online harms. These include the Alannah and Madeline Foundation, YSafe, Cybersafety Solutions, Safe on Social, Project Rockit, and Screen Sanity, just to name a few.

Conclusion

Regulating digital media technologies including online platforms is a bit like trying to capture a moving target. Established social media platforms (e.g. MySpace) disappear, while new ones emerge. New technologies have the potential to fundamentally change the way some things are done (e.g. generative AI). Some give rise to new risks not previously considered (e.g immersive and augmented realities (Gray et al., 2024), deep fakes/online pornography). Governments are often one step behind industry, and parents are often one step behind their children. Enforcing basic online safety expectations that apply to retrospective and prospective platforms is essential.

Online safety education remains absolutely crucial, as I will continue to argue throughout this book. Currently, however, I suggest that much (but not all) of the online safety educational material retains a primary focus on risk and harm, and does not appear to take into account either parents' or children's varying practices and perspectives. Parents are implicated in these educational resources in various ways and in varying degrees, to manage, restrict, monitor, guide and/or support their children's digital media use. These resources form part of the discourse that constructs the 'good' parent as one who actively mediates their children's media use, the subject of the next chapter.

Notes

1 The Australian Broadcasting Authority merged with the Australian Communications Authority in 2005, creating the Australian Communications and Media Authority.
2 The Australian Classification Board is a body of independent assessors (or 'censors') administered by the Australian Government, who classify film, computer games and certain publications. See https://www.classification.gov.au/about-us/classification-board.
3 Content was determined to be 'potentially prohibited' by ACMA staff and thus negated the need to have every piece of content formally classified by the Office of Film and Literature Classification.
4 The Big Brother 'turkey slap' incident is one such example. More recent examples of 'public shocks' include the livestreaming of acts of violence, sexual assaults and murder, including in 2019 when the murder of 50 people at a Mosque in Christchurch was livestreamed via Facebook (Flew, 2021).
5 Interestingly, this roadmap was developed as part of the previous government's response to the House of Representatives Standing Committee on Social Policy and Legal Affairs report, which was titled 'Protecting the age of innocence'.
6 https://raisingchildren.net.au/?gclid=Cj0KCQjwjpjkBRDRARIsAKv-0O1EhckUoHe9WkzBj yjSGTb4gggV6n8lCfmC0A1YUVcmy84BQqQ01zgaAjOHEALw_wcB.
7 https://www.thinkuknow.org.au/about-thinkuknow.

References

Albury, K., & Crawford, K. (2012). Sexting, consent and young people's ethics: Beyond Megan's Story. *Continuum, 26*(3), 463–473.

Australian Government Department of Infrastructure, T., Regional Development, Communications and the Arts. (2024 April). *Statutory review of the online safety act 2021: Issues paper*. Australian Government Retrieved from https://www.infrastructure.gov.au/sites/default/files/documents/online-safety-act-2021-review-issues-paper-26-april-2024.pdf

Australian Law Reform Commission. (2012, 29 February). Overview of the RC category. Retrieved from https://www.alrc.gov.au/publication/classification-content-regulation-and-convergent-media-alrc-report-118/11-the-scope-of-prohibited-content/overview-of-the-rc-category/

Australian Law Reform Commission. (n.d.). Broadcasting services act. Retrieved from https://www.alrc.gov.au/publication/national-classification-scheme-review-dp-77/2-the-current-classification-scheme/broadcasting-services-act/

Broadcasting Services Act. (1992). (Cth) (Austl). Retrieved from http://classic.austlii.edu.au/au/legis/cth/consol_act/bsa1992214/

Cunningham, K. (2020, 1 February). 'It was pretty scary': The Big Brother 'turkey slap' that rocked reality TV. *The Guardian*. Retrieved from https://www.theguardian.com/tv-and-radio/2020/jan/31/it-was-pretty-scary-the-big-brother-turkey-slap-that-rocked-reality-tv

Department for Science, I.T. (2024, 8 May). Guidance. Online Safety Act: Explainer. Retrieved from https://www.gov.uk/government/publications/online-safety-act-explainer/online-safety-act-explainer

Dooley, J., Thomas, L., Falconer, S., Cross, D., & Waters, S. (2011). Educational evaluation of Cybersmart Detectives: Final report: Presented to the Australian Communications and Media Authority (ACMA). Child Health Promotion Research Centre, Edith Cowan University. Perth, Western Australia https://ro.ecu.edu.au/ecuworks2011/862/

Enhancing Online Safety Act. (2015).

eSafety Commissioner. (2023). *Roadmap for age verification and complementary measures to prevent and mitigate harms to children from online pornography*. Retrieved from https://www.esafety.gov.au/sites/default/files/2023-08/Roadmap-for-age-verification_2.pdf

eSafety Commissioner. (2024). eSafety submission to the Joint Select Committee on Social Media and Australian Society. Retrieved from https://www.aph.gov.au/Parliamentary_Business/Committees/Joint/Social_Media/SocialMedia/Submissions

eSafety Commissioner. (2024). Industry codes and standards at a glance. Retrieved from https://www.esafety.gov.au/industry/codes#:~:text=These%20classes%20cover%20the%20most,commenced%20on%201%20July%202024

European Commission. (2024, 25 July). The digital services act package. Retrieved from https://digital-strategy.ec.europa.eu/en/policies/digital-services-act-package

Flew, T. (2021). *Regulating platforms*. Cambridge: Polity.

Gray, J. E., Carter, M., & Egliston, B. (2024). Regulating social VR: Limitations and tensions in global policy and governance. In *Governing social virtual reality: Preparing for the content, conduct and design challenges of immersive social media* (pp. 77–89). Switzerland: Springer Nature.

Humphry, J., Boichak, O., & Hutchinson, J. (2023). Emerging online safety issues – Co-creating social media with young people – Research report. Retrieved from https://ses.library.usyd.edu.au/handle/2123/31689

Mavoa, J., Gibbs, M., & Carter, M. (2017). Constructing the young child media user in Australia: A discourse analysis of Facebook comments. *Journal of Children and Media, 11*(3), 330–346.

Nash, V. (2021). Gatecrashers? Freedom of expression in an age-gated internet. In A. Duff (Ed.), *Research handbook on information policy* (pp. 277–291): Cheltenham, UK: Edward Elgar Publishing.

Ofcom. (2023, 5 December). Implementing the Online Safety Act: Protecting children from online pornography. Retrieved from https://www.ofcom.org.uk/online-safety/protecting-children/implementing-the-online-safety-act-protecting-children

Online Safety Act. (2021). Retrieved from https://www.legislation.gov.au/Details/C2021A00076

Page Jeffery, C. (2021). '[Cyber] bullying is too strong a word...': Parental accounts of their children's experiences of online conflict and relational aggression. *Media International Australia, 184*(1), 150–164. doi:10.1177/1329878X211048512

Rowland, M. (2022). Release of the 2022 National Online Safety Survey. *Media release*. 14 November. https://minister.infrastructure.gov.au/rowland/media-release/release-2022-national-online-safety-survey

Rowland, M. (2024). Ensuring our online safety laws keep Australians safe [Press release]. Retrieved from https://minister.infrastructure.gov.au/rowland/media-release/ensuring-our-online-safety-laws-keep-australians-safe

Telefonica. (2024, 15 May). Protection of minors and online age verification: The case of France. Retrieved from https://www.telefonica.com/en/communication-room/blog/protection-of-minors-and-online-age-verification-the-case-of-france/

Think U Know. (2019). Think U Know. Retrieved from https://www.thinkuknow.org.au/about-thinkuknow

Third, A., Collin, P., Walsh, L., & Black, R. (2019). *Young people in digital society: Control shift*. London, UK: Palgrave Macmillan Nature.

Third, A., & Idriss, S. (2013). *Online risks, cybersafety campaigns and young people*. A briefing paper for the Technology and Wellbeing Roundtable. September. https://www.westernsydney.edu.au/__data/assets/pdf_file/0003/703794/ARC_Linkage_Project_Roundtable_Cybersafety_Briefing_Paper.pdf

UK Public General Acts. (2023). *Online Safety Act*. c. 50 https://www.legislation.gov.uk/ukpga/2023/50

Zaman, B., Holloway, D., Green, L., Jaunzems, K., & Vanwynsberghe, H. (2020). Opposing narratives about children's digital media use: A critical discourse analysis of online public advice given to parents in Australia and Belgium. *Media International Australia*, *176*(1), 120–137.

3

PARENTAL MEDIATION AND CONSTRUCTION OF THE 'GOOD' PARENT

We're up against a lot of parents out there that don't care, they're not monitoring, they're not looking at internet histories.

42-year-old mother of 12-year-old boy

Despite increasing pressure on platforms to ensure the safety of their users, parents are still ultimately responsibilised for ensuring the safety of their children online. The mother quoted above was a participant in one of my parent focus groups exploring parental anxieties about their children's use of digital media. Here, she draws a distinction between 'good' parents that engage in monitoring their children's media use, and other (implicitly 'bad') parents who don't. What constitutes a 'good' parent in this instance, according to this participant, is a parent who actively monitors their children's online activities, including looking at their internet histories. Other parents, however, indicated that they did not, nor would not, monitor their children's online activities, arguing for their child's right to privacy, or simply that it 'was just another thing to look at' within an already long list of parenting duties. For some parents, being a good digital parent meant imposing rules and restrictions, including the use of filtering and other technical tools. Yet for the majority of participants, trust, dialogue and open communication with their child had become the stated default.

Thus, for the parents who I engaged with, good parenting involved *some* kind of intervention in their children's media use – whether that be monitoring, imposing rules and restrictions, or actively discussing digital media technologies with their children. The ways in which parents engage with their children's media use is known as parental mediation. Parental mediation theory was originally developed in response to concerns about children's television viewing (Clark, 2011). It has evolved over time to capture the various ways in which parents mediate their children's use of the internet and digital media to not only minimise risk, but increasingly to 'maximise the opportunities' afforded by digital

DOI: 10.4324/9781003346708-4

media (Livingstone et al., 2017; Nathanson, 2001a; Valkenburg et al., 1999). Livingstone and Helsper (2008, p. 3) state:

> mediation is widely seen to capture the parental management of the relation between children and media, usefully, it extends the parental role beyond simple restrictions to encompass also conversational and interpretative strategies.

Much of the contemporary parental mediation literature theoretically draws upon earlier influential studies about television. These studies identified three primary strategies through which parents monitored and regulated their children's television viewing: active mediation[1] (talking with children), restrictive mediation (setting rules), and co-viewing (watching television with children) (Bybee et al., 1982; Nathanson, 1999, 2001b; Valkenburg et al., 1999). Parental mediation theory in a contemporary media environment recognises that parents attempt to manage not only (and probably to a lesser extent) television, but increasingly children's use of digital media technologies including the internet, mobile phones, laptops, tablets and gaming.

There is now an extensive body of literature about parental mediation of children's media use, and at least ten parental mediation models of children's internet use have been proposed during the last decade (Kuldas et al., 2021). For example, active mediation includes practices such as talking about children's online activities, and sitting nearby while the child is online; technical restriction includes the use of software and technical surveillance tools, and monitoring involves checking up on children's online practices after use (Livingstone et al., 2015). A survey of 400 European parents, however, found that parents typically adopted one of two mediation styles: 1) restrictive mediation, which involves parents restricting, banning or insisting on supervising any of a long list of online activities; and 2) enabling mediation, whereby parents undertake active strategies such as talking to their children about what they do online or encouraging their activity as well as giving safety advice; as well as activities that might appear restrictive (use of technical controls and parental monitoring) but are better interpreted as building a safe framework so that positive uses of the internet can be encouraged (Livingstone & Byrne, 2018; Livingstone et al., 2017).

Parental mediation in the digital age, however, is no straightforward task. In contrast to one or two televisions in the home, children are typically using multiple devices both within and outside the home, using technologies in multiple ways – some of which are deemed beneficial by parents and tacitly sanctioned (such as schoolwork and 'FaceTiming' grandparents), and some of which are deemed problematic (e.g. social media). The opacity around children's online activities, as well as children's capacity for simultaneously toggling between various activities such as homework, entertainment, and socialising, makes parental attempts to regulate their children's media use even more difficult. The difficulties of mediating adolescent media use within a contemporary context where digital devices are used for an increasing range of everyday tasks and media panics are front and centre presents a difficult dilemma for many contemporary parents.

Problematising the 'good' parent

Parenting has traditionally been distinguished from the practice of child-rearing, and has been understood in terms of protecting children from harm and nurturing and stimulating and socialising the child (Furedi, 2002). The verb 'to parent' is relatively new, and interest in the practice of parenting has escalated within the context of a broader shift in the sociocultural context in which parents raise their children (Lee, 2014). In the last few decades there has been a shift in the care and governance of children within middle-class and professional families away from a primary focus on the safety and welfare of the child (and by extension the state) towards more aspirational objectives concerned with maximising opportunity and securing competitive advantage for children. There is a significant body of contemporary literature, both scholarly and popular, that documents this transformation. Rose (1990) notes the shift away from preventing 'psychological maladjustment through correct procedures of child rearing to new objectives: maximising both the emotional adjustment and the cognitive efficiency of the child through proper management of early relations with the parents and the environment' (pp. xi–xii). Furedi (2002, p. 106) draws a distinction between 'child-rearing' and 'parenting', where parenting is endowed with 'profound importance' because it is purported to essentially determine the traits necessary for a successful life. More recently, Nelson (2010) argued that acute economic uncertainty and the precarity of middle and professional families' class status have resulted in 'parenting out of control' by concerned adults anxious to secure their children's educational and competitive advantage in the world. Lareau (2011) describes the 'concerted cultivation' of children by parents, to actively foster the child's talents, opinions and skills. And Hays (1998) identifies a parenting ideology of 'intensive mothering', a 'gendered model that advises mothers to expend a tremendous amount of time, energy and money in raising their children' (Hays, 1998). There has also been a recent explosion in popular texts, activities, and games geared towards helping parents achieve this. Many scholars agree that contemporary discursive constructions of 'good' parenting have expanded the expectations placed upon parents so that they are tasked not only with protecting their children from harm, but increasingly with ensuring that they reach their full potential (Faircloth, 2014; Faircloth & Murray, 2015; Furedi, 2002; Hays, 1998; Nelson, 2010).

Shifts in the construction of 'good' parenting are also linked to media and technological change and are discursive constructions of what a 'good' childhood and 'good' education look like (Drotner, 2022; Mavoa et al., 2017). In part, this is about actual changes to technology and their affordances, but it also refers to different ways of understanding technology as a result of discourses of technological innovation framed in terms of opportunity and risk. For example, Willett (2015) points out that 'good' parents were expected to limit their children's exposure to 'commercial' television content while attending to their children's educational needs within the home. Sesame Street, she argues, was a quintessential example of 'good' television because it was not commercial and was explicitly educational. Complicating this was the stated original goal of Sesame Street to 'master the addictive qualities of television and do something good with them' (Davis, 2008, p. 8). Livingstone (2017, p. 3) explicitly acknowledges the competing discourses of risk and opportunity in relation to young people's use of digital media technologies and its effects on parents, suggesting that '[D]igital media somehow intensify parental hopes, fears and ambivalences about risks and opportunities, now and for the future'.

The rapid acquisition of internet-enabled PCs throughout Australian homes in the 1990s and the discourse that accompanied these technological changes left little doubt that it is the parents' responsibility to regulate and manage their children's digital media use. A media analysis of newspaper articles about the internet in the late 1990s revealed that parents were expected to take responsibility for mitigating the dangers of the internet to children and young people (Turow, 1999), and those that are seen to shirk their responsibilities are subjected to judgement and blame. Parenting has thus become a highly moralised affair (Faircloth & Murray, 2015). The comments sections of parenting blogs are replete with criticisms – usually from other parents who consider themselves much more assiduous in this regard – heaping judgement and blame on the actions of parents-at-fault.[2] In addition to government regulators and cyber safety organisations, the media, and other parents, it seems that even children themselves think that it's the job of their parents to monitor and regulate their own media and technology use through setting limits and rules (Vaterlaus et al., 2014). Parents and carers therefore bear the brunt of responsibility for enacting and enforcing much of the cyber safety advice, guidelines and recommendations within the domestic sphere.

Dominant discourses about young people and technology represent antinomies that have been constructed by technology evangelists and dissenters (Thomas, 2011), and have been variously referred to as eliciting mild euphoria vs panic (Buckingham, 2007), or optimism vs pessimism (Drotner, 1992). Buckingham (2013, pp. 7–8) is critical of these polarised approaches whereby the discussion oscillates between 'moral panic and wild euphoria'. He argues:

On the one hand the internet is portrayed as a repository for paedophiles and pornography (along with the occasional terrorist). On the other, it is seen to be all about creativity, liberation and empowerment. Similarly, computer games are either a provocation to violence and a form of mindless 'dumbing down', or they are a wonderful new tool for learning. The public debate about these issues often shifts awkwardly between these two registers, with both making alarmist overinflated claims that have little basis in evidence.

This dichotomy has been typically framed in cyber safety and scholarly discourse in terms of risk vs opportunity. Livingstone describes maximising digital opportunities while simultaneously minimising online risks for young people as the 'holy grail' of contemporary parenting (Livingstone et al., 2017). Yet, as I argue later in this book, online risks and opportunities are not always clearly distinguished, and are fluid, overlapping and context dependent, necessitating a move away from this binary.

Anxious parenting and a 'culture of fear'

There is a growing body of contemporary literature, spanning both academic as well as more popular realms, that posits that fear, risk, and anxiety are becoming the dominant principles around which the public and its institutions organise their lives (Barr et al., 2012). The notion of risk as an organising principle originated with Ulrich Beck's influential Risk Society thesis, in which he argued that rapid development and industrialisation have brought about a suite of global risks the likes of which we have not previously seen (Beck, 1992). However, contemporary constructions of risk, increasingly position children as a primary locus of concern.[3] Media commentary and public discourse, including moral panics, invoke the notion of childhood in crisis (Kehily, 2010), as well as a sense of nostalgia that things were easier and safer before (also not a new phenomenon), contributing to a general, unfocused fear that pervades discussions about children and thus the notion that danger and risk have become a central feature of everyday life (Altheide, 2002).[4] Lee et al. (2014) argue that the concept of risk in recent years has expanded to resonate with parenting culture, and describe the various feelings and responses of parents in terms of 'risk consciousness', which is marked by a preoccupation with unwanted or dangerous outcomes that *might* happen, rather than what is *likely* to happen.

Some scholars argue that fear and anxiety have become standard ingredients in contemporary parenting culture in which parents feel they have less control over their own lives as well as their children's (Clark, 2013). Parents are said to be increasingly uncertain, overanxious (Nelson, 2010) fearful and paranoid, (Furedi, 2002) as they attempt to fulfil a role considered to encompass not only a process of 'risk management' whereby parents must mitigate the risks associated with rapid social change, but also to ensure that they embrace the possibilities that such change affords (Barr et al., 2012). Within this context, media increasingly gives voice to a range of 'experts', including – but not limited to government, online safety experts, and academics – who appear to know what they are talking about and who tell parents what to do – sometimes in contrast or conflict with parents' better instincts.

Amongst these discourses of risk and danger, and discursively constructed ideals around 'good parenting', it is not surprising that parental anxiety emerges as parents struggle to avoid feelings of guilt, worry, failure and shame (Faircloth & Murray, 2015), along with a perceived deficit in parents' own knowledge and competencies.

The practice of parenting is often described in terms of different sets of practices or 'ways'. There has been a general shift in the ways that parents (especially those from middle and upper class backgrounds) govern their children's internet activities, away from an authoritarian style whereby parents control their children's online activities through rules and rewards, towards an approach based on agreement, trust and negotiation (Livingstone & Bober, 2006).[5] This is reflective of the broader shift in parenting foregrounded earlier, whereby parents are investing more time and effort into maximising their children's opportunities and educational advantages. This style of parenting is increasingly egalitarian and focused on trust and negotiation rather than command and control. As Livingstone and Bober (2006) noted more than a decade ago:

> In late modernity, as Beck (1992) and others have argued, power relations within the family have shifted from a model of authority and generational hierarchy, to the more egalitarian, 'pure relationship'. Parental authority exercised through control over the rules and rewards is giving way, though not without a struggle, to a parent-child relationship that prioritises trust and negotiation, as mediated by the discourse of rights, including children's rights. Parental regulation of media provides, on this view, an occasion for relationship 'work' rather than a response to an external threat.
>
> *(p. 14)*

There is little doubt that parenting has undergone a significant shift since the turn of the century, and that the rapid adoption and domestication of the internet, and the pervasiveness of mobile phones and social media, have intensified 'risk anxiety' (Scott et al., 1998), ignited numerous moral panics about children and technology (Marwick, 2008), and generated a new set of potential dangers and concerns for parents (Barr et al., 2012; Nelson, 2010). These concerns have engendered a new parenting and cyber-safety discourse focusing on 'parenting in the digital age'. This discourse has shifted – although not entirely displaced – the locus of parental concern away from physical spaces, such as the 'street' articulated in terms of 'stranger danger' or as the site (away from the 'good' family home) of alcohol and substance abuse, towards technologies such as smartphones and the internet. The dominant discourse is one of 'safety', whereby it is the 'good' parent's responsibility to have knowledge of 'risks'.

Parenting and the 'knowledge gap'

Parents are often contradictorily positioned in popular discourse. Sometimes they are portrayed as quasi-victims as a result of their assumed ignorance, other times they are portrayed as partly responsible due to a perceived lack of knowledge about the potential harms which renders them unable to protect their child from them. This contradiction is often expressed through popular discourse, which typically frames digital risk issues in terms of a deficit in parental (as well as child) knowledge. Thus sometimes parents are seen as the solution, sometimes they are seen as part of the problem (Bragg & Buckingham, 2013).

Early parental concerns about the internet arose in part due to a perceived *lack* of parental knowledge about this new media technology that was rapidly being adopted in domestic households throughout the country. Not only were parents concerned about the risks posed by contemporary technologies, they were also anxious about whether or not they possessed the requisite skills and knowledge to manage them (Clark, 2009; Green et al., 2004; Lally, 2002; NetRatingsAustralia, 2005; Shepherd et al., 2006; Valentine & Holloway, 2002; Yardi & Bruckman, 2011). Modes of parental governance are premised on an assumed hierarchy of expertise and knowledge within the traditional family. Traditional family relations consist of an asymmetrical power relation between parents and their children, elevating the status of parents due to their assumed knowledge, experience and expertise relative to their children. However, the notion of a media-related knowledge gap between older and younger generations, premised on the idea that children and teenagers are more knowledgeable, and possess greater expertise about all things digital compared to their parents, disrupts this hierarchical structure, threatens to undermine parents' power base, and may reconfigure power relations within the home (Green et al., 2004, p. 90). In short, parents have long been concerned that they lack the required technical knowledge to manage digital media use in the home which has undermined their sense of authority and control and contributed to parental anxiety. Additionally, discursively constructed generational rhetoric which contrasts 'digital native' children with their 'digital immigrant' parents may serve to sustain parental concerns about a generational knowledge gap.

Various sources aim to address this perceived parental knowledge deficit. As foreshadowed in the previous chapter, online safety resources and educational programs often serve to provide the necessary risk-related information to parents, implicitly tasking them with managing the risks of digital media to their children. The notion of a 'knowledge gap' between older and younger generations, including parents and their children, is one that is in part constructed and sustained through public discourse about young people and technology. The discourse of 'media generations' frames the challenges and problems of use in terms of knowledge and expertise about how to use and access media technology. The original conceptualisation involved the idea of children and teenagers being more knowledgeable, and in possession of far greater expertise,[6] about all things digital compared to their parents. The observation that generations are no longer defined by war or depression but by media use continues to ring true (Buckingham, 2006; Wark, 1993). For example, Tapscott (2009) referred to young people born in the 1980s and 1990s as the 'net generation', and the term 'iGeneration' has been used to describe those children born in the 1990s, so called because of their use of iPhones, iPods, iPads and other similar technologies (Waldron, 2012). Generational discourses premised on digital media frame children both positively and negatively in terms of their digital media use and expertise, yet conceptualisations of older generations (including parents) appear more static. Tapscott (1998, pp. 1–2) conceptualised parents as ignorant, and 'reeling from the challenges of raising confident, plugged-in, and digital savvy children who know more about technology than they do'. This common (mis)conceptualisation is compounded by a more general presumption of parental incompetence which has a history pre-dating the 1970s (Lee, 2014).

Despite these assertions about the generational divide with respect to digital media now being decades old, the notion of a generational gap nonetheless remains. Popular discourse assumes that parents lack knowledge about what their children do online, including the kinds of apps and social media platforms they are using, the internet sites they are visiting, their online behaviours and the potential risks of their behaviours. Teenage children, on the other hand, are taken to be knowledgeable about digital media and assumed to possess the required expertise to navigate various online environments, including the internet, social media and online gaming, from various devices, but are assumed to lack knowledge about the risks and *consequences* of their online behaviours.

Generational discourses predicated on technology use are problematic for three key reasons. First, they adhere to an overly simplistic homogenising logic which paints entire generations with the same brush without accounting for diverse practices and backgrounds. Second, they typically adopt a technologically determinist view, an approach which has long been criticised within the academic literature for oversimplifying and overstating the effects of technology (Buckingham, 2006). As Buckingham (2006) argues, these changes are seen to be *produced* by technology, and do not take into account the social, historical and cultural factors which shape technology use. Third, such discourses tend to construct a firm binary between old and new forms of media (such as television and the internet), whereas old and new media come to co-exist, with new media rarely entirely displacing the old (Buckingham, 2006).

The contradictory positioning of parents in relation to their children's use of digital media highlights a dichotomy between the figure of the powerful, agentic parent who is able to (and therefore must) exert an authoritarian command and control style of parenting to mitigate risk, and the figure of the relatively powerless, permissive parent struggling against the broader forces of consumerism, sexualisation and technological change. As I discuss later, it is a dichotomy that exists in tension with contemporary parenting discourse, which denounces both authoritarian and permissive styles of parenting, espousing instead an *authoritative* parenting style, characterised by responsiveness, warmth, trust and dialogue (Clark, 2013; Nelson, 2010).

'Responsibilisation' of parenting

Parents are tasked with developing their own understanding and knowledge-based practices for mediating their children's media technology access and use. Sue Palmer (2006, p. 18) argues in her popular book, *Toxic Childhood*:

> Responsibility for rearing children lies, as it always has, with parents. They have to wise up, stop being paralysed by a combination of rapid change, uncertainty and guilt, and concentrate on providing a secure, healthy environment in which their children can grow.

Palmer's text is an example of what theorists of governmentality describe as 'responsibilisation', which has been described as:

> [P]rocesses of individualisation and standardisation ... [that] incite and encourage the 'individual as enterprise' to conduct themselves in accordance with the appropriate (or approved) model of action.
>
> *(Burchell, 1993, p. 29)*

With respect to parenting this entails displacing the burden of mitigating the risks to children downward, usually to individual parents, and even children themselves (Oswell, 2008). As argued in the previous chapter, the complexities of digital media regulation have meant that parents are still deemed primarily responsible for keeping their children safe from online dangers. Oswell (2008) suggests that the devolution of regulatory authority downward is indicative of 'privatisation' and 'responsibilisation', rather than actual parental autonomy and control.

Parents' actual knowledge about media technology may be far more extensive than that of their children. For example, Livingstone (2017) challenges the notion that parents are digital immigrants,[7] arguing that parents are increasingly confident users of technology, using it in their professional lives and also for socialising and entertainment. My own research indicates that far from the anxious parents of 15 years ago who felt that they lacked the requisite knowledge and skills about the internet, for the most part parents demonstrated considerable competence related to digital media. With a few notable exceptions,[8] most participants enthusiastically shared the various ways in which they used their devices, social media platforms, and apps and programs for work as well as pleasure. Some participants possessed specific IT expertise and knowledges from working in related fields, and others who did not possess such expertise and knowledge often had spouses who did. Thus, in many cases the household technology expert was a parent. Many parents admitted that they themselves probably used their devices too much and were wary of the behaviours that they were modelling to their children, particularly within the context of their significant concerns about the amount of time that their children spent engaging with devices.

As one mother in my study pointed out, implicitly critiquing the 'digital native/immigrant' construct:

> We are to a certain extent, setting an example. We talk about our kids now being digital natives, but when I reflect back now, from the time my son was small I either had a computer or laptop. Then when I was working, I had the Blackberry, I'd be checking emails and things like that for work and stuff. They've watched us do it.

Indeed, in 2024 arguments that parents today are 'digital immigrants' or incompetent technologically no longer hold much sway as many if not most of today's new parents have themselves been born into and grown up in the digital age. The knowledge, or generation, gap is far from uniform, and varies greatly depending on numerous factors, including the socio-economic, educational and professional background of parents (Livingstone et al., 2015). Similarly, Plowman and McPake (2013) suggest that the assertion that all children are digital natives is a myth, with many children learning about digital media from their parents. As Livingstone (2017) argued several years ago, we are likely undergoing a generational shift, and as such should leave the 'deficit model' of parenting behind.

I suggest that the existence of a knowledge gap between parents and their children has been and is still posited so as to 'responsibilise' parenting as a mode of governmental control. Knowledge of parenting and parenting subjectivities is thus 'responsibilised' as a technique of governmental control (Burchell, 1993; Kelly, 2001). Despite most parents that participated in my research demonstrating, either explicitly or tacitly, strong competencies and knowledges of digital media, many still drew on the digital native/immigrant discourse as a way of making sense of their perceived deficits.

The logic of responsibilisation draws on normative understandings of what it means to be a 'good' parent. Being a good parent in this governmental discourse means performing parenting in such a manner so as to minimise the risks posed by digital media to young people. Within the context of digital media, the acquisition of parental knowledge is often framed in terms of parental monitoring, supervision, and research about various apps and platforms that children are using. Digital media knowledges are also sold to parents through various expert advice delivered via seminars, presentations, popular books, and other cyber safety resources. Good parenting includes, for example, the expectation that parents monitor and control children's experiences with media (Mazmanian & Lanette, 2017); and in some circumstances that parents engage in what Lim (2018, pp. 32–33) calls transcendent parenting, whereby parents must 'transcend every media consumption environment their children enter,' and 'harness these multiple modes of communication to keep watch over and keep in touch with their children wherever they may be.' The expectation that good parents monitor their children's media use is also evident in cyber safety discourse. Popular Australian cyber safety author Susan McLean (McLean, n.d.), for example, argues that parental monitoring and research about children's online activities is 'vital' and prominent Australian child psychologist Michael Carr-Gregg states that 'It's imperative that parents continue to teach, monitor and protect their children when it comes to cyber safety' (Carr-Gregg, n.d.). The modern parent is thus expected to have full knowledge of their children's activities and whereabouts in online spaces, as well in physical spaces outside of the home.

Early parental concerns about the internet arose in part due to a perceived *lack* of parental knowledge about this new media technology that was rapidly being adopted in domestic households throughout the country. Not only were parents concerned about the risks posed by contemporary technologies, they were also anxious about whether or not they possessed the requisite skills and knowledge to manage them (Clark, 2009; Green et al., 2004; Lally, 2002; NetRatingsAustralia, 2005; Shepherd et al., 2006; Valentine & Holloway, 2002; Yardi & Bruckman, 2011), often leading to a 'fundamental anxiety' that their natural power base will be diminished (Green et al., 2004, p. 90), and a perceived reconfiguration of power relations within the home (Savic et al., 2016). In short, parents have long been concerned that they lack the required technical knowledge to manage digital media use in the home which has undermined their sense of authority and control and contributed to parental anxiety. The discursively constructed generational rhetoric which contrasts 'digital native' children with their 'digital immigrant' parents may serve to sustain parental concerns about a generational knowledge gap.

The internet and other digital media technologies, however, are no longer new and unfamiliar. Parents are no longer 'terrified' (Lally, 2002) of computers, or view them as 'potentially dangerous technology that is out of their control' (Holloway & Valentine, 2003).

Indeed, computers and other digital media now occupy a familiar presence, and as most participants agreed, absolutely necessary place, within family homes. Despite the enduring popularity of the 'digital native/immigrant' construction, many parents of the current era are in fact technologically knowledgeable and skilled (Blum-Ross, 2015; Livingstone, 2017). It is evident that many families, including those that participated in my research, have come to rely on digital media not just for entertainment, socialising, and for educational and professional purposes, but also for managing the business of contemporary family life which is increasingly characterised by two working parents and children juggling multiple extra-curricular activities. Participants in my study reported using private family Facebook groups and WhatsApp as a way of communicating with family members and making logistical and practical arrangements. Digital family calendars were created to ensure family members knew where they needed to be and when. Parents used Facebook pages to follow their children's extra-curricular activities. Digital media was used to maintain relationships between children and their grandparents who were often located interstate or overseas. And importantly, mobile phones were seen as important tools for ensuring (largely through parental monitoring) the safety of their children.

The media panics documented in Chapter 1 have led to an extension of the risks and dangers threatening children's safety beyond physical spaces such as the street – articulated in terms of stranger danger – to encompass virtual spaces accessible via smartphones and the internet which can be accessed within the previously safe, but now media rich confines of children's bedrooms. Questions about parental monitoring of children's whereabouts and activities in physical spaces, and concerns about children's activities in online spaces have coalesced with the advent of the smartphone, which has become the monitoring tool of choice amongst parents who provide these devices to their children out of concern for their children's safety (Hofer & Moore, 2011; Kim & Davis, 2017; Nelson, 2010). Paradoxically however, it is children's use of these devices which has become a key locus of concern in media and panic discourses (Lim, 2013; Page Jeffery, 2017; Twenge, 2017), some cyber safety advice, as well as amongst parents themselves. Thus the monitoring device has become something that parents in turn are expected to monitor, resulting in the smartphone becoming something of a double-edged sword for parents concerned about their children's safety.

The responsibilisation of parenting as a mode of governmental discourse extends the logic of a deficit of parenting knowledge to include opportunities. Many scholars have noted the contradictory framings – or what Drotner calls 'discursive dichotomies' (2005, p. 40) – of digital media and young people, as screen-based technologies are presented both as a site of danger and of exciting potentialities. Within discourses of opportunity, digital media and the internet are presented in celebratory terms, framed as beneficial, empowering and emancipating (Buckingham, 2007), and providing opportunities and advantages for young people. Much of the rhetoric is based on the alleged 'transformative potential of ICTs' (Buckingham, 2007), whereby technology is portrayed as a necessary ingredient in raising 'successful' children. Good parenting thus is seen to involve the provision of digital devices for children, but good parents must simultaneously protect their children from risk and harm (the inherent tension between these discursive dichotomies is discussed in more detail in the next chapter). As Mavoa et al. (2017, p. 341) note, the result is:

two distinct and largely opposing constructions of childhood and of technology. Children are at risk of having their childhoods completely erased by technology and simultaneously, are hailed as future masters of the technology that will redeem humankind. This contrasting set of realities gives real-world backing to Jenkins' (1998) positioning of children as 'caught somewhere over the rainbow – between nostalgia and utopian optimism, between the past and the future'.

(p. 5)

Maintaining this delicate balance between the discursively constructed opportunities and risks is fundamental to the construction of 'good' parenting in the digital age (Livingstone & Bober, 2006; Willett, 2015).

Within the context of the 'good' parent as one who monitors and is knowledgeable about their children's digital practices, various studies have sought to document the various implications associated with a deficit in parental knowledges, contrasted with those parents who more actively monitor their children's digital practices. A lack of parental knowledge about the nature of their children's online activities can lead to incorrect assumptions, misunderstandings and blanket restrictions which can result in family conflict (Livingstone, 2021; Kim & Davis, 2017). Parents with greater knowledge and experience with their children's digital media activities are more likely to see value in them (Kim & Davis, 2017). Parental knowledges within the context of digital media, however, extend beyond knowledge about their own children's online activities. Some parents are hindered by a perceived lack of technical knowledge and skills, as well as knowledge pertaining to the various apps and platforms that their children are using, the characteristics of these networks, and the potential risks involved (Symons et al., 2017). Without these knowledges, it is difficult for parents to impose clear and informed expectations on their children in relation to their media use (Symons et al., 2017).

Parents are thus expected to possess multiple knowledges: those pertaining to digital media devices, platforms, apps, and software; the risks and the range of opportunities afforded by digital media, and also their own child's digital media activities. The rest of this chapter builds on and expands the scope of parental mediation research by drawing on my research with parents to examininge in more detail parental techniques of surveillance and their various knowledge acquisition practices in relation to their children's digital media practices.

How do parents acquire knowledge about their children's media use?

Parents that I interviewed identified five primary ways in which they sought to monitor and acquire knowledge about their children's online activities: 1) physical observation; 2) digital surveillance; 3) trust-based and discursive strategies; 4) restriction and control through social or technical means; and 5) talking with other parents.

While the perceived knowledge about their children's activities was highly variable amongst participants, all parents, including those who claimed to have 'no clue' about their children's online activities, demonstrated basic knowledge about the devices their children were using (or not using), how frequently they were using them, some of their favourite apps, and what they believed were their favoured online activities.

Physical observation

The basic knowledge demonstrated by all parent participants was acquired primarily through physical observation of their children as they engaged in their practices of daily life and was not necessarily the result of concerted parental monitoring efforts. It was difficult for parents to ignore, for example, their daughters 'glued to their phones' or posing for selfies, their sons sitting on the couch gaming, or the constant ping of messages being received. For example, one 45-year-old mother of daughters aged 15 and 18 said of her younger daughter, 'When she's sitting having breakfast she's got her phone in one hand, spoon in the other, just constantly looking at this screen hunched over.'

Most parents also engaged in more deliberate, conscious forms of surveillance to actively observe what their children were doing online or on their devices. This included placing the home computer in a high-traffic area, prohibiting device use in bedrooms, looking over children's shoulders while they were on devices, or randomly walking into their bedrooms to check what they were doing. One 53-year-old father of a 15-year-old girl and a 17-year-old boy said:

> [My wife is] actively monitoring it. And part of our philosophy has been to have the computers in public spaces. They're meant to be using their devices in the public areas of the house rather than in their bedrooms. It hasn't always worked.

Digital surveillance

Almost all participants also engaged in some form of digital surveillance – both overt and covert – of their children, even if they didn't define their behaviour in these terms. In some cases, these practices were the result of practical arrangements rather than deliberate surveillance strategies, even though parents admitted that they also served a useful purpose for monitoring their children's activities. For example, younger children who had not yet acquired smartphones frequently used their parents' devices to access social media and send text messages to friends, rendering their activities highly visible to their parents. In some households all devices in the home were linked to parent accounts. For one mother of 12 and 15-year-old daughters, these practical arrangements enabled covert surveillance:

> Our youngest daughter doesn't have a phone, so she uses mine and so she asked if she could put [Instagram] on mine. And I said sure, and that means that I can look at it … They don't even know that I look at their Instagram accounts and their friends' Instagram accounts!

Parents also used third parties such as siblings or extended family members to follow or become friends with their child on social media, and report back in the event of any inappropriate behaviour – a practice that was implicitly deemed more acceptable by parents than covert surveillance. In the majority of cases however, parents engaged in overt digital surveillance techniques to purposefully acquire knowledge about their children's technology activities, and some participants (but not all) implied that that's what good parents do, as implied in the opening quote to this chapter.

Overt digital surveillance techniques that were most common amongst participants included requiring their children's passwords, following or friending their child on social media, regularly checking their child's text messages and internet browsing history, and using browsers or software that emailed reports about the child's internet activities to parents. The few parents that engaged in these forms of surveillance disclosed these practices to their children as a disciplinary technique. For example, one 40-year-old mother to four children aged 8 to 15, took a much more restrictive approach to mediation than other parents in the study, utilising a whole suite of technical surveillance tools:

> We have our modem set so it filters out a certain level of content. Then we have family sharing, so we've set up another device. Then all the children's devices are linked in under my device. Then within that, they can't delete their internet browsing content. I'm the only one who can actually delete it, so it's screened on a daily basis if need be.

Consistent with other studies, covert digital surveillance techniques, or what children might term snooping, were less common amongst parents, and included secretly monitoring their child's social media accounts, reading text messages, and checking their child's browser history. Many parents indicated disapproval of such techniques, indicating that it was a breach of their child's privacy and trust.

Trust-based and discursive strategies

Most participants highlighted trust, communication and dialogue as essential ingredients of good parenting, as well as a way of acquiring knowledge and mitigating risk. For many parents in this study, trust, dialogue and communication were cited as their main mediation strategy. Parents discussed the importance of teaching their children right from wrong, trusting them to do the right thing, and being available if things went wrong to help and support their children. As one mother said:

> It's like teaching your kids to drive. It's like, alright I've taught you everything that I can, now here are the keys off you go, and you hope that they just don't crash the car. And if they do then you have to be there and support them and try to make it better.

Parental accounts such as this one indicate that such approaches are characterised by dialogue with their children about what is acceptable, unacceptable, appropriate and inappropriate, and then leaving their child to their own devices (literally) and trusting/ hoping that they behave appropriately. Part of this approach, according to parents, involves keeping the lines of communication open so that if their child does the wrong thing or finds themselves in a difficult situation, the child will come to the parent for help and guidance. As one 47-year-old mother to a 14-year-old girl said:

> We have this similar sort of trusting relationship. We can talk about things and I ask her what she's looking at and if there's ever anything nasty or upsetting she will tell me about it.

One possible reason for the popularity of this approach, which was adopted to some extent by almost all participants, is the perceived impossibility of constant, or even regular, mediation and monitoring. Thus parents felt that they had no choice but to simply trust their children. Yet discursive strategies, especially child-initiated disclosure of information, do not appear to be a comprehensive source of knowledge for parents. This is especially the case in relation to exposure to inappropriate online material or behaviours, where parents only rarely reported children discussing feelings of exclusion by peers online or concern around their encounters with unpleasant or confronting experiences. This suggests, and is supported by findings discussed in later chapters, that these discursive practices primarily involve parents talking to their child about online safety, rather than listening to them about their practices, experiences and perspectives. Indeed, where parents discovered concerning incidents involving their children this was not generally a result of children volunteering this information. Parents noted, however, that their children were often happy to discuss what they had watched on YouTube or their recent gaming conquests.

The vast majority of parents had initiated discussions with their children about online risks, and frequently used real events reported in the media to raise issues about inappropriate behaviours and conduct. These discussions served an important knowledge generation tool for parents, who used them to ascertain how their own children might act in similar situations.

Parents sometimes went online with their children, both to find out what their children did and to create opportunities to talk about their activities. Instead of, or as well as, being a technique of surveillance, this kind of mediation can constitute active or enabling mediation (Livingstone et al., 2017), evaluative guidance (Livingstone et al., 2015) or participatory learning (Clark, 2011). These engagements took the form of parents and children playing games with each other online, watching YouTube videos together or as a family, and shared engagement in social media. While the knowledge that these practices generated for parents was somewhat limited, it served other important functions for parents, including parent/child bonding, and provided a practical foundation for discussions about appropriate online behaviours.

Restriction and control through social or technical means

A minority of parents adopted what has come to be known as a restrictive approach to parental mediation. These restrictive practices also afforded parents some (limited) knowledge about their children's online activities. Such practices were typically defined by strict limitations and prohibitions in relation to devices: not being allowed a mobile phone or tablet device until a certain age; content: not being allowed social media accounts; context: not being allowed to use devices in certain situations (for example, at the dinner table), or at certain times (for example after 9 pm); and time: imposing strict daily time limits on technology use.

Almost all participants engaged in some of these restrictive practices in their mediation of their children's device use. For example, not allowing devices at the dinner table or in bedrooms after a certain hour were common rules imposed by almost all participants. A small proportion of parents, however, sought to more tightly control their children's use of digital media. One 43-year-old father of a 13-year-old boy and 15-year-old girl, for example, had imposed strict one-hour time limits on his children's computer use and utilised software to shut off the computer once the time limit had been exhausted. These restrictive practices can be viewed as a form of knowledge generation for parents, as they it defined the remit of activities that children could engage in, and therefore to some degree, parents knew what their children weren't (or at least shouldn't) be doing. It is perhaps not surprising that parents who engaged in these more restrictive forms of mediation appeared to demonstrate less knowledge about their children's online activities. As such, the concerns and practices of more restrictive parents were more heavily influenced by external discourses about technological risk, as parents adopted a set of rules or methods in response to the perceived risks in an attempt to ameliorate them.

Talking with other parents

Parents indicated that general knowledge gleaned from other parents, often acquired incidentally through discussions at the school gate or social gatherings among friends, was particularly valuable. Indeed, it quickly became evident that the majority of participants had volunteered (in the absence of any monetary incentives) to participate in my research study so that they could tap into other parental knowledges via the focus groups. Many parents, armed with a pen and paper, diligently jotted down concerns, risks and tips from other parents that they themselves had not thought of. For example, one 43-year-old mother to a 10-year-old boy and 12-year-old girl who was observed taking notes throughout the focus group, said 'I really think that the knocking of heads among parents is really valuable, and the combining of resources.' And while some parents admitted to attending cyber safety information sessions run by their child's school or the Australian Federal Police, participants suggested that it was the discussions with and insights from other parents also attending these events that parents found particularly useful. One 44-year-old mother to an 11 year-old-boy and 14-year-old girl, said:

> It was interesting telling a lot of my friends about coming here [to the focus group] tonight. So many said, 'Tell me, tell me all about what other people talk about!' Because everybody wants to know what other people are doing. My mother … can't give me any guidance on this. All she can tell me is how much easier parenting was in her day, because the digital revolution had not yet happened. So it's really difficult, we've only got each other to talk to.

These accounts suggest that parents rely on other parents as communities of practice to learn about and work through the various challenges of mediation and monitoring of digital media. Parents appeared to invoke a sense of solidarity with each other, unable, as the quotes above suggest, to talk about these challenges with their own parents. One 45-year-old mother to three children aged between 6 and 13, highlighted the value of discussions with other parents as a form of knowledge acquisition, but also suggested that such parental exchanges served another useful function of establishing consistent rules, and presenting a 'united front'.

> Something that's helped is talking to other parents with kids the same age, and we're all checking what we allow. Because I've got an eight-year-old watching the screens when my son's on X-box, so my boys aren't allowed to play MA[9] or higher games like GTA.[10] We check with the other parents what the kids are playing with, that we're all on the same page in games and content.

Lack of parental knowledges

Despite the various techniques of knowledge acquisition and monitoring outlined above, a number of parents still expressed concern about their perceived lack of knowledge about their children's specific online activities. For example, twenty-six parents highlighted the popularity of Instagram and Snapchat amongst their children, particularly amongst their daughters, but beyond a general knowledge about what the apps actually do (for example 'I know Instagram is about photos, and with Snapchat they disappear'), few claimed to have little knowledge about the specific affordances of the apps. One 47-year-old mother to a 6-year-old girl and 14-year-old boy noted that 'there isn't much crossover between what they're interested in using and what I'm interested in using. I think it's almost deliberate.' When asked about the kinds of things that their children were doing on their devices, a few participants responded with something like, 'I thought you might ask me this, and I really should have checked before coming along!' One or two had actually checked prior to the interview or focus group.

One likely reason for the perceived deficit in parental knowledge is the lack of visibility around individualised media use, as well as an apparent desire to foster the growing independence and autonomy of their adolescent children. Some parents, particularly those with older children, said that their children were entitled to privacy, and that therefore they shouldn't know everything that their children were doing. Some parents indicated they were comfortable not knowing the details and expressed little desire to bridge the knowledge gap, preferring instead to immerse themselves in other aspects of their children's lives or rely primarily on more restrictive methods to manage risk, while for others it appeared to be a significant cause of concern. One 46-year-old mother to four children aged 12–20, for example, was particularly anxious about her perceived lack of knowledge, despite her best attempts to monitor her children's activities:

> To tell you the truth I have no idea what they're doing online, and I focus my work hours around being able to be there when they get home from school. So it's not like I'm not there in their face, trying to know what they're doing. But if someone's on the device I can't see what they're doing all the time. And I certainly can't see it with four kids.

A minority of parents indicated that they felt obligated to address their perceived knowledge deficit, while others were either comfortable not knowing, didn't have the time, or didn't want to know. One 43-year-old mother to an 8-year-old boy and 14-year-old girl indicated that she felt a particular burden to acquire knowledge about the programs and apps that her son was using:

> I feel like I have to learn about them all. I probably should look at the apps and understand them a bit better if they're using apps that I don't use … I just Google different apps and see what other people are scared about.

Many other parents, however, confessed to having neither the time, interest or inclination to acquire knowledge about the apps and platforms that their children were engaging with online, and, as indicated above, many saw little point in doing so considering the rate of technological change. One postgraduate-educated mother to two teenage daughters said, 'Because I'm so time poor, I actually don't want to Google all that stuff in my own time.' Another mother expressed a similar view, confessing that the apps and platforms that her son took such an interest in 'bored [her] shitless most of the time.' One 46-year-old mother, when asked if she looked at her 21-year-old and 14-year-old daughters' Instagram accounts replied, 'Occasionally, I'm just a bit lazy. It's just another thing to look at.' Perhaps for these reasons, cyber safety materials and resources were not a significant source of information and knowledge for most parents. The vast majority of participants indicated that they made little use of cyber safety resources and literature, with many demonstrating no interest in accessing these materials, and others indicating that they found them only 'a bit' useful. Parents instead indicated that they relied on what they termed common sense or gut feel, as well as trust and discursive strategies. As one 41-year-old mother to three children aged 10–13 said:

> I don't read anything [cyber safety materials]. I don't want to. So I just tell them gen-erally, 'This is how you should be using social media.' New apps come out all the time, and I don't want to spend the time researching the app. And I'm not going to and they are going to know better than me anyways.

These accounts indicate that time, or lack thereof, was an important determinant of par-ents' approach to knowledge acquisition and mediation. Even those parents who wanted to be more involved in their children's online activities acknowledged the significant time investment in doing so, with many admitting that they didn't want to spend time learning about the details of their children's digital media habits, particularly when most partici-pants in this study were full-time professionals. Many parents also wanted to foster their children's independence and grant them the privacy they thought their children were enti-tled to. Thus, these parents privileged guidance, dialogue and trust over more restrictive methods.

'Parenting is a gradual process of letting go of all your principles.' The challenges of good parenting in the digital age

While it is clear that almost all parents felt that some level of monitoring and mediation was a requirement of good parenting, it was evident that the reality of doing so not only took time and significant effort, but was also fraught with difficulty. Overwhelmingly, the vast majority of participants in this study pointed to various challenges associated with mediat-ing their children's device use. Study participants indicated that they had started out with rules and regulations and the best intentions to regulate, monitor and restrict their child's digital media use, but that these had since 'gone out the window,' 'all gone to pot,' and were 'completely unsustainable.' One 45-year-old post-graduate educated mother to three boys aged 12–18 conceded that 'parenting is a gradual process of letting go of all your principles.' Another 44- year-old mother to a 12-year-old girl and 10-year-old boy expressed the difficulties of mediation as follows:

> We started out with rules, and I have to say that we haven't really been very good at sticking with it. And one of them was 'asking if you're going on the internet' and that's just laughable. The second one was 'internet use in the public space,' but she wanted to do her schoolwork in the quiet place in her bedroom. It's been very difficult to negoti-ate them.

One mother's account below highlights a number of the challenges experienced by parents in this study: young people's circumvention of the rules and the ensuing conflict that often arose from parental attempts to enforce the rules, leading to the eventual abandonment of rules and regulations on the part of parents.

We did try initially to say at 9 pm devices go off and they go onto the family charging station, but neither of them would do it, so every single night we would have arguments about switching off. It became a point of real friction. And we did things like cut off their internet access at a particular time, but then they would just use the download allowance on their phones, and then we'd need to top up their credit because we need them to have their phones ... They clearly really, really wanted to still be able to be online twenty-four hours a day, so in the end we gave up, we said 'fine, you've worn us down. It's pretty fucked frankly that you guys can't control your addiction to your things, but we've tried.' We did, we tried lots of variations.

The challenges of mediation that were shared by participants suggest that the trust-based and discursive strategies favoured by so many parents in this study, rather than being the preferred sole method of mediation, were instead the fall-back position that parents adopted when all else had failed. Thus while parents were aware of, and had initially tried to live up to, the expectations of the good parent as one that monitors and regulates their children's media use, they had eventually come to accept that it was a near impossible task. As one parent conceded, 'you can't always be watching. In any normal house you can't actually be over the shoulder looking at the screen.' Monitoring is especially difficult where children are older, parents are working, and there are multiple children in the household using their own devices for the completion of tasks such as homework, which was the typical scenario across participants. What parents referred to as trust-based strategies were somewhat paradoxically operationalised by parents as a governmental strategy, as many parents often disclosed their intent to randomly check their children's online activity to their children as a disciplinary technique, expecting that they would then 'do the right thing.' At the same time, parents indicated that they were not entirely satisfied with trust and discursive strategies as the primary forms of mediation, as Michelle said:

We do rely on trust a lot. I feel pretty comfortable with that because of the relationships we have with both the kids. I do still see a better way. I haven't worked out what that is yet.

Conclusion

The parental accounts documented in this chapter indicate that the trust-based strategies employed by most parents in the study are, in reality, not actually about trust, but rather a pragmatic acceptance of the near impossibility of monitoring and regulating their children's digital media use. Participants found that their best intentions with regard to managing digital media in the home were not so easily achieved in practice. Consistent with other studies (Mazmanian & Lanette, 2017) it became clear that parental monitoring and mediation strategies consist of a set of diverse, adaptable and in some cases negotiated tactics and practices that parents utilise in their everyday domestic activities.

Yet despite the apparent dissatisfaction and frustration expressed by some parents for their perceived failure to effectively monitor their children's digital media use, their ensuing fall-back strategy of trust and negotiation is, to some degree, legitimised by contemporary dominant narratives of good parenting. As foreshadowed earlier in this chapter, the trust-based approaches favoured by parents in this study align with a broader cultural shift towards more egalitarian and child-empowered approaches to parenting, particularly amongst middle-class parents, as opposed to what might be considered a command-and-control style of parenting (Clark, 2013; Lareau, 2011; Livingstone & Bober, 2006; Nelson, 2010). What is interesting is that trust-based parenting can either be framed to conform to a particular ideal of good parenting, or conversely as a pragmatic acceptance of incapacity (as participants in this study tacitly suggested), which might be constructed as laissez-faire, inadequate or simply bad parenting. Furthermore, contemporary discourses of child-empowered ideal parenting exist in tension with the discursive construction of the good parent as one that monitors their child's online activities. Thus, practices of trust and dialogue co-exist in tension with practices of monitoring and surveillance. These discourses, and the near impossibility of fulfilling the competing and contradictory expectations placed upon the good parent in the digital age, produced a tension and apparent anxiety amongst parents in this study. Such tension is just one of many experienced by parents as they attempt to monitor and mediate their children's digital practices, as I explore in the next chapter.

Parts of this chapter have been published as follows: Page Jeffery, C. (2021). 'It's really difficult. We've only got each other to talk to'. Monitoring, mediation, and good parenting in Australia in the digital age. *Journal of Children and Media*, 15(2), 202–217.

Notes

1 Active mediation is also sometimes known as instructive or evaluative mediation (Valkenburg et al., 1999).
2 Clark (2013) cites the example of the comments section of the *New York Times* blog *Motherlode* for examples of how quickly parents judge the parenting practices and philosophies of others. Similarly, Bragg and Buckingham (2013) discuss the UK media 'blaming the moronic mothers' (p. 4) in response to the alleged sexualisation of children, a topic that was fiercely debated throughout the Anglophone West in the early 2000s. You do not need to go far to find similar discourses of parental blame within the Australia context.
3 Altheide (2002) found through a newspaper analysis that media discourses of fear have increased.
4 A contemporary manifestation of this fear of 'childhood in crisis' cited by Kehily (2010) is the UK-based Daily Telegraph Campaign in 2006 to 'halt the death of childhood'. The basis of this movement was that children had been damaged due to over-exposure of electronic media, lack of play space, and an over-emphasis on academic testing in schools (p. 172).
5 Class and the sociocultural backgrounds of parents do still, however, determine to a large extent parenting styles and mediation (Clark, 2013; Lareau, 2011).
6 Lee et al. (2014) draw on Hays (1996) here who in her observations about the 'intensification of motherhood' observes that the questioning of maternal capabilities has been built into modern American society. They note also that Furedi demonstrates 'how the 'targeting' of parental authority is a core theme in discussions of 'the problem family' from at least the nineteenth century.
7 The 'Digital Native' / 'Digital Immigrant' analogy was coined by Marc Prensky (2001) to describe what he considered to be the key differences between generational computer users. Prensky explains that the children and young people of the day were all 'native speakers' of the digital language of computers, video games and the internet. He contrasts this with the 'digital immigrants' who were not born into the digital world but who later adopted many aspects of the new technology. As 'immigrants', this older generation, including parents, must learn and adapt to their environment. However, as Prensky argues, they always retain to some degree, their 'accent' – they always have some foot in the past and have an 'outdated' language.

8 One mother for example, described herself as a 'bit of a luddite' and another had only recently acquired a smartphone after being pressured by her family. Another participant admitted that she was 'glued to her phone' mainly for work purposes, but was less interested in social media, admitting that she had been led 'kicking and screaming' to join Facebook.

9 MA15+ is an Australian classification category which restricts content to 'Mature Adults' aged 15 and over.

10 GTA stands for Grand Theft Auto, a video game series known for strong violence and sexual content, and which was given an R18+ rating in Australia, restricting it to adults 18 and over.

References

Altheide, D. L. (2002). Children and the discourse of fear. *Symbolic Interaction, 25*(2), 229–250.

Barr, J., De Souza, M., Harrison, C., Hyde, B., Van Vliet, H., & Saltmarsh, S. (2012). Parenting the 'Millennium Child': Choice, responsibility and playing it safe in uncertain times. *Global Studies of Childhood, 2*(4), 302–318.

Beck, U. (1992). *Risk society: Towards a new modernity.* London: Sage Publications.

Blum-Ross, A. (2015). Parents are now 'digital natives' too–thoughts from the 2015 family online safety institute conference. *Parenting for a digital future.* New York: Oxford.

Bragg, S., & Buckingham, D. (2013). Global concerns, local negotiations and moral selves: Contemporary parenting and the "sexualisation of childhood" debate. *Feminist Media Studies, 13*(4), 643–659.

Buckingham, D. (2006). Is there a digital generation? In D. Buckingham & R. Willett (Eds.), *Digital generations: Children, young people, and new media* (pp. 1–13). Mahwah, New Jersey, London: Lawrence Erlbaum Associates Inc.

Buckingham, D. (2007). *Beyond technology: Children's learning in the age of digital culture.* Cambridge: Polity Press.

Buckingham, D. (2013). Making sense of the 'digital generation': Growing up with digital media. *Self & Society, 40*(3), 7–15.

Burchell, G. (1993). Liberal government and techniques of the self. *Economy and Society, 22*(3), 267–282.

Bybee, C. R., Robinson, D., & Turow, J. (1982). Determinants of parental guidance of children's television viewing for a special subgroup: Mass media scholars. *Journal of Broadcasting & Electronic Media, 26*(3), 697–710.

Carr-Gregg, M. (n.d.). Social media and staying safe online. Retrieved from https://schooltv.me/searcher?search_api_fulltext=social+media

Clark, L. S. (2009). Digital media and the generation gap: Qualitative research on US teens and their parents. *Information, Communication & Society, 12*(3), 388–407.

Clark, L. S. (2011). Parental mediation theory for the digital age. *Communication Theory, 21*(4), 323–343.

Clark, L. S. (2013). *The parent app: Understanding families in the digital age.* New York: Oxford University Press.

Davis, M. (2008). *Street gang: The complete history of Sesame Street.* New York: Viking.

Drotner, K. (1992). Modernity and media panics. In M. Skovman & K. C. Schroder (Eds.), *Media cultures reappraising transnational media* (pp. 42–62). New York, London: Routledge.

Drotner, K. (2005). Mediatized childhoods: Discourses, dilemmas and directions. In J. Qvortrup (Ed.), *Studies in modern childhood: Society, agency, culture* (pp. 39–58). Basingstoke and New York: Palgrave Macmillan.

Drotner, K. (2022). The co-construction of media and childhood. In D. Lemish (Ed.), *The Routledge international handbook of children, adolescents, and media* (pp. 17–24). Abingdon: Routledge.

Faircloth, C. (2014). Intensive parenting and the expansion of parenting. In E. Lee, J. Bristow, C. Faircloth, & J. Macvarish (Eds.), *Parenting culture studies* (pp. 51–75). Basingstoke and New York: Palgrave Macmillan.

Faircloth, C., & Murray, M. (2015). Parenting: Kinship, expertise, and anxiety. *Journal of Family Issues, 36*(9), 1115–1129.

Furedi, F. (2002). *Paranoid parenting: Why ignoring the experts may be best for your child.* Chicago: Chicago Review Press.

Green, L., Holloway, D., & Quin, R. (2004). Australian family life and the Internet. In G. Goggin (Ed.), *Virtual nation: The internet in Australia* (pp. 88). Sydney Australia: UNSW Press.

Hays, S. (1996). *The cultural contradictions of motherhood.* USA: Yale University Press.

Hays, S. (1998). *The cultural contradictions of motherhood.* New Haven and London: Yale University Press.

Hofer, B. K., & Moore, A. S. (2011). *The iConnected parent: Staying close to your kids in college (and beyond) while letting them grow up.* New York: Simon & Schuster.

Holloway, S. L., & Valentine, G. (2003). *Cyberkids: Children in the information age.* London: RoutledgeFalmer.

Kehily, M. J. (2010). Childhood in crisis? Tracing the contours of 'crisis' and its impact upon contemporary parenting practices. *Media, Culture & Society, 32*(2), 171–185.

Kelly, P. (2001). Youth at risk: Processes of individualisation and responsibilisation in the risk society. *Discourse: Studies in the Cultural Politics of Education, 22*(1), 23–33.

Kim, A. S., & Davis, K. (2017). Tweens' perspectives on their parents' media-related attitudes and rules: An exploratory study in the US. *Journal of Children and Media, 11*(3), 358–366.

Kuldas, S., Sargioti, A., Milosevic, T., & Norman, J. O. H. (2021). A review and content validation of 10 measurement scales for parental mediation of children's Internet use. *International Journal of Communication, 15,* 23.

Lally, E. (2002). *At home with computers.* Oxford and New York: Berg Publishers.

Lareau, A. (2011). *Unequal childhoods: Class, race, and family life* (2nd ed.). Berkeley, Los Angeles, London: University of California Press.

Lee, E. (2014). Introduction. In E. Lee, J. Bristow, C. Faircloth, & J. Macvarish (Eds.), *Parenting Culture Studies* (pp. 1–22). Basingstoke and New York: Palgrave Macmillan.

Lee, E., Faircloth, C., Macvarish, J., & Bristow, J. (2014). *Parenting Culture Studies.* Basingstoke and New York: Palgrave Macmillan.

Lim, S (2018). *Transcendent parenting. Raising children in the digital age.* New York: Oxford University Press.

Lim, S. S. (2013). On mobile communication and youth "deviance": Beyond moral, media and mobile panics. *Mobile Media & Communication, 1*(1), 96–101.

Livingstone, S. (2017). Beyond digital immigrants? Rethinking the role of parents in a digital age. *LSE parenting for a digital future.* Retrieved from http://eprints.lse.ac.uk/76204/1/Parenting%20for%20a%20Digital%20Future%20E2%80%93%20Beyond%20digital%20immigrants_%20Rethinking%20the%20role%20of%20parents%20in%20a%20digital%20age.pdf

Livingstone, S. (2021). The rise and fall of screen time. In V. C. Strasburger (Ed.), *Masters of media: Controversies and solutions* (pp. 89–104). Maryland and London: Rowman & Littlefield.

Livingstone, S., & Bober, M. (2006). Regulating the internet at home: Contrasting the perspectives of children and parents. In D. Buckinham & R. Willett (Eds.), *Digital generations: Children, young people, and new media* (pp. 93–113). Mahwah, New Jersey, London: Lawrence Erlbaum Associates Inc.

Livingstone, S., & Byrne, J. (2018). Parenting in the digital age: The challenges of parental responsibility in comparative perspective. In Giovanna Mascheroni, Cristina Ponte & Ana Jorge (Eds.), *Digital parenting. The challenges for families in the digital age* (pp. 19–30). Göteborg: Nordicom.

Livingstone, S., & Helsper, E. J. (2008). Parental mediation of children's internet use. *Journal of Broadcasting & Electronic Media, 52*(4), 581–599.

Livingstone, S., Mascheroni, G., Dreier, M., Chaudron, S., & Lagae, K. (2015). *How parents of young children manage digital devices at home: The role of income, education and parental style.* London: EU Kids Online, LSE.

Livingstone, S., Ólafsson, K., Helsper, E. J., Lupiáñez-Villanueva, F., Veltri, G. A., & Folkvord, F. (2017). Maximizing opportunities and minimizing risks for children online: The role of digital skills in emerging strategies of parental mediation. *Journal of Communication, 67*(1), 82–105.

Marwick, A. E. (2008). To catch a predator? The MySpace moral panic. *First Monday, 13*(6). doi:10.5210/fm.v13i6.2152

Mavoa, J., Gibbs, M., & Carter, M. (2017). Constructing the young child media user in Australia: A discourse analysis of Facebook comments. *Journal of Children and Media, 11*(3), 330–346.

Mazmanian, M., & Lanette, S. (2017, February). "Okay, one more episode" an ethnography of parenting in the digital age. In *Proceedings of the 2017 ACM conference on computer supported cooperative work and social computing* (pp. 2273–2286).

McLean, S. (n.d.). Fact sheet: Internet safety tips for parents, teachers & carers. Retrieved from https://www.cybersafetysolutions.com.au/downloads/Internet-Safety-Tips-for-Teachers-Parents-and-Caregivers.pdf

Nathanson, A. I. (1999). Identifying and explaining the relationship between parental mediation and children's aggression. *Communication Research, 26*(2), 124–143.

Nathanson, A. I. (2001a). Mediation of children's television viewing: Working toward conceptual clarity and common understanding. *Annals of the International Communication Association, 25*(1), 115–151.

Nathanson, A. I. (2001b). Parent and child perspectives on the presence and meaning of parental television mediation. *Journal of Broadcasting & Electronic Media, 45*(2), 201–220.

Nelson, M. K. (2010). *Parenting out of control: Anxious parents in uncertain times.* New York and London: NYU Press.

NetRatingsAustralia. (2005). *kidsonline@home: Internet use in Australian Homes* Sydney. Prepared by NetRatings Australia Pty Ltd for the Australian Broadcasting Authority and NetAlert Limited. http://www.netalert.net.au/02010-kidsonline@home---Internet-use-in-Australia-homes---April-2005.pdf

Oswell, D. (2008). Media and communications regulation and child protection: An overview of the field. In K. Drotner & S. Livingstone (Eds.), *The international handbook of children, media and culture* (pp. 475–492). Los Angeles: Sage.

Page Jeffery, C. (2017). Too sexy too soon, or just another moral panic? Sexualisation, children, and 'technopanics' in the Australian Media 2004–2015. *Feminist Media Studies.* doi:10.108 0/14680777.2017.1367699

Palmer, S. (2006). *Toxic childhood: How the modern world is damaging our children and what we can do about it.* London: Orion Books.

Plowman, L., & McPake, J. (2013). Seven myths about young children and technology. *Childhood Education, 89*(1), 27–33.

Prensky, M. (2001). Digital natives, digital immigrants part 1. *On the Horizon, 9*(5), 1–6.

Rose, N. (1990). *Governing the soul: The shaping of the private self.* London: Taylor & Francis/Routledge.

Savic, M., McCosker, A., & Geldens, P. (2016). Cooperative mentorship: Negotiating social media use within the family. *M/C Journal, 19*(2). https://journal.media-culture.org.au/index.php/mcjournal/article/view/1078

Scott, S., Jackson, S., & Backett-Milburn, K. (1998). Swings and roundabouts: Risk anxiety and the everyday worlds of children. *Sociology, 32*(4), 689–705.

Shepherd, C., Arnold, M., & Gibbs, M. (2006). Parenting in the connected home. *Journal of Family Studies, 12*(2), 203–222.

Symons, K., Ponnet, K., Emmery, K., Walrave, M., & Heirman, W. (2017). Parental knowledge of adolescents' online content and contact risks. *Journal of Youth and Adolescence, 46*(2), 401–416.

Tapscott, D. (1998). *Growing up digital: The rise of the net generation.* New York, London: McGraw-Hill.

Tapscott, D. (2009). *Grown up digital.* New York : McGraw-Hill.

Thomas, M. (2011). *Deconstructing digital natives: Young people, technology, and the new literacies.* New York: Routledge.

Turow, J. (1999). The Internet and the Family: The View from Parents: The View from the Press. *The Annenberg Public Policy Center of the University of Pennsylvania. Report No. 27.* May 1999. https://cdn.annenbergpublicpolicycenter.org/wp-content/uploads/19991201_Internet_and_family2.pdf

Twenge, J. M. (2017). Have smartphones destroyed a generation? *The Atlantic.* September 2017. https://www.theatlantic.com/magazine/archive/2017/09/has-the-smartphone-destroyed-a-generation/534198/

Valentine, G., & Holloway, S. L. (2002). Cyberkids? Exploring children's identities and social networks in on-line and off-line worlds. *Annals of the Association of American Geographers, 92*(2), 302–319.

Valkenburg, P. M., Krcmar, M., Peeters, A. L., & Marseille, N. M. (1999). Developing a scale to assess three styles of television mediation:"Instructive mediation," "restrictive mediation," and "social coviewing". *Journal of Broadcasting & Electronic Media, 43*(1), 52–66.

Vaterlaus, J. M., Beckert, T. E., Tulane, S., & Bird, C. V. (2014). "They always ask what I'm doing and who I'm talking to": Parental mediation of adolescent interactive technology use. *Marriage & Family Review, 50*(8), 691–713.

Waldron, K. A. (2012). The iGeneration: Technology guidelines for parents and teachers. *Education Faculty Research, 2*. Retrieved from http://digitalcommons.trinity.edu/educ_faculty/2

Wark, M. (1993). Suck on this, planet of noise! *Media Information Australia, 69*(1), 70–76. doi:10.1177/1329878X9306900113

Willett, R. J. (2015). The discursive construction of 'good parenting'and digital media–the case of children's virtual world games. *Media, Culture & Society, 37*(7), 1060–1075.

Yardi, S., & Bruckman, A. (2011). Social and technical challenges in parenting teens' social media use. Paper presented at the *Proceedings of the SIGCHI Conference on Human Factors in Computing Systems*.

4

'IS THAT APPROPRIATE?'

How do parents make sense of their anxieties
and concerns?

Against the backdrop of media panics, risk discourse, online safety policy and regulation, and constructions of the 'good' parent, how do parents feel about, and make sense of, their children's digital media use? What concerns them? How are these concerns framed? Do these concerns align with the risks and opportunities that are identified in mass media and online safety discourse? Drawing on the qualitative data from the interviews and focus groups with parents in Project One this chapter argues that parents make judgements about the appropriateness of their children's digital activities, not in terms of the risk versus benefit binary which has been promulgated via both cyber safety and scholarly discourse, but rather in terms of whether it is perceived to enhance or disrupt their child's development. The process of child development cuts across two trajectories: the socio-biological development of children into adults, and socio-technological discourses of progress and opportunity. Across these two trajectories, parents are tasked with protecting their children from harm to ensure that their 'natural' development is not disrupted. At the same time, and as foreshadowed in Chapter 3, parents are increasingly encouraged to actively cultivate their child's development to ensure that they reach their full potential. Contemporary media is implicated in both of these processes in various ways.

As argued in Chapter 1, the perceived risks posed by digital media to young people have historically stemmed from concerns about exposure to adult or 'inappropriate' content or situations, thought to corrupt young people's 'innocence' and thus their normal development from innocent child to mature adult. The locus of concern has shifted away from questions of passive exposure to content towards active engagement using digital media. The interactivity and individualised use afforded by contemporary portable networked devices have granted young people a degree of agency and autonomy not previously available to them, nor necessarily deemed appropriate, while subverting power relations between children and their parents (Savic et al., 2016) and undermining parents' traditional gatekeeping function. Collective concerns about the online conduct of teenagers are in part mobilised by assumptions that children lack the judgement, common sense and

DOI: 10.4324/9781003346708-5

developmental maturity to understand the potential harm that they may inflict on themselves and others through such behaviours. Thus, young people are often conceptualised as posing a risk to their own development by engaging in online conduct and behaviours deemed to be inappropriate.

In addition to protecting their child's natural development, parents are increasingly expected to actively cultivate their child's development (Lareau, 2011; Nelson, 2010) to ensure that they reach their full potential and capability. Contemporary digital media technologies have, since the early 2000s, been sold as an important ingredient in this process. As foreshadowed in the previous chapter, socio-technological discourses of progress and innovation espouse the benefits of digital media technologies and frame computers, digital media, and the requisite digital competencies as essential to a prosperous future, suggesting that children cannot afford to be left behind and must embrace the opportunities afforded by this 'digital revolution'.

The parents interviewed implicitly invoked two distinct models of development when discussing the risks and opportunities afforded by their child's digital media use: natural development which requires protection, and enhanced development (or reaching their latent capacity and potential) which requires activation and cultivation. This chapter documents several examples to demonstrate the ways in which parents frame their concerns about their child's engagement with digital media technologies in terms of the tension between these two processes.

The developmental paradigm

Collective concerns and parental hopes and fears about children's use of digital media are tied to broader expectations about children's 'normal' development. Theorists including Hall (1904), Piaget (1969), and Erikson (1963) have posited that children progress through various stages of psycho-social development throughout their school years – from early childhood through puberty to adolescence. The developmental process has several dimensions – including physiological and psychological – and has traditionally followed a discursively constructed linear trajectory comprising a set of norms for each development phase, social and behavioural expectations, and milestones marking the transition between phases. Jackson and Scott (1999) argue:

> It is still taken for granted that the process of maturing from child to adolescent to adult unfolds as a series of naturally occurring stages, that there is a 'right age' at which children should develop certain competencies and acquire particular freedoms and responsibilities. These assumptions are so pervasive that it is difficult to think outside them, so widely accepted that they have become unquestioned 'truths'.
>
> *(p. 92)*

The 'developmental paradigm' is central to modern constructions of childhood (Holloway & Valentine, 2003). Physiological development is an obvious component of this process, typically marked by milestones such as puberty and the onset of menstruation in girls. The milestones associated with psychosocial development, however are historically and culturally contingent and have shifted in recent years. The age at which children might first walk or ride to school on their own, for example, may be considered a milestone in a child's development, one which appears to have been delayed by parents in recent years due to apparent (probably misguided) safety concerns likely mobilised by mass media discourse, resulting in shifting 'norms' about what activities are considered safe and appropriate for young children to do.

More recently, technology and digital media practices and device ownership have become embedded within models of childhood development, and digital media ownership and use are increasingly signalling the transition between different phases of childhood. These milestones may include, for example, the child's acquisition of their first mobile phone and their own social media accounts. These 'technological' milestones often coincide with other milestones such as starting high school, where children were travelling to school alone for the first time. Many parents reported purchasing their children mobile phones for their child's safety and for the parents' peace of mind.

The discursively constructed psychological norms around 'desirable' childhood development are disseminated in numerous ways – through the education of social workers and health professionals, but also through popular literature and mass media debate, in advertising and culture more generally (Rose, 1990). Developmental perspectives are also prominent in professional and public discourse and help shape risk assessment in relation to children (Scott et al., 1998). This developmental discourse is premised upon the notion that children should stick to activities (or consume media content) that are appropriate to their developmental age (Buckingham, 2007), and thus places obligations upon parents to ensure that their children only undertake and view age-appropriate activities and content. With respect to media such as movies and games, the Australian Classification Guidelines provide guidance to parents about what types of content may be suitable (or indeed, unsuitable) for children of particular ages.[1] Popular social media sites such as Facebook and Instagram state that children have to be 13 to open accounts with the services. In practice, of course, these restrictions are easily and widely circumvented (and these age limits have of course attracted significant debate in recent times).

Deviations from developmental norms often elicit concern and heighten risk anxiety (Jackson & Scott, 1999). Rose (1990, p. xii) argues that gaps between the actual behaviours of children and the ideals of these norms are inevitable, suggesting that some level of concern about children and their correct development is almost unavoidable. The discourse of development largely underpins parental judgements about what they consider to be appropriate (or not) activities for their children to be participating in. Deviations or transgressions from the discursively constructed developmental trajectory typically elicit parental anxiety and concern about the wellbeing of their child.

Socio-technological development of the child

Existing alongside discourses of development and constructions of risk/panic is the technological development paradigm, the 'socially shaped' (McKenzie & Wajcman, 1999) process by which new media technologies are created and adopted. Discourses of technological development are often framed in positive terms such as progress, innovation, benefit and opportunity (Selwyn, 2016). As such, their incorporation into children's education has come to be seen as essential. Discussions about computers, digital media and education have frequently been imbued with a persuasive rhetoric and 'visionary utopianism' or 'ed-techtopian' discourse (Buckingham, 2007).

As I have argued elsewhere (Page Jeffery, 2022b), much has been written about ed-tech. Selwyn (2016) argues that this optimism has historically been expressed through enthusiastic, exaggerated and hyperbolic 'ed-tech' speak. Sellar (2016), more moderately, argues that education is oriented for a desire for progress and a view to the future. In either case, computers and digital technologies have come to be seen as important tools for children's education and future success (Buckingham, 2007; Loveless et al., 2001). Governments throughout the developed world have sought to remove barriers to technological take-up in schools (Buckingham, 2007; Moran-Ellis & Cooper, 2000) and technology-assisted learning has become the norm within all Australian schools (Graham & Sahlberg, 2021). Governments throughout the developed world have promoted the opportunities provided by digital media technologies in terms of the growth, development and competitiveness of young people – and by extension, the nation (Silcock et al., 2016). This is especially the case in Australia, where government policy has sought to provide the necessary infrastructure, remove barriers to technology uptake and provide students with access to devices which have come to be considered essential ingredients of a contemporary education (see for example, the Australian Government's 2007 Digital Education Revolution, Gillard, 2008). In response to the presumed benefits of technology for education, many developed nations have enacted policies to provide children with the technologies deemed necessary for their future success in the global marketplace. Parents are anxious to ensure that they acquire the necessary technical skills for the jobs of the future (Livingstone & Sefton-Green, 2016).

As already foreshadowed, the growing body of parental mediation literature holds some promise for both recognising, and helping parents negotiate, the tension between these discursively constructed risks and opportunities. The shift away from exposure-related 'risks' towards a greater recognition of the various 'opportunities' complicates but helps us to better understand the realities of parenting in a digital world which is constructed simultaneously as both a risk society and an innovative, progressive, and technologically driven one. Within this context there is an implicit acknowledgement that good parenting is multifaceted, complex and significantly more onerous than merely limiting children's exposure to inappropriate media content. While increasingly recognising online 'opportunity', much of the cyber safety, media and government policy discourse still reduces online risk and opportunities to distinct, separate categories.

Parents in this study implicitly drew on the developmental paradigm when framing their concerns about their children's digital media use. Parents made judgements about the appropriateness or otherwise of their children's online activities, within the context of the discourse of development that shapes normative expectations about 'proper' child development. Yet parents also indicated the importance and benefits of digital skills. Their accounts indicate that parents are navigating a socially constructed tightrope, balancing a desire for the advancement of their child's digital skills to help them realise their potential, with protecting them from the potential harms that technological development necessarily present.

Development and appropriateness

Parents articulated and negotiated the tension between their child's normal development and the perceived inevitability of technological development in terms of the appropriateness of a given activity. The notion of appropriateness, a vague and subjective label, was not explained or defined by parents, but was used to explain a range of digital activities. Activities that were seen to disrupt their child's natural development were deemed, either explicitly or tacitly, to be inappropriate. By contrast, activities that were seen to enhance their development, in terms of their ability to activate their child's inherent capacity and potential, were deemed appropriate. Explicit articulations of inappropriateness amongst participants were almost always raised when discussing depictions of girls' bodies and sexual self-representations. Sexual behaviour or expression is considered to transgress the boundaries of childhood entirely, corrupting innocence (Egan, 2013) and accelerating children's natural development into adolescence and adulthood before they are deemed ready.

There are multiple dimensions to parental concerns and perspectives regarding this discourse of development and how it is understood in terms of the perceived risks and opportunities of networked media technologies. Most participants implied that their children weren't mature enough, or in possession of the required judgement and common sense, to manage the risks of digital media. One participant, a post-graduate educated senior executive who was father to a 14-year-old girl, suggested that schools, in their apparent haste to adopt digital media and exploit its purported educational benefits, had failed to protect their students from the risks:

> The facilitation of everything good and bad that's out there through the way schools now do business … you've got to have an iPad, you've got to have a computer, you've got to have connection to the cyberworld, to the digital world, to function. I am sure, I'm quite confident in saying that the extent to which education is facilitated has far and away outstripped the educational fraternity's ability to create the protections for kids. They've really been thrown to the wolves I think in very large measure.

Many participants drew explicit distinctions between their children and the 'developed' faculties of adults which allegedly bestowed upon them the maturity, self-discipline and common sense to enable them to manage risks and control their media use. Another highly educated male executive, acknowledged that digital media was 'fun and addictive', but suggested that adults 'had a few emotional tools' to manage their device use, compared to children who didn't 'have those internal control mechanisms yet through a lack of maturity to be able to say "enough of that" and put it to one side'.

Participants raised a number of issues of concern that they considered posed a threat to their child's natural development, some of which are outlined below. It should be noted, however, that a lack of concern about certain risk issues was also framed by some parents in developmental terms. For example, while some parents expressed concern about sexting because their daughters were approaching a 'particular age of sexual experimentation', others weren't worried because 'their children weren't at that stage yet'.

The sections that follow explore the ways parents articulated their concerns about different dimensions of childhood development and how these normative understandings are threatened, but in some instances enhanced, by digital media technologies. It is unsurprising that we see parallels between some of these concerns and the media panics outlined in Chapter 1. From time management to educational opportunities, sociality, and reputation management, parents talked about how there was always a judgement about the value of a given activity and whether it was appropriate for their child's level of development in the context of the risks and opportunities of the media technology.

Mental capacities, attention and critical thinking

The growing brain and capacity for distraction

Anxieties about digital media technologies disrupting normal child development have often been framed, both within media and popular discourse as well as from parents themselves, in terms of the potential impact on children's growing brains. As argued in Chapter 1, concerns about the 'dumbing down' effects of media have a history that predates the internet (see, for example, Drotner, 1992; Horkheimer et al., 2002; Mosley, 2000; Postman, 1985).

While parents in this study acknowledged the various benefits of digital media within educational contexts, they were more concerned about the impact of digital media use – including for educational purposes – on their child's physical brain development, their capacity to concentrate on tasks for extended periods of time without distraction, their critical thinking skills, and their ability to achieve balance in their lives. The perception that a child's teenage brain was still developing physically, and therefore had the capacity to be affected, moulded and impacted in a way that fully developed adult brains couldn't, was also apparent amongst participants.[2] One mother, a post-graduate qualified professional, articulated this in terms of the 're-wiring' of her 16-year-old daughter's brain:

> I think it's changed the wiring of their brains. The wiring in her brain and her ability to think deeply... She argued madly to get Facebook when she was in year six, and that was probably my biggest mistake that I let her do that. Because since then she has basically, I think that her framing of herself, her attention span, her ability to use her brain is all wired to the short-term, quick returns of social media. Getting her to concentrate is hard.

Parental concerns that their children's schools were increasingly deploying digital media across various elements of their child's education highlight the contradictory framing of children's use of digital media in terms of negative health discourses and positive educational discourses, the blurred boundaries between opportunity and risk, and the challenges faced by parents responsibilised for mediating their use. Parents framed their concerns primarily in terms of the potential for digital media to compromise their child's ability to deeply engage with tasks and focus for long periods of time, as they observed their child (allegedly) completing their homework on devices while simultaneously toggling between various other online activities such as social media, instant messaging, and entertainment apps such as YouTube. Thus, parents were worried not only that it was affecting their child's ability to complete their schoolwork in a timely manner, but also that it was compromising their inherent capacity to do so. As one post-graduate educated father of a 15-year-old daughter and 16-year-old son, articulated:

> Just reading really short things all the time, and not being able to focus on a long piece of writing, it's detrimental to your thought processes in some ways. It kind of stunts your mental capacities.

> He [my son] procrastinates a lot, and he's supposed to work, and he'll just spend all his time ... He'll do a little bit of work, and then he'll be like, 'I need to relax and have a break'. It's really difficult because the work tool is the distraction tool.

While getting children to complete their homework is hardly a new problem, the requirement that homework be completed on digital devices creates new challenges for parents concerned that their children lack the self-discipline to successfully manage their workloads on devices that also provide access to YouTube and social media (Page Jeffery, 2022b). As articulated by many parents in this study, different aspects of teenagers' lives – from their educational responsibilities, to socialisation and entertainment – are merging spatially and temporally via digital technologies. As one post-graduate educated mother stated:

> My daughter is 14 and she's in year 8 and has an iPad and an iPhone. She had to have an iPad for school …. That's where, for me, the whole thing started to go a bit out of control, because she's expected to do her homework but I'm just not sure how much homework is actually getting done, with this Snapchat thing constantly popping up. And that is what happens, it's a real interruption to her… She struggles in school and reading and writing is not fun, it's an absolute chore. She has a visual processing disorder, which I think is the nice new name for Dyslexia. So, she battles, concentrating is hard and sticking with it is hard … I go in and say after half an hour, "Is that all you've done?" "Well, my friends keep chatting," … She doesn't want to be left out of the conversation. It's really difficult for her.

Participant concerns about 'dumbing down' reflect collective concerns, outlined in Chapter 1, about the 'dumbing down' effect of the internet more broadly. Their concerns parallel the broader shift away from 'dumbing down' as a result of exposure to 'debased' commercial content, towards a more 'active' abandonment of cognitive effort. Many parents echoed popular narratives about young people being easily distracted and coming to depend on the instant answers and intellectual shortcuts provided by the internet, whereby thinking has been outsourced, or delegated to a device.

A minority of parents did, however, suggest that their children's negotiation of various online contexts may actually help their child develop the skills to manage competing demands. Thus, while parents were clearly concerned about digital media disrupting learning and development, some parents did concede that digital media might provide their children with a valuable opportunity to develop the self-control and multi-tasking skills needed for future study and work. A father of three boys aged 3–13, observed that the boundaries between work and play were increasingly blurred, and suggested that 'it's good for them to start learning that from a young age – self-control'.

Critical thinking

Parental concern about digital media potentially compromising their children's critical thinking skills similarly highlights the challenges faced by parents in maximising the educational potential of digital media, while managing the risks. Such concerns were framed by parents in developmental terms, as parents implied that the ability to think critically is a skill that is learned and developed through childhood. One mother of 11 and 13-year-old daughters, said:

> The technology is so tactile and user-friendly, I think this rush to embrace it, particularly in primary school is actually detrimental because they don't know how to be critical about what they're seeing.

In sharing similar accounts, many parents implied that children were developmentally more susceptible to the dumbing down effects of the internet because it was 'all they knew', and 'no-one used books anymore'. In contrast, while many parents tacitly recognised that the internet provided a valuable source of information that enhanced their children's education, many parents felt that children's critical thinking skills were being compromised because they only used the internet, in their implicit view an inferior source of information to books. One mother enthusiastically recalled an experiment that her 13-year-old daughter had done at school which involved 'testing liquid and stuff' and did not involve computers or technology. She implied that such activities were important because she didn't 'want them seeing that everything's online, because they will forget how to write. And I think they lose a bit of critical thinking about what's put in front of them'.

Many other participants framed their concerns about their child's capacity for critical thinking and analysis in terms of the perceived surface engagement with digital media, which did not, in their minds, accord with deep thinking and analysis. As one father to a 12-year- old son, said:

> My key concern is the modes of thinking, the modes of engaging are very different… I think it's that thing of having a lot of surface engagement with something but no depth…but my concern more is that a very broad surface level of thinking without any depth or critical understanding, that's a very different experience when you're reading a book or reading something in a different format…And I just wonder what the effect is going to be on this generation.

Such views imply a belief that children need to firmly establish the key foundations of learning offline before migrating to digital technologies. In other words, children must be allowed to follow the normal developmental learning trajectory, which encompasses mastering fundamental offline tasks such as handwriting, reading books, and completing homework using a pen and paper first. Parental concerns about the introduction of digital media into their children's school lives appear to be premised upon a belief that digital media were interrupting and thus jeopardising their normal developmental trajectory, resulting in 'intellectual laziness' and 'stunted' mental capacities. As one mother said, 'I think they've got to get the foundations right, and I think they can skip that if they're just given a tablet'.

Concern about digital media compromising children's mental capacities and critical thinking skills highlights the tension between child development and socio-technical development. Parents' anxieties about dumbing down were challenged by their acknowledgement of the benefits of digital media, as well as its inevitability and the ease with which information could be accessed and verified, and thus its capacity to enhance their child's intellectual development. Yet, for parents, their children were not yet capable of using digital media to minimise its risks to critical thinking, while maximising its opportunities (e.g. access to information) by virtue of their age and relative lack of developmental maturity. Perhaps more importantly, parents were evidently concerned about the perceived threats to their children's capacity to develop these skills, considered so important for their future success.

Mediated play, sociality and social development

Childhood play and socialisation are accepted as normal and necessary features of contemporary childhood, however many parents suggested that the increasing technological mediation of their child's play may not be appropriate for their normal development. One participant – a psychologist and mother of four teenage children – was particularly anxious about the increasing role that digital media was playing in her children's lives. She expressed concern that mediated play had 'numbed' her children and 'stifled their creativity'. She lamented that her children were no longer interested in painting, drawing and all 'the amazing things that they used to do before'. Another mother observed that her 13-year-old daughter and her friends 'face-time each other in the group, even when they're all in the same room'. One mother recalled her daughter's 12th birthday party sleep-over, and observed the girls 'sitting side-by-side, at two in the morning, instagramming', and appeared dismayed that they weren't doing as she had done as a child, 'staying up late with friends and being noisy and ridiculous'.

These accounts from parents invoke a nostalgic ideal of friendship based on developing and cultivating relationships in person and engaging in shared play and activities which are co- located. However, the affordances of social networking and networked gaming have seen the emergence of a different kind of friendship, where the very act of 'friending' someone is different from traditional notions (boyd & Heer, 2006). The psychologist mother quoted above expressed concern about the ways in which mediated sociality was compromising a more natural and organic way of socialising, and the potential developmental effects of this:

> I do think that the way that a person socialises online is very different from the way that you socialise in person, and developmental stages that you go through in socialising with friends, they're being hindered by thinking that texting and online talking is actually as real. The way that monitors and alters their speech pattern, that sort of self-filtering "I'd better say this, or I'd better not say that", or to write something and then to write something and delete it and try again… editing it. All of these are things that you should be able to manage in your speech and talking to people face to face, but people aren't … I think it's altering people's cognitive and emotional development.

Parental concern about the increased mediation of friendships and other social and familial relations and concerns about isolation are consistent with earlier studies (see, for example, Sergi et al., 2017). However, participant accounts suggest that such concerns appear to have additional dimensions, including the potential erosion of young people's social skills, and that digital media displace face-to-face sociality, disrupts family relationships and is less authentic than relationships cultivated offline.

Anxieties about the developmental effects of the increasing mediation of young people's social relationships were also framed by parents in terms of problematic social behaviours such as cyberbullying and online conflict and exclusion, with some expressing concern that their children may not be mature enough to deal with the potentially negative mediated interpersonal interaction afforded by social networking platforms. For example, one mother to 13 and 17-year-old sons, talked about how her younger son had experienced bullying in the past. As a result, she was delaying purchasing a device for him out of concern for his wellbeing and emotional and social development (although she admitted this was difficult due to homework requirements). Yet many more parents were ambivalent about this issue, suggesting that interpersonal conflict, although not necessarily cyberbullying, was an inevitable part of adolescence, and by extension, an intrinsic part of normal child development. Here, parents shared a much more nuanced account of online bullying and drama than has been publicised through mass media and online safety discourse. As one post-graduate educated father to a 14-year-old girl stated:

> There's a great tendency to overreact because there's so much out in the media, things like the 11-year-old boy committing suicide because he was being bullied. And god, we're all going to commit suicide, well no, we're not.

Without excusing or justifying bullying behaviours, parents tacitly delineated between the common covert behaviours of drama and exclusion, considered to be part of natural adolescent development, and more overt, targeted, 'serious' cyberbullying intended to cause harm. The latter was seen as a transgression of normal, acceptable and appropriate peer interaction, although in reality the distinction is often far less clear, and contemporary definitions of cyberbullying do little to elucidate these boundaries. In drawing this distinction, parents implied that exclusion, drama and relational aggression were (and had long been) a normal and inevitable feature of adolescent life. Such perspectives are consistent with contemporary cyberbullying literature, which suggests that rather than constituting an entirely new problem that remains independent and separate from more traditional forms of bullying, 'cyberbullying' is a 'reconfiguration' of traditional bullying (Livingstone et al., 2016), and an 'extension of the school environment' (Juvonen & Gross, 2008, p. 497).

It is understandable that participants were concerned about their children being hurt as a consequence of negative online social interactions, however most were pragmatic in their responses. Parents recognised that the affordances of digital media may have shifted the character of negative interpersonal relations in troubling ways, in particular, that online bullying 'followed children home' and thus extended beyond the spatial and temporal confines of the school. However, while acknowledging that digital media had shifted the character of peer sociality, it was evident that parents considered that the networked sociality that their children were engaging in was generally replicating and extending offline peer group dynamics. As one mother said while sharing an experience recounted to her by her 16-year-old daughter:

> A couple of years ago a couple of the girls would be having an [online] conversation and she could see that she was being excluded from the conversation, or someone would post a photo of a party on Instagram ... That happened a couple of times. Is that any worse than when you go to school on Monday and you realise that everyone had a party? You have to deal with that. Maybe it's the immediacy of it, that right now they're all over at so and so's house having a party and I'm not there, why not?

Thus, while parents acknowledged that peer conflict, exclusion and drama were distressing and hurtful, they conceded that these experiences provided an important learning and development opportunity for children, who need to build resilience, navigate peer relationships, and learn how to cope with hurt, betrayal and exclusion, both online and offline. Indeed, in many ways, the affordances of digital media, specifically the visibility of mediated social exchanges, enabled parents to help their children navigate peer conflict. As one mother of a 12-year-old girl and 10-year-old boy said:

> In a way having it [conflict/bullying] happen on text and having the authority to read it means I can see some of it sometimes. We've had conversations that we wouldn't have been able to have because I wouldn't have known exactly what was going on. I don't think it's any worse because it's on social media. It's just it's there and you can see it. The only thing that makes it worse is that it's written down and other people can see it and it stays there.

Navigating the complexities of interpersonal relationships, and the joys and heartache that they invariably bring, was therefore seen to be a necessary part of child development and maturation. In this way, online conflict was seen by parents to provide an opportunity for enhancing their child's development by cultivating and nurturing their capacity for resilience and conflict resolution.

Mediated self-representation, identity development and reputation

The tension between technological development and child development has also been framed in terms of young people's practices of self-representation. Collective concerns about the digital footprint young people are creating, and the potential reputational consequences, are premised on assumptions of a deficit in young people's judgement and common sense by virtue of their age and concomitant lack of maturity. Popular advice and cyber safety resources seek to address this alleged deficit by imploring young people to think before they post, or employ the 'grandma test' (to prompt them to consider if their post is something they would be comfortable with their grandmother seeing) before sharing online. Such concerns were echoed by study participants, who were worried that their child's inappropriate practices of self-representation might compromise their future opportunities. Parents were evidently aware of some of the unique affordances of digital media, such as the persistence, visibility and spreadability of content (boyd, 2014), and thought that their children did not yet have the capacity or maturity to fully appreciate the possible consequences of expressing themselves, or 'oversharing', online. This awareness, coupled with the common concern that their children privileged the valorisation that they received via 'likes' and comments in response to content shared, over reticence and restraint, was a source of anxiety for many parents.

For some participants such as one working professional and mother of 12 and 15-year old daughters, reputational concerns were the primary reason for not allowing her daughters to have social media accounts. This mother noted, along with other participants, that 'angsty rants' were typical of teenagers, yet she was concerned about the reputational effects of documenting them:

> You read stories about employers trawling social media of potential employees, and I'm sure there's heaps of things that people have put on there that they'd never want an employer to see. And I don't think at 13 to 20 you have the emotional maturity to understand that.

This participant's account implies that angsty rants are a normal phase of teenage development, however expressing them via social media is implicitly inappropriate due to the affordances of social media which mean that the rant remains long after the teen has moved on developmentally as a permanent record of the 'storm and stress' (Hall, 1904) of adolescence. Most participants were similarly concerned about the construction and expression of identity online, as well as representations or information disclosure by their child or third parties that may have reputational repercussions. These anxieties expressed by participants were disproportionately concerned with representations that could be considered to be sexualised, and other representations considered to connote a precociousness deemed inappropriate, like drinking or partying. As one post-graduate educated mother to a 16-year-old daughter said:

> My major concerns were that she did not fully understand the reputation that she was creating for herself, and then the ramifications of that. So essentially that she was going to make things harder for herself than they needed to be.

Underlying these concerns was an assumption on the part of parents that their children lacked the maturity, judgement and common sense to consider the potential long-term consequences of such behaviours. Indeed, according to Gabriel (2014, p. 105), many of the fears associated with young people's online behaviours are premised on:

> dominant assumptions informed by developmental psychology and developmental neuroscience … that children and young people have limited capacity to critically reflect on their own development, and that to expect this of them is to harm their 'natural' cognitive and emotional growth.

Parents related many experiences where their child had shared information or images via social media which had threatened their child's reputation. In one particularly extreme example, one mother shared a story involving her 17-year-old-son in which a depiction of him engaged in sexual activity with a younger girl was uploaded to social media. She described the ongoing legal and social implications which had 'dragged on for months'. Yet this mother was still doubtful that her son had learned from the experience at all, noting:

> He still doesn't get it … I'm pretty sure that since then he has still shared images and asked for images and got images. They have no clue what they're doing. That is the incredible danger of it.

Conclusion

As already foreshadowed, parental mediation and online safety literature have tasked parents with minimising the risks posed by digital media to their children, while maximising opportunities. In Australia, the opportunities have been framed in terms of the educational potential of digital media, while many of the dangers have typically been presented as a discrete set of risks which include, for example, cyberbullying and exposure to inappropriate content, as well as a range of negative health impacts (Scott et al., 2019). Dominant discourses have predominantly framed young people's use of digital media in terms of this reductive binary of risk and opportunity.

Yet, as parental accounts in this chapter show, parents reflect on various reflexive processes when judging the appropriateness or otherwise of their children's online activities, drawing on the discourse of development. The accounts reproduced by parents are indicative of a particular position held by middle-class Australian parents, in which parents navigate a tension between two developmental trajectories: socio-biological development whereby children progress through childhood to adolescence and adulthood; and technological development which is socially shaped (McKenzie & Wajcman, 1999) as progressing in a positive direction, with increasing opportunities and benefits to children, particularly with regards to their education, connectivity and self-expression. The accounts suggest that various activities or practices which have historically been framed as a risk which parents might be expected to mitigate, in fact provided valuable opportunities to cultivate and enhance their child's development, as they facilitated learning, growth and resilience. By contrast, parents considered that various tasks typically conceptualised as an opportunity, such as technology for learning and education, in their view had the potential to impede their child's learning and development. Further, some activities or behaviours implicitly existed on a continuum, only transgressing the boundaries of normal and appropriate once a particular (subjective and fluid) threshold had been crossed: for example, crossing the threshold from normal peer conflict that is a part and parcel of child development and helps develop resilience, into inappropriate cyberbullying which may disrupt development. These accounts thus highlight the deficit of the risk versus vs benefit binary which have has to date framed both young people's use of digital media, and parents' responsibility to mediate it, and point towards a need for a more nuanced approach to both conceptualising and negotiating young people's media use.

Parts of this chapter have been published in: Page Jeffery, C. (2021). Parenting in the digital age: Between socio-biological and socio-technological development. *New Media & Society, 23*(5), 1045–1062.

This chapter also draws on some of the findings published in: Page Jeffery, C. (2022). '[Cyber] bullying is too strong a word…': Parental accounts of their children's experiences of online conflict and relational aggression. *Media International Australia, 184*(1), 150–164 and Page Jeffery, C. (2022). 'It's just another nightmare to manage:' Australian parents' perspectives on BYOD and 'ed-tech' at school and at home. *Learning, Media and Technology, 47*(4), 471–484.

Notes

1 Changes to the classification categories and guidelines over the years demonstrate the shifting 'norms' and standards regarding media content.
2 Note that these interviews and focus groups were undertaken several years before Jonathan Haidt's bestselling book 'The Anxious Generation' was published in 2024 which argues that digital technologies are rewiring young people's brains. This suggests that parents have long been primed to be receptive to such claims.

References

boyd, d. (2014). *It's complicated: The social lives of networked teens.* London, New York: Yale University Press.

boyd, d., & Heer, J. (2006). Profiles as conversation: Networked identity performance on Friendster. *Paper presented at the Proceedings of the 39th annual Hawaii international conference on system sciences (HICSS'06).*

Buckingham, D. (2007). *Beyond technology: Children's learning in the age of digital culture.* Cambridge: Polity Press.

Drotner, K. (1992). Modernity and media panics. In M. Skovman & K. C. Schroder (Eds.), *Media cultures reappraising transnational media* (pp. 42–62). New York, London: Routledge.

Egan, R. D. (2013). *Becoming sexual: A critical appraisal of the sexualization of girls.* Cambridge: Polity Press.

Erikson, E. (1963). *Childhood and society* (2nd ed.). New York: W W. W Norton and Company Inc.

Gabriel, F. (2014). Sexting, selfies and self-harm: Young people, social media and the performance of self-development. *Media International Australia, 151*(1), 104–112.

Gillard, J. (2008). Budget education revolution 2008–09. Statement by the Honourable Julia Gillard, MP 13 May. https://archive.budget.gov.au/2008-09/ministerial_statements/education.pdf

Graham, A., & Sahlberg, P. (2021). Growing Up Digital Australia: Phase 2 technical report (Phase 2). Gonski Institute for Education. UNSW, Sydney. https://www.gie.unsw.edu.au/sites/default/files/documents/GONS5000%20Growing%20Up%20Digital%20Report_FINAL.pdf

Hall, G. S. (1904). *Adolescence.* New York: Appleton-Century-Crofts.

Holloway, S. L., & Valentine, G. (2003). *Cyberkids: Children in the information age.* London: Routledge Falmer.

Horkheimer, M., Adorno, T. W., & Noeri, G. (2002). *Dialectic of enlightenment.* Stanford: Stanford University Press.

Jackson, S., & Scott, S. (1999). Risk anxiety and the social construction of childhood. In D. Lupton (Ed.), *Risk and sociocultural theory: New directions and perspectives* (pp. 86–107). United Kingdom: Cambridge University Press.

Juvonen, J., & Gross, E. F. (2008). Extending the school grounds? – Bullying experiences in cyberspace. *Journal of School health, 78*(9), 496–505.

Lareau, A. (2011). *Unequal childhoods: Class, race, and family life* (2nd ed.). Berkeley, Los Angeles, London: University of California Press.

Livingstone, S., & Sefton-Green, J. (2016). *The class: Living and learning in the digital age.* New York: New York University Press.

Livingstone, S., Stoilova, M., & Kelly, A. (2016). Cyberbullying: Incidence, trends and consequences. *LSE Research Online.* Retrieved from http://eprints.lse.ac.uk/68079/

Loveless, A., DeVoogd, G. L., & Bohlin, R. (2001). Something old, something new... Is pedagogy affected by ICT? In A. Loveless & V. Ellis (Eds.), *ICT, pedagogy, and the curriculum: Subject to change* (pp. 63–83). London and New York: RoutledgeFalmer.

McKenzie, D., & Wajcman, J. (1999). *The social shaping of technology.* Buckingham, UK: Open University Press.

Moran-Ellis, J., & Cooper, G. (2000). Making connections: Children, technology, and the national grid for learning. *Sociological Research Online, 5*(3), 46–57.

Mosley, I. (2000). *Dumbing down: Culture, politics and the mass media.* Thorverton UK: Imprint Academic.

Nelson, M. K. (2010). *Parenting out of control: Anxious parents in uncertain times.* New York and London: NYU Press.

Page Jeffery, C. (2022a). '[Cyber] bullying is too strong a word...': Parental accounts of their children's experiences of online conflict and relational aggression. *Media International Australia, 184*(1), 150–164.

Page Jeffery, C. (2022b). 'It's just another nightmare to manage': Australian parents' perspectives on BYOD and 'ed-tech' at school and at home. *Learning, Media and Technology, 47*(4), 471–484.

Piaget, J. (1969). *The psychology of the child.* London: Routledge and Kegan Paul.

Postman, N. (1985). *Amusing ourselves to death: Public discourse in the age of show business.* United States: Viking Penguin.

Rose, N. (1990). *Governing the soul: The shaping of the private self.* London: Taylor & Francis/Routledge.

Savic, M., McCosker, A., & Geldens, P. (2016). Cooperative mentorship: Negotiating social media use within the family. *M/C Journal, 19*(2). https://journal.media-culture.org.au/index.php/mcjournal/article/view/1078

Scott, H., Biello, S. M., & Woods, H. C. (2019). Social media use and adolescent sleep patterns: Cross-sectional findings from the UK millennium cohort study. *BMJ Open, 9*(9), e031161.

Scott, S., Jackson, S., & Backett-Milburn, K. (1998). Swings and roundabouts: Risk anxiety and the everyday worlds of children. *Sociology, 32*(4), 689–705.

Sellar, S. (2016). Leaving the future behind. *Research in Education, 96*(1), 12–18.

Selwyn, N. (2016). Minding our language: Why education and technology is full of bullshit… and what might be done about it. *Learning, Media and Technology, 41*(3), 437–443.

Sergi, K., Gatewood Jr, R., Elder, A., & Xu, J. (2017). Parental perspectives on children's use of portable digital devices. *Behaviour & Information Technology, 36*(11), 1148–1161.

Silcock, M., Payne, D., & Hocking, C. (2016). Governmentality within children's technological play: Findings from a critical discourse analysis. *Children & Society, 30*(2), 85–95.

5
FAMILY CONFLICT AND DIGITAL MEDIA

So far, I have demonstrated that parents have a range of concerns about their children's digital media use – some of which are shaped by media panics – and that they attempt to monitor and mediate their children's digital practices in different ways as they endeavour to mitigate their anxieties and enact 'good' parenting. Yet, as parents explained, this is no easy task, as parental attempts at mediation are frequently met with hostility and resistance. The 'storm and stress' (Hall, 1904) associated with adolescence often coincides with young people acquiring their first phone or other devices, often resulting in a perfect storm of parent/adolescent conflict. This chapter builds on the data from Project One which indicated that attempts to mediate children's media use was a cause of family conflict, and documents the findings from Project Two – the participatory action workshops that were conducted with parents and their children to reduce digital family conflict. It must be said that parent/adolescent conflict is hardly new, yet in a digital era in which the screen is ever-present, there is a growing tendency to blame digital media for a growing number of family issues and conflicts. It is worthwhile, therefore, to remind ourselves that parent/child conflict during adolescence has a much longer history.

The 'storm and stress' of governing adolescents

Governing children in the liminal space between childhood and adulthood raises many issues and challenges for parents. The period of adolescence, like childhood more generally, is socially and culturally constructed (Arnett, 2014; Buckingham, 2000; James & James, 2004; James et al., 1998). It has been described as a time of challenge and turbulence (Roth & Brooks-Gunn, 2000) and 'storm and stress' (Hall, 1904) as young people negotiate the boundaries between dependence and autonomy (Kurz, 2002). A period of liminality and transition, adolescence is characterised by self-discovery, identity-seeking, concern with the self, growing independence, greater engagement with consumer culture, increasing autonomy and risk taking (Arnett, 2014; Livingstone, 1998, 2007; Owen, 2014; Strasburger et al., 2009)[1]. The liminality of adolescence is typically conceptualised with reference to developmental psychology which seeks to explain how young people

DOI: 10.4324/9781003346708-6

transition into adulthood. As documented in the previous chapter, theories of development have been heavily influenced by the work of Stanley Hall (1904), Jean Piaget and Inhelder (1969) and Erik Erikson (1963). Maturation into adulthood is framed in terms of a number of natural stages of physical, emotional and cognitive development (Gabriel, 2014).

Teenagers seeking to enact independence by testing boundaries established through parental governance can be contrasted with the younger child in need of protection. As documented earlier, the period of transition from 'childhood innocence' to the 'autonomous adolescent,' signals a shift in the locus of concern away from primarily external threats, where harm may be 'done to' children, towards adolescent children putting themselves and others at risk due to their own behaviours and decisions as well as presenting a potential threat to the 'moral fabric of society' (James & James, 2004). The partial independence and self-determination enacted by adolescents, as well as the process of puberty and sexual maturation, means that adolescents in particular are viewed as requiring policing for the 'knowledge they may acquire and the sexual or disruptive behaviours they may enact' (Livingstone, 1996, p. 11). Thus, the young, passive 'child in danger' in need of protection can be contrasted with the older, active 'dangerous' child (Oswell, 1998) in need of control and containment (James & James, 2004).

Personal ownership of media dramatically increases in the early teenage years as part of the development of identity (Livingstone, 2007). This reflects an underlying process of 'individualisation', whereby audiences, and the media that service them, are increasingly fragmented and individualised. The contemporary smartphone is the key individualising, privatising, device (Morley, 2006). Within this context, the bedroom, and what Livingstone (2007, p. 1) calls 'bedroom culture' has become a 'central location – both physically and symbolically – of media use and the mediation of everyday life'. 'Bedroom culture' is characterised by a set of conventional meanings and practices closely associated with privacy, identity and the self. The rise of 'bedroom culture' accompanies a broader shift in the consumption of media away from the communal spaces of the living room (for example, where families watched television as a family) towards the consumption of media in the private space of the bedroom (Livingstone, 2007). This shift from communal to private consumption of media presents significant challenges for parents who are expected to monitor and mediate their children's digital media use. Further, much of the contemporary online safety advice continues to advise parents to prohibit young people from using their devices and accessing the internet in their bedrooms. However, the perceived need for parental mediation of young people's digital media use decreases as children grow older and parents generally engage in less mediation of older children (Clark, 2011; Duerager & Livingstone, 2012; Yardi & Bruckman, 2011).

A number of studies indicate that parent-adolescent digital conflict is common (Beyens et al., 2016; Blackwell et al., 2016; Hadlington et al., 2019; Kim & Davis, 2017; Lauricella et al., 2016; Mesch, 2006; Tammisalo & Rotkirch, 2022; Yang & Zhang, 2021). It is generally accepted that parent-adolescent conflict is a normative feature of adolescence (Beyens & Beullens, 2017; Steinberg, 2001), and the period of adolescence has long been considered a difficult time for families as children increasingly seek privacy, autonomy and independence. However, digital media technologies have been found to present additional challenges and complexities for families. As argued in Chapter 1, the focus on online risk in Australia coupled with increasing media use amongst young people creates anxiety for many parents who, understandably, want to secure their children's wellbeing and thus attempt to monitor, regulate or restrict their children's media use (Page Jeffery, 2021).

Scholars have found that one primary source of conflict between parents and their teenagers stems from the tension between parental desire for authority and children's desire for autonomy and to maintain jurisdiction over their own lives (Smetana, 1988). While younger children are more accepting of parental interventions, older children have been found to increasingly question the legitimacy of parental authority (Soenens & Vansteenkiste, 2010). As I have argued elsewhere (Page Jeffery et al., 2022), digital media have become an important means through which adolescents develop independence and test boundaries. Their behaviours, peer relationships, and practices of self-representation – all elements which would be considered within the personal domain of parental authority and potential sources of family conflict in their own right – are also enacted in online spaces in ways which can amplify or create additional conflict. Parental attempts to monitor or regulate their children's media use are often interpreted by adolescents as threatening their autonomy, and commonly result in child psychological reactance (Brehm, 1966), whereby young people respond by doing the opposite of what they are expected (Symons et al., 2020; Yardi & Bruckman, 2011).

Digital media technologies have also been found to reconfigure traditional parent-child power relations, which may also lead to conflict. As already foreshadowed, many adolescents are considered to be more knowledgeable about digital technologies than their parents, thus leading to what has been termed 'child effects' (Bell, 1979) and what Correa (2014) terms 'bottom-up technology transmission' whereby children are socialising their parents. Despite a lack of empirical evidence to support a competence gap, it appears that parents and children have different digital knowledges and competencies. This may present a challenge to parental authority (Ribak, 2001), a disruption to the established 'hierarchy of expertise', and thus a subversion of traditional family power relations (Mesch, 2006; Savic et al., 2016). Research has found that families where the child was viewed as the computer expert, and where children are more likely to guide their parents how to use digital media, report more intergenerational conflict about media (Mesch, 2006; Nelissen & Van den Bulck, 2018).

Parent-adolescent digital conflict can also arise in relation to a wide range of other issues. Conflict often emerges around disagreements about the 'appropriate' age to get a smartphone or social media accounts (Ammari et al., 2015; Rideout, 2015; Rudi et al., 2015, cited in Kim & Davis, 2017). More frequent device use amongst adolescents has also been found to negatively impact family relationships, often leading to parent-child conflict (Beyens & Beullens, 2017; Mesch, 2006; Tammisalo & Rotkirch, 2022; Yang & Zhang, 2021). Consistent with psychological reactance theory,[2] more restrictive forms of mediation also lead to more conflict (Beyens & Beullens, 2017; Nathanson, 2002). Time displacement also affects family cohesion, as time spent using digital devices not only displaces family time, but also affects the quality of that family time (Mesch, 2006).

Underpinning much of this tension and conflict are different perspectives between parents and their children about the purpose and value of digital media technologies, what constitutes legitimate use, and differing skills, knowledge and expectations between parents and their children (Blackwell et al., 2016; Kim & Davis, 2017; Mesch, 2006; Ouvrein & Verswijvel, 2021). For example, parents often expect digital media technologies to be used for educational purposes, whereas adolescents use it for social and entertainment purposes (Mesch, 2006). Further, for many parents, providing their children with a mobile device helps them to monitor their children and ensure their safety (Devitt & Roker, 2009; Wei & Lo, 2006, cited in Kim & Davis, 2017), although many adolescents may not appreciate this kind of surveillance. Adolescents, in contrast, are more likely to see their mobile phone as an opportunity to connect with their peers and assert their personal autonomy (Weinstein & Davis, 2015 cited in Kim & Davis, 2017). A real or perceived lack of parental knowledge about what their children are doing online contributes to these often conflicting views and perspectives (Page Jeffery, 2022).

As documented in Chapter 3, a perceived lack of parental knowledge and understanding makes it difficult for parents to set boundaries for effective parenting (see also, Yardi and Bruckman, 2011). Kim and Davis (2017) and Blackwell et al. (2016) also found that parents were often unaware of what their children were doing on their devices, and that parents and children placed different values on online activities such as gaming. There is now, however, some evidence that pandemic-related lockdowns and increased use of digital devices at home have led to greater parental understandings and appreciation of their children's digital practices and online activities (Healy et al., 2024), although in many cases the extended lock downs exacerbated parental anxiety about their children's screen time (Willett & Zhao, 2024). Children have also expressed frustration with limits related to screen time, particularly when they believed their parents were not aware of their actual online activities, did not understand the value of those activities, or underestimated their school and work responsibilities (Blackwell et al., 2016). Conflict often reduced as parenting knowledge increased, especially when parents had direct experience with their child's digital media activities (Kim & Davis, 2017).

Parental mediation of children's media use is a parental practice as it is specific to a particular context or domain (media use). Parenting style is a broader concept encompassing the emotional nature of parenting, and represents the 'constellation of attitudes towards the child that are communicated to the child and create an emotional climate in which the parents behaviours are expressed' (Darling & Steinberg, 1993, p. 488). Studies show that an open, authoritative and communicative parenting style, which often lends itself to more enabling mediation practices and greater parental understanding of their children's online activities, is more likely to lead to acceptance of parental authority, mutual respect, and thus less parent-child conflict (Byrne & Lee, 2011; Kim & Davis, 2017; Lau et al., 1990; Symons et al., 2020)

The initial qualitative research findings from the first project which involved interviews and focus groups with 40 parents of 12–16-years-olds revealed that digital media was a significant source of conflict between parents and their children. Parents expressed frustration and exasperation as their attempts to mediate their children's media use frequently resulted in family conflict. Parents indicated that as a result, they had slowly given up on enforcing many of their previously held rules, as the following quotes from parents demonstrate:

We had that no phones at the dinner table [rule]. We did try initially to say at 9pm devices go off and they go onto the family charging station which we had in the office at home. But neither of them would do it, so every single night we would have this back and forth, the 'Come on, time to power down, go and plug your device in,' or if we didn't remind them they would just hang on to it until we came in and said, 'It's ten o'clock what the hell are you doing?' So it became a point of friction. My husband would get very frustrated when they were staying online. We did things like cut off their internet access at a particular time.

The problem is we try and instigate things and then we get a bad night and it all goes to pot…. I just can't have this fight.

I've got daughters who are 12 and 10, we have a lot of battles around this. I don't feel I enforce the rules very well. We've tried no devices in the bedroom and they sneak around or have various arguments as to why this is necessary…. So, we tried and limit time, not always successfully, we try and limit the rooms, but also not successfully.

Until about a year ago I think we had some pretty strict, like, we would literally physically confiscate the devices after nine o'clock, just 'Give us your devices,' but it's more difficult when you have a person who's almost an adult, who is older…You don't have the same relationships like, just give me your thing. You don't talk back, you just do it because you're a child. When they get to a certain age and maturity level and size it becomes more difficult, you have to try and have a discussion to explain our concerns and that they understand and agree, because it's harder to just impose your will on people who are 16 or 17 than when they're 14 or even 15. And even my daughter, she'll just refuse. You can have a massive confrontation, or you can just say, 'OK, whatever'. Yeah, it's hard.

Minimising conflict

In response to these findings, I designed a project aimed at minimising parent/child digital conflict through enhancing intergenerational understanding about media use. As documented in the introduction, this project consisted of several workshops bringing parents and their children together to separately share their perspectives, concerns, and practices, with the explicit aim of facilitating mutual understanding of each other's views and perspectives. We wanted parents to understand the value of media in the lives of young people, while we wanted young people to understand the nature of their parents' concerns (and the concern for their children's safety and wellbeing which underpinned rules and restrictions). We also wanted to provide young people with the opportunity to demonstrate their existing knowledge and mitigation strategies in relation to online risk, to challenge widely held beliefs that young people are risk-takers and generally ill-equipped to identify and manage online risks.

The workshops provided participants the opportunity to share their perspectives in separate, facilitated groups (whereby parents and young people were separated from each), which were then shared with the whole group via facilitators. Participant responses were shared in a variety of ways depending on the size of the workshops. In many workshops, parents individually documented their answers on post-it notes which were then collected, collated and transcribed. Amongst larger groups, parents discussed their responses in smaller groups, with one scribe from each group documenting the most common responses for their groups. Amongst children, in some cases they documented their responses on post-it notes which were then collected and transcribed, and at other times they were discussed as a group and a facilitator and research assistant wrote down the answers in front of the group on a whiteboard. All data generated by participants was collated and transcribed for later analysis. A full description about how the family workshops were run can be found at Page Jeffery et al. (2022).

Four major causes of family digital conflict were identified by the majority of parents and children separately: screen time/time displacement/balance; inappropriate content; children's behaviour; and sibling conflict and influences related to device use. This fourth issue, however, was not as prevalent amongst the child participants. The issues of screen time/time displacement unequivocally emerged as the major cause of parent/child digital conflict and appeared to be a significant recurring source of family tension. Before discussing these themes further, it should be noted that while parents and children identified their concerns in ways which facilitated this fairly straightforward coding and categorisation, in reality the issues are overlapping, intertwined, and manifest in more complex ways which relate to overarching issues of autonomy and resistance to parental authority, and differences in values, knowledge and practices.

Screen time and time displacement/balance

It is perhaps little surprise that the perennial issue of screen time was identified by parents as a key cause of family conflict, a finding which is consistent with findings from the first research project involving parents. Studies examining parental concerns about their children's media use and general wellbeing frequently reveal screen time to be parents' main concern (The Royal Children's Hospital National Child Health Poll, 2021). This concern was expressed by parents in various, but unequivocal, ways:

> 'Time spent online', 'Time', 'Time on devices', 'loss of time', 'time to get off – just five more minutes!' 'overuse', 'time limits: Do countdowns – realise I hate being told to stop too', 'just one more minute!' 'Always on a device', 'inability to walk away from device'; 'time to turn off at bedtime'; 'one more one more one more', and so on.

Parents' widespread concern about their children's screen time emerged as a key issue which led to other related concerns and conflicts – namely that time spent online means less time engaging in other tasks which parents deem to be necessary, more worthwhile or legitimate. The displaced activities identified by parents varied, but the most common more activities deemed more important included schoolwork, spending time with family, undertaking household chores, reading, physical play, and basic daily tasks such as eating, brushing teeth, and sleeping. Parents often talked about this in terms of 'balance' in their children's lives. Some of the main responses were as follows:

> 'Not doing homework', 'not stopping to do other important tasks'; 'not helping with housework', 'decreased family time', 'not doing other valuable things/activities', 'less time on study/other work', 'balance', 'on iPad without having done homework and chores', 'lack of balance with other things, reading, music practice, physical play', 'kids stuck to devices and not helping out and meeting responsibilities', 'watching TV instead of reading', 'not showing interest in other activities', 'not attending to basic needs (toileting, eating, getting ready', 'don't do anything else – cycle of eat sleep and conflict'.

Young participants similarly identified time spent on devices as by far the most common cause of parent/child digital conflict. Adolescents were acutely aware that their screen time was an issue for their parents, and that their parents were concerned that screen time was displacing other 'more important' activities. Adolescents framed the issue of digital conflict related to screen time in the following ways:

> 'Time limits', 'spending too much time', 'me saying "just 5 more minutes"', 'I argue about asking for more screen time', 'time management', 'when I ask for four more minutes my device gets taken away', 'calling me down when I want to finish something', 'how much time I have', 'how much time I've had previously', 'nagging about games and nagging about having devices on weekdays', 'annoying. They make me get off and I lose my level in the game', 'pausing when you can't pause – online game'.

Relatedly, adolescents also demonstrated that they were aware of their other responsibilities which were often displaced by screen time, such as homework, chores, sleep, exercise and family time. Some examples include:

> 'Not doing chores', 'not able to sleep at night', 'not feeding pets', 'family movie night', 'when I don't get ready for school in time', 'whether I've done my chores', 'family time', 'don't do enough exercise'.

Parental concern about their children's failure to complete chores, homework and basic self-care activities are, I would suggest, a legitimate concern is, I would suggest, legitimate. Yet it was also clear that many parents did not appreciate the value their children derived from digital media, or how important media was to them. Indeed, some parents implied that many of their children's online activities were a waste of time. This particular concern typically emanates from middle and upper class families whose educational aspirations for their children do not accord with 'excessive' device use (Clark, 2013), and can also be interpreted in terms of parental desire to cultivate young people's 'healthy' development (see Chapter 4). By suggesting that much of the time spent on screens is wasteful, parents did, either implicitly or explicitly, designate time spent engaged in other tasks as more worthwhile or valuable, suggesting the existence of a hierarchy of value which applies to both activities undertaken online or on devices and more broadly in relation to how teenagers choose to spend their time. Generally, parents ascribe more value to tasks that are deemed educational, creative, interactive, and social, although there were of course variations across families regarding which activities were deemed to be of greater value than others, reflecting each family's own priorities, and their particular attitudes to work, study, and play (Green et al., 2004; Sheppard et al., 2024; see also Mesch, 2006).

Inappropriate/'rubbish' content

The second area which parents and children identified as a source of conflict related to the content that young people were engaging with online, as well as online purchases that they were making. As argued in Chapter 1, concerns about media content have a long history, particularly in relation to violence, sex and other content deemed inappropriate for children, and these concerns were regularly cited by participants. Parents also indicated concern about 'dumbing down' as a result of the online content that their children consumed. Such concerns once again reflect an implicit hierarchy of value not just in relation to activities, but also content. Parents framed these concerns in the following ways:

'Content quality/credibility', 'content – bad language, mind numbing activities', 'what they watch', 'what content is appropriate (disagreement)', 'inappropriate messages and content', 'types of games', 'choice of videos on YouTube', 'wanting apps that friends have but Mum doesn't allow', 'paying for certain apps or microtransactions', 'buying Minecraft add-ons!', 'kids watching content that isn't 'inappropriate' but is just annoying to the adults', 'Snapchat, Instagram because their friends have', 'money saved is spent on Roblox bux', 'listening to content with bad language'.

Like their parents – but to a lesser extent – adolescents also identified the content that they engaged with, as well as the content and platforms that they were and were not allowed, as sources of family conflict. Children framed their responses in the following ways:

'What I watch online – absolute rubbish', 'the games we are allowed to play', 'they don't let me have social media and other apps', 'not having apps other people have', 'looking at inappropriate content', 'getting in trouble asking for a game or cryptocurrency', 'content on YouTube', 'age appropriate content', 'spending money – in app purchases', 'buying things online'.

The effects of digital media use on children's behaviour

Another major source of conflict according to parents, and to a slightly lesser extent their children, was the effects of digital media use on children's behaviour. Parents suggested that when their children were on devices they were distracted, 'zoned out' and paid little attention to their parents. Many parents suggested that their children's moods were affected by device use, that their children were often rude or disagreeable when their devices were taken away, and that their children often broke the rules or engaged in deceitful or sneaky behaviour. Parents framed these issues as follows:

'Zoned out and not listening', 'attitude/tantrum', 'mood/attitude', 'breaking of rules', 'lack of co-operation', 'attention span and focus', 'not listening or responding', 'rude when device taken away', behaviour – lack of response', 'kids flouting rules', 'trust (sneaking devices)', 'kids hiding what's on screens', 'ignoring friends/family in favour of screens', 'attitude after long usage', 'late nights – ignoring instructions', 'switching off totally when watching devices', 'meltdowns', 'lack of patience', 'always thinking and talking about games', 'reducing communication', 'aggression', 'lack of respect', 'bad attitude'.

Young people demonstrated a degree of self-awareness in identifying their own, at times, problematic behaviour as a source of family conflict about device use. Many young people acknowledged their own tendencies to break the rules, argue and get angry when their device use was curtailed by their parents. They said:

'They get cranky when I get angry at a game', 'yelling!', 'angry', 'probably when I call friends and don't tell them and they walk in', 'not accepting when they tell me to get off', 'smart responses', 'nagging'.

Sibling conflict and influence

One cause of conflict that parents identified, but to a lesser extent than other issues, was conflict amongst their children in relation to access to devices. This issue, however, was not identified by many of the child participants. Sibling conflict over shared devices is well documented (Lally, 2002; Mesch, 2006), but appears to have been much more common when networked devices such as home computers were shared, rather than individually owned. Still, the issue was identified by some families in the study. In addition to conflict related to accessing shared devices, parents were also concerned about their younger children's exposure to their older children's digital content or practices. Parents framed this issue as follows:

'Competition for devices', 'younger siblings growing up too fast – exposure to older siblings' content', 'kids fighting between themselves who gets to use the favourite device/computer', 'sibling fights over preferred devices', 'sharing devices – one iPad, 3 kids', 'older child has a device, younger child wants one', 'he had more than me', 'arguing between siblings over games'.

Conclusion

The main sources of parent/child conflict identified above suggest a lack of shared understanding between parents and their children about each other's perspectives. Parents' responses indicate a different set of perceptions regarding the value of technology and the role that it should play in children's lives. What is also clear from these findings is that, for the most part, it is parental attempts at mediation, particularly restrictive practices and attempts at rule enforcement that lead to the conflict, as parents seek to guide behaviours which they consider to be 'balanced', 'appropriate', and in the best interests of their child in terms of their wellbeing and safety. It should be noted that conflicts related to mood, tantrums, not listening, 'getting pushback', and sibling conflict, while notionally about digital media use, could in fact occur in relation to any domain in which adolescents seek to maintain jurisdiction over their own lives and activities. The underlying tension and conflict arise as a result of the push/pull of adolescent autonomy with parental authority – adolescent resistance to parental control, and parental exasperation as a result of their failure to control their children's behaviours and activities. Through these exchanges, parents attempt to impose their own values and perspectives – which are shaped in part by multiple factors including discourses of online risk and opportunity and 'good' parenting – about what are valuable and legitimate digital practices. In most cases, it appears that parents do this without seeking to understand what their children are doing or what they gain from their online activities. It stands to reason therefore that parental attempts to understand their children's digital practices, including what they value and the things that they like to do online, as well as young people's existing knowledge and skills for identifying and managing online risks is a necessary first step towards mutual understanding, increased parent/child trust, and reduced conflict.

The findings put forward in this chapter indicate that parental attempts at mediation which result in child reactance and conflict stem in part from an assumed deficit in young people's knowledge about online risks and their skills for mitigating them. The next chapter explores whether there is any justification for such an assumption.

Parts of this chapter have been published as follows:

Page Jeffery, C. (2024). 'Trust us! we know what we are doing!' Parent-adolescent digital conflict in Australian families. *Journal of Children and Media*, 1–17.

Notes

1 Whilst constructions of 'adolescence' are historically and culturally determined, it is nonetheless generally acknowledged that the phase denoted by the term is starting earlier than it did a century ago, as puberty begins at a much earlier age in industrialised countries than it previously did. However, if we measure the end of adolescence in terms of accepting adult roles and responsibilities such as marriage, parenthood and full-time work, adolescence ends much later than it did in the past, as these transitions are now typically postponed (Arnett, 2014).
2 Psychological reactance theory states that if individuals' behavioural freedoms are threatened, they will experience motivational arousal to regain them (Brehm, 1966).

References

Arnett, J. J. (2014). *Adolescence and emerging adulthood*. New Jersey: Pearson Boston, MA.

Bell, R. Q. (1979). Parent, child, and reciprocal influences. *American Psychologist, 34*(10), 821.

Beyens, I., & Beullens, K. (2017). Parent–child conflict about children's tablet use: The role of parental mediation. *New Media & Society, 19*(12), 2075–2093.

Beyens, I., Frison, E., & Eggermont, S. (2016). "I don't want to miss a thing": Adolescents' fear of missing out and its relationship to adolescents' social needs, Facebook use, and Facebook related stress. *Computers in Human Behavior, 64*, 1–8.

Blackwell, L., Gardiner, E., & Schoenebeck, S. (2016). Managing expectations: Technology tensions among parents and teens. *Paper presented at the Proceedings of the 19th ACM Conference on Computer-Supported Cooperative Work & Social Computing.*

Brehm, J. W. (1966). *A theory of psychological reactance*. UK and USA: Academic Press.

Buckingham, D. (2000). *After the death of childhood: Growing up in the age of electronic media*. Cambridge, UK: Polity Press.

Byrne, S., & Lee, T. (2011). Toward predicting youth resistance to internet risk prevention strategies. *Journal of Broadcasting & Electronic Media, 55*(1), 90–113.

Clark, L. S. (2011). Parental mediation theory for the digital age. *Communication theory, 21*(4), 323–343.

Clark, L. S. (2013). *The parent app: Understanding families in the digital age*. New York: Oxford University Press.

Correa, T. (2014). Bottom-up technology transmission within families: Exploring how youths influence their parents' digital media use with dyadic data. *Journal of communication, 64*(1), 103–124.

Darling, N., & Steinberg, L. (1993). Parenting style as context: An integrative model. *Psychological Bulletin, 113*(3), 487.

Duerager, A., & Livingstone, S. (2012). How can parents support children's internet safety? EU Kids Online. *LSE Research Online*. Retrieved from http://eprints.lse.ac.uk/42872/1/How%20can%20parents%20support%20children%E2%80%99s%20internet%20safety%28lsero%29.pdf

Erikson, E. (1963). *Childhood and society*. New York: W Norton and Company.

Gabriel, F. (2014). Sexting, selfies and self-harm: Young people, social media and the performance of self-development. *Media International Australia, 151*(1), 104–112.

Green, L., Holloway, D., & Quin, R. (2004). Australian family life and the Internet. In G. Goggin (Ed.), *Virtual nation: The internet in Australia* (pp. 88). Sydney Australia: UNSW Press.

Hadlington, L., White, H., & Curtis, S. (2019). "I cannot live without my [tablet]": Children's experiences of using tablet technology within the home. *Computers in Human Behavior, 94*, 19–24.

Hall, G. S. (1904). *Adolescence*. New York: Appleton-Century-Crofts.

Healy, S., Willett, R., & Zhao, X. (2024). Temporalities and changing understandings of children's use of media: Australia, China, and the United States. In R. Willett, & X. Zhao (Eds.), *Children, media, and pandemic parenting* (pp. 48–64). London: Routledge.

James, A., & James, A. (2004). *Constructing childhood: Theory, policy and social practice*. Basingstoke: Macmillan.

James, A., Jenks, C., & Prout, A. (1998). *Theorizing childhood*. Cambridge: Polity Press.

Kim, A. S., & Davis, K. (2017). Tweens' perspectives on their parents' media-related attitudes and rules: An exploratory study in the US. *Journal of Children and Media*, 11(3), 358–366.

Kurz, D. (2002). Caring for teenage children. *Journal of Family Issues*, 23(6), 748–767.

Lally, E. (2002). *At home with computers*. Oxford and New York: Berg Publishers.

Lau, S., Lew, W. J., Hau, K.-T., Cheung, P. C., & Berndt, T. J. (1990). Relations among perceived parental control, warmth, indulgence, and family harmony of Chinese in mainland China. *Developmental Psychology*, 26(4), 674.

Lauricella, A. R., Cingel, D. P., Beaudoin-Ryan, L., Robb, M. B., Saphir, M., & Wartella, E. A. (2016). The Common Sense census: Plugged-in parents of tweens and teens. *San Francisco, CA: Common Sense Media*.

Livingstone, S. (1996). On the continuing problems of media effects research. In J. Curran & M. Gurevitch (Eds.), *Mass Media and Society* (2nd ed., pp. 305–324). London: Edward Arnold.

Livingstone, S. (1998). Mediated childhoods: A comparative approach to young people's changing media environment in Europe. *European Journal of Communication*, 13(4), 435–456.

Livingstone, S. (2007). From family television to bedroom culture: Young people's media at home. In E. Devereux (Ed.), *Media studies: key issues and debates* (pp. 302–321). London, UK: SAGE Publications.

Mesch, G. S. (2006). Family characteristics and intergenerational conflicts over the Internet. *Information, Communication & Society*, 9(4), 473–495.

Morley, D. (2006). What's home' got to do with it? Contradictory dynamics in the domestication of technology and the dislocation of domesticity. In T. Berker, M. Hartmann, Y. Punie, & K. J. Ward (Eds.), *Domestication of media and technology* (pp. 21–39). Berkshire, England: New York: Open University Press.

Nathanson, A. I. (2002). The unintended effects of parental mediation of television on adolescents. *Media Psychology*, 4(3), 207–230.

Nelissen, S., & Van den Bulck, J. (2018). When digital natives instruct digital immigrants: Active guidance of parental media use by children and conflict in the family. *Information, Communication & Society*, 21(3), 375–387.

Oswell, D. (1998). The place of 'childhood'in Internet content regulation: A case study of policy in the UK. *International Journal of Cultural Studies*, 1(2), 271–291.

Ouvrein, G., & Verswijvel, K. (2021). Child Mediation: Effective education or conflict stimulation? Adolescents' child mediation strategies in the context of sharenting and family conflict. *Journal of e-Learning and Knowledge Society*, 17(3), 70–79.

Owen, S. (2014). Framing narratives of social media, risk and youth transitions: Government of 'not yet'citizens of technologically advanced nations. *Global Studies of Childhood*, 4(3), 235–246.

Page Jeffery, C. (2021). "It's really difficult. We've only got each other to talk to." Monitoring, mediation, and good parenting in Australia in the digital age. *Journal of Children and Media*, 15(2), 202–217.

Page Jeffery, C. (2022). 'It's just another nightmare to manage: 'Australian parents' perspectives on BYOD and 'ed-tech' at school and at home. *Learning, Media and Technology*, 47(4) 471–484.

Page Jeffery, C., Atkinson, S., & McCallum, K. (2022). The safe online together project: A participatory approach to resolving inter-generational technology conflict in families. *Communication Research and Practice*, 1–16. doi:10.1080/22041451.2022.2056426

Piaget, J., & Inhelder, B. (1969). *The psychology of the child*. New York: Basic Books.

Ribak, R. (2001). Like immigrants' negotiating power in the face of the home computer. *New Media & Society*, 3(2), 220–238.

Roth, J., & Brooks-Gunn, J. (2000). What do adolescents need for healthy development? Implications for youth policy. *Social Policy Report*, 14, 3–19.

Savic, M., McCosker, A., & Geldens, P. (2016). Cooperative mentorship: Negotiating social media use within the family. *M/C Journal*, 19(2).

Sheppard, L., Zhao, X., & Coulter, N. (2024). Space, time and families' relational media practices. In R. Willett & X. Zhao (Eds.), *Children, media and pandemic parenting. Family life in uncertain times* (pp. 47–66): London: Routledge.

Smetana, J. G. (1988). Adolescents' and parents' conceptions of parental authority. *Child Development, 59*(2), 321–335.

Soenens, B., & Vansteenkiste, M. (2010). A theoretical upgrade of the concept of parental psychological control: Proposing new insights on the basis of self-determination theory. *Developmental Review, 30*(1), 74–99.

Steinberg, L. (2001). We know some things: Parent–adolescent relationships in retrospect and prospect. *Journal of Research on Adolescence, 11*(1), 1–19.

Strasburger, V. C., Wilson, B. J., & Jordan, A. B. (2009). *Children, Adolescents, and the Media.* Thousand Oaks, London, New Delhi: Sage.

Symons, K., Ponnet, K., Vanwesenbeeck, I., Walrave, M., & Van Ouytsel, J. (2020). Parent-child communication about internet use and acceptance of parental authority. *Journal of Broadcasting & Electronic Media, 64*(1), 1–19.

Tammisalo, K., & Rotkirch, A. (2022). Effects of information and communication technology on the quality of family relationships: A systematic review. *Journal of Social and Personal Relationships, 39*(9), 2724–2765.

The Royal Children's Hospital National Child Health Poll. (2021). *Top 10 child health problems: What Australian parents think. Poll Number 20.* Retrieved from Melbourne: The Royal Children's Hospital. https://rchpoll.org.au/polls/top-10-child-health-problems-what-australian-parents-think/

Willett, R., & Zhao, X. (2024). *Children, media, and pandemic parenting: Family life in uncertain times.* London: Taylor & Francis.

Yang, X., & Zhang, L. (2021). Reducing parent-adolescent conflicts about mobile phone use: The role of parenting styles. *Mobile Media & Communication, 9*(3), 563–583.

Yardi, S., & Bruckman, A. (2011). Social and technical challenges in parenting teens' social media use. *Paper presented at the Proceedings of the SIGCHI Conference on Human Factors in Computing Systems.*

6

WHAT DO YOUNG PEOPLE UNDERSTAND ABOUT ONLINE RISK?

As documented at the beginning of this book, the paradigm of risk and harm which has long framed media discourse, education and policies related to children's use of digital media technologies, has led to a deficit approach to much of the online safety discourse and materials in Australia. This paradigm of risk and harm is premised on an assumed deficit in the knowledge and skills of children – and to a lesser extent their parents – in relation to online risks. Within this paradigm, children are often constructed as a 'protected species' – innocent, corruptible and at risk. Various responses to panics over the years have adopted a particular rhetoric which emphasises, and even valorises, this deficit by framing it in terms of the sacred 'innocence' of childhood. For example, the UK Government Report into the alleged sexualisation of children titled its enquiry 'Letting Children Be Children' (Bailey, 2011), variations of which we have heard in relation to many other media panics over the years. More recently, the Australian House of Representatives Standing Committee on Social Policy and Legal Affairs released a report titled 'Protecting the Age of Innocence' which contained a number of recommendations in relation to age verification trials in Australia to protect children from exposure to online pornography (Australian Government, 2023). While some of these assumptions about a lack of knowledge and skills in relation to younger children are legitimate, the imaginary older adolescent who is presumed to lack the skills and maturity to safely negotiate digital spaces justifies approaches aimed at restriction and control – an approach that I have repeatedly critiqued.[1] Parents, while assumed to possess greater life knowledge and skills than their children (Coulter, 2020), are nonetheless frequently portrayed as being one step behind them technologically (Nelissen & Van den Bulck, 2018; Savic et al., 2016) and lacking the specific knowledge and skills to mitigate online risks despite evidence that shows varying levels of parental expertise.

All of this begs the question: Are concerns about the vulnerability and corruptibility of children online justified? Are they immature, lacking judgement and skills to identify, and effectively respond to, online risk? The answer to this is, of course, likely complex and dependent on a number of factors, including age, maturity, and experience. One might

DOI: 10.4324/9781003346708-7

also argue that young people who do have the knowledge and competencies to identify and mitigate online risk likely do so precisely because of online safety education that fills the 'gap' in young people's knowledges. Indeed, there is likely some truth to this, and online safety education is without doubt an important ingredient in developing young people's skills and knowledge. However I suggest that we need to recognise that young people are not one homogenous group, but diverse in their ages, cultural backgrounds, knowledge, competencies and relative maturity. They acquire knowledge and skills in a range of ways, including through their family environment and their own experiences. In order to help young people thrive in their use of digital technologies while effectively navigating potential negative dimensions, we need to understand and account for young people's existing knowledges, competencies and skills.

We sought to do this through a 'story completion' exercise that was one of the activities during the family workshops involving both parents and their children. During this activity, parents and their children were provided one of seven potential risk scenarios, or 'story stems' and asked to complete the story individually. The story completion method is a form of narrative enquiry that gives participants the opportunity to apply first-hand experiences in a hypothetical context which in turn, provides objective insights into how participants perceive their immediate environment (Lupton, 2020). Narrative inquiry is an approach to socio-cultural research that privileges the role of the story in helping people to make sense of and articulate their lived experiences (Clandinin, 2006, cited in Lupton, 2020). The story completion method provides insights into participants' 'lived experiences in a way that does not directly question people about their own feelings or practices' (Lupton, 2020, p. 3). The method differs from traditional forms of narrative inquiry in that it creates stories about people who are not themselves but instead are fictional and asks participants to respond to a story stem rather than creating the entire narrative themselves. Nonetheless, participants must draw on their own experiences and knowledges to develop the narrative (Lupton, 2020).

The story completion method encompasses two distinct characteristics: (1) it involves the creation of fictional characters rather than solely focusing on first-hand experiences, and (2) the researchers prompt participants through story stems (Lupton, 2020). Braun and colleagues affirm the notion of stories as vehicles for an accurate representation of the sociocultural factors that influence a participant's predisposed value and belief system, and how this equips researchers with a nuanced understanding throughout the development of strategies or interventions.

Our project devised several scenarios described within story stems, each of which depicted a child protagonist faced with a potential online risk (see Appendix A for details). These scenarios corresponded to high profile risks that have been the subject of media panics and online safety discourse – for example, online predators and unwanted online contact, inappropriate online content, and online bullying. Some of the scenarios were sourced from the Office of the eSafety Commissioner, and others were written by the project team. Seven scenarios were used across 13 family workshops, with one scenario selected for each workshop based on two main factors: the concerns raised by parents in the first workshop activity which asked parents to discuss their main concerns about their children's online activities; and the average age of the child participants. As the issues of inappropriate online content and contact were two key concerns raised by parents in the workshops, these scenarios account for most story stems used in the workshops (Table 6.1).

TABLE 6.1 Online risk scenarios distributed to participants in the form of story 'stems'

Scenario	Risk issue	Number of responses
Scenario 1 Annabelle and Lily – aged 15 – are best friends. As a symbol of their friendship and trust for each other, they have shared their mobile phone passcodes and social media passwords with each other. After an argument, Annabelle logged on to Facebook to discover that Lily used her password to access her account and post a number of embarrassing status updates, pretending to be Annabelle.	Password sharing/ privacy breach/ reputational threat	8 child responses, 7 adult responses
Scenario 2 George, age 10, was watching videos of dogs playing on YouTube. Because YouTube was on autoplay, it kept recommending new videos for George. After watching several cute videos, a video appeared showing someone throwing stones at a dog. George loves dogs and was very confused and upset by what he saw (source, Office of the eSafety Commissioner)	Distressing online content	22 child responses, 16 parent responses
Scenario 3 Mandy, aged 11, has started playing an online game that includes chatting with people she doesn't know outside the game. It's fun and her big brothers do it all the time so she thinks it must be safe. The game has an age recommendation of 10+. Recently, someone has been sending her lots of messages, and it's beginning to make her feel uncomfortable.	Unwanted online contact	20 child responses, 17 parent responses
Scenario 4 Marcus, aged 13, loves playing his Nintendo Switch. In one of his favourite games, players can play and communicated online with other players anywhere in the world. One evening. Marcus received a message from someone called 'Booty' who asked Marcus his name, age, home town and where he went to school. He also asked Marcus for a photo.	Unwanted online contact	12 Child responses, 13 adult responses
Scenario 5 Phoebe, aged 13, was sent an email from a classmate asking her to check out a link to a site called www.boredatschool.com.au The site had links to entertaining videos, games and memes. Some of the links were funny, but Phoebe came across one which linked to a video of a child being hit and hurt. Afterwards, Phoebe couldn't get the image out of her mind (source, eSafety Commissioner)	Distressing online content	23 child responses, 27 adult responses

(Continued)

Table 6.1 (Continued)

Scenario	Risk issue	Number of responses
Scenario 6 Riley, aged 15, loves fan fiction and is an active member of an online forum where members share and discuss their work. Riley has been chatting with another forum member, named Vibes, and they have discovered that they share many interests. They have been chatting regularly, and Vibes has suggested that they meet in real life.	Meeting online contacts in real life	8 child responses, 11 adult responses
Scenario 7 Thanh, aged 11, has been sharing videos of his cake creations on his parents' YouTube account. He and his parents decided it would be safe because YouTube doesn't allow comments on videos featuring kids under the age of 13. However, some children in his class posted links to his videos in a Google doc and are making mean comments on it (source, Office of the eSafety Commissioner).	Online bullying	6 child responses, 7 adult responses

Participants were instructed to read the scenario and consider how the main character might feel and act in this situation and finish the story in the space provided. Participants were asked to complete the activity independently but were told that they would share and discuss their responses with their accompanying family members on completion. Parents and children were provided with the same story stems on colour-coded paper (orange for children, blue for adults). Participants were given ten to fifteen minutes to complete the story, and another ten minutes to discuss their responses with their families. Time permitting, we then facilitated a whole group discussion.

What do we already know about young people's responses to online risk?

Several studies show that adolescents adopt a range of 'coping' strategies in relation to online risks. Most of this research focuses on adolescents, with research about parents and online risk typically adopting a parental mediation theoretical approach (see Chapter 3 for more details on parental mediation theory). Relatedly, a number of studies examine the extent to which children – and to a lesser extent their parents – reproduce public scripts about online risks and safety which may in turn influence their risk responses.

Mass media discourses have been found to shape, sometimes (but not always) powerfully, parents' and young people's knowledge about online safety, however existing research yields contradictory findings. Several studies have found that young people reproduce public scripts and sensationalist discourses about online dangers. Mascheroni et al. (2014) argue that young people define, negotiate and adopt preventative measures in response to that which is socially constructed as risky and problematic. This is especially the case with high profile risks such as online predators and cyberbullying, where young people distance themselves from their own positive online experiences to reproduce sensationalist media panics (Mascheroni et al., 2014). Third et al. (2017, 2019) found that young people and their parents reproduce public scripts and mainstream narratives about digital technologies, focusing on the adult-centric concerns of online safety initiatives, and articulating views on online safety that echo the concerns framed in the mass media. Spišák (2016) similarly found that young people internalised to an extent public risk narratives about the harmful effects of pornography which led to feelings of guilt and shame.

In contrast, Mýlek et al. (2021) found that information about meeting online acquaintances offline (a risk often framed in terms of 'stranger danger' and 'grooming') from news media and preventive programs do not influence adolescents' risk perception of that particular risk. Research that I conducted as part of my first research project with Australian parents found that they were ambivalent in this regard, with some parental concerns about online risks heavily informed by mass media and popular discourse, and other parents eschewing panic discourses altogether.

A significant body of literature indicates that young people utilise various coping mechanisms when bothered or threatened by a situation. Coping can be defined as 'efforts to adapt to stress or other disturbances by a stressor or adversity to protect oneself from the psychological harm of risk experiences' (Masten & Gewirtz, 2006, cited in Vandoninck et al., 2013, p. 61). These strategies can be emotional, cognitive, or behavioural responses to manage the internal and external demands of stressful situations (Skinner & Zimmer-Gembeck, 2007, cited in Vandoninck et al., 2013).

Two distinct approaches to coping dominated the early literature: problem-focused coping which strives to tackle the problem directly; and emotion-focused coping, which addresses the negative emotional consequences of the problem and attempts to evoke more positive feelings (Lazarus & Folkman, 1984, cited in Vandoninck et al., 2013). These models, however, have attracted some criticism for their overlapping categories, and recent research has updated adolescent coping typologies, including devising those specifically adapted for online risk situations.

Online coping has been described as 'internet-specific problem-solving strategies children adopt after a negative experience online, such as deleting the message or blocking the sender' (Vandoninck et al., 2013). Scholars have identified various online coping typologies, some of which have been developed in relation to distinct risks such as cyberbullying (see, for example, Parris et al., 2012), while others have been applied to online risks more generally. Adolescents typically employ three types of coping strategies: 1) Fatalistic/passive/indifference – where the child does not take any action; 2) communicative – which involves talking about the problem with trusted others; and 3) proactive or problem-solving, where the child takes action to reduce or eliminate harmful outcomes, such as blocking people online (Livingstone et al., 2011; Vissenberg & d'Haenens, 2020). Problem solving and communicative strategies are considered more effective than passive strategies and have been found to be adopted by more resilient children who demonstrate higher levels of wellbeing (Vissenberg & d'Haenens, 2020). Behavioural avoidance (e.g. going offline for a while) in situations that are not extremely harmful (i.e. content risks) may also be an effective strategy, particularly if combined with communicative strategies (Vandoninck & d'Haenens, 2015). Adolescents have been found to combine two or three coping strategies, particularly problem-solving approaches, when responding to online risks (d'Haenens et al., 2013).

Previous studies show that adolescents are, in general, proactive in addressing online risks and are sanguine about online consequences, in many cases downplaying online risks and treating them as 'no big deal' (Humphry et al., 2023; Staksrud & Livingstone, 2009;

Vandoninck & d'Haenens, 2015; Wisniewski et al., 2016). Even younger children aged 6–10 have demonstrated that they are able to recognise inappropriate online content, threats from strangers and oversharing (Zhao et al., 2019). Humphry et al. (2023) found that young people have a wide repertoire of online safety skills and self-regulation tactics and like to feel in control of their online safety. Additionally, young people control who and how they connect with people online, demonstrate agency over their algorithmic feeds, and actively use social media privacy settings. While responses to risk vary across cultures, gender and age, the most common responses to offensive online content are to talk about the problem with trusted others, delete or ignore it, block offending users, or 'fix' the issue (Staksrud & Livingstone, 2009; Vandoninck & d'Haenens, 2015; Vandoninck et al., 2013; Wisniewski et al., 2016). Discursive/communicative approaches whereby young people discussed their risk encounters with parents, other trusted adults, and peers were a particularly common coping strategy utilised by adolescents (Staksrud & Livingstone, 2009; Vandoninck & d'Haenens, 2015; Vandoninck et al., 2013; Wisniewski et al., 2016).

During the family workshops, parent and child participants documented a range of responses and strategies for addressing the risks presented in the story stems and demonstrated empathy for the protagonists depicted in the scenarios. Story responses were categorised according to seven codes:

1　affective responses (e.g. anger, sadness, upset, worried, 'started to cry')
2　remedial/problem solving strategies (e.g. block content, turn off Autoplay, delete content, report them to the authorities)
3　communicative/discursive strategies (e.g. tell parents or a teacher, talk to friends/siblings, ask the person to leave them alone)
4　retaliative action (e.g. 'do it back, but worse', 'post a mean comment', 'doxx them')
5　humorous/creative responses (e.g. 'George turned to chess and became a grand master at the age of 14').
6　consequences of incident (e.g. parents wouldn't let her on screens anymore, friendship was over)
7　lessons learned/overt advice (e.g. 'never share passwords', 'play only with people you know', 'be more careful next time', 'remember Stranger Danger!!!')

From these codes, three themes which encompass shared patterns of meaning across the data were generated: 1) Empathy and compassion: participants expressed empathy and compassion towards the character, putting themselves in the protagonist's place and acknowledging the emotional impact of the scenario; 2) 'Block, delete, ignore': Participants identified potentially risky situations and demonstrated a range of appropriate practical/technical and remedial strategies in response to the issue; and 3) 'Tell a parent or trusted adult': Participants' responses document discursive/communicative strategies to cope with the incident. In most cases, parents and trusted adults were identified, however some responses named friends or siblings as potential confidantes. The three themes encompassed the first three codes which were the most prevalent across both child and parental responses. The remaining four codes were not developed into themes as they were not considered to represent shared patterns of meaning, and in many cases were scenario-specific. In many ways, children's responses were not dissimilar to parents', however parental responses tended to be longer and more didactic.

It should be acknowledged that the source content – i.e. the scenario depicted in the story stems – would have shaped the nature of the participant responses. A breakdown of the codes – from which the three main themes were developed – for each scenario can be found in Table 6.2, noting that the majority of story responses contained more than one code. While it is evident that some codes were more prevalent in some scenarios, likely due to the nature of the scenario, the three main themes were nonetheless recurrent across all scenarios.

The responses that are quoted below have been included because they are broadly representative of a larger number of responses across the entire dataset, although extracts from all scenarios have not been included.

Empathy and compassion

Participants were asked to describe how the protagonist might feel about the situation. While participants documented a range of affective responses, including anger, betrayal and confusion (see 'affective responses' code in Table 6.2), scenarios depicting young people encountering confronting content, or upsetting experiences such as online bullying, elicited considerable empathy and compassion. Children were especially empathetic, documenting a range of emotional responses and acknowledging the distress that may arise in some of the situations. George and Phoebe (see Scenario 2 and Scenario 5), who both encounter distressing violent content online and are aged 10 and 13 respectively, elicited considerable empathy amongst children.

'Phoebe felt worried. She felt like that might happen to her'.

'Phoebe thought about it for days and she couldn't think about anything else'.

'[George] would feel rather upset about seeing dogs get abused like that. He would probably not feel very good and not watch any videos about dogs on YouTube for a long time.... He would probably think, is that dog ok as well'.

Most parents also expressed empathy for the protagonists, demonstrating an awareness of how upsetting some online content can be for children.

'George cried at first then became very angry. He started throwing things at the screen that had been playing, hoping to defend the dog. He continued to be quite disturbed over the next few days, and behaved in ways he wouldn't normally, until he eventually talked to his Mum and Dad about it'.

'Phoebe was scared and upset. She was worried that she might see things like that again even when she didn't want to, and she was confused because she didn't know what links she could trust and which ones she couldn't'.

Scenarios which depicted young people being approached by strangers online, while eliciting some affective responses, did not elicit the same level of empathy from participants, especially young people. Such responses suggest that while being contacted by strangers online may be confusing and sometimes scary, it is less likely to be emotionally distressing. Further, young people demonstrated that unwanted online contact is something that can

TABLE 6.2 Distribution of codes

Code	S.1 C (8)	S.1 P (7)	S.2 C (22)	S.2 P (16)	S.3 C (20)	S.3 P (17)	S.4 C (12)	S.4 P (13)	S.5 C (23)	S.5 P (27)	S.6 C (8)	S.6 P (11)	S.7 C (6)	S.7 P (7)	Total
Affective responses	3	6	14	11	8	8	9	6	15	18	4	6	3	3	114
Remedial strategies	3	4	14	9	17	9	10	3	7	6	1	3	6	1	93
Communicative strategies	7	5	17	13	17	13	10	5	16	23	1	4	5	7	143
Retaliative action	4	2	2	1	0	1	0	0	1	2	0	0	1	0	14
Humorous/creative responses	1	1	1	1	0	0	0	0	2	1	0	0	0	1	8
Consequences	4	2	0	1	0	0	1	3	0	1	2	1	0	0	15
Overt advice/lessons learned	2	4	3	0	1	2	0	2	2	2	2	1	2	2	25

be promptly addressed through a range of strategies (see Theme 2). See, for example, the following responses to Scenario 4:

'Marcus would feel confused as he just wants to play Nintendo, he wouldn't be expecting this. Marcus would either block this user or tell an adult '.

'Marcus might feel unsafe and scared. He should block and report 'Booty'. He should tell a trusted adult, ignore the message and do things how he usually does after that (get on with his life) '.

Parents' responses were not dissimilar to those of their children, and for the most part documented pragmatic responses to being approached by an online stranger. The exception was three responses in one workshop documenting worst-case scenarios where Marcus met the online stranger and was attacked, kidnapped, and/or never heard from again (such responses were coded as 'consequences'). However, these responses were exceptional, with parents as well as their children demonstrating an apparent reluctance to reproduce panic discourses about online strangers, as the following responses from parents indicate:

'Mandy would feel like this is not appropriate, and that she should not feel uncomfortable online. She could block the person from sending messages, and tell an adult that she trusts'.

'Marcus was not sure about this request. Nobody has asked for so much personal information before. I ask Booty, why? but he would not say. I told my parents about this. After talking about it with them, I did not respond his request'.

There are clear differences in the affective responses to distressing online content and unwanted online contact. The risk of unwanted online contact, often referred to as 'grooming' and amplified by the mass media via its framing of the folk-devil figure of the paedophile, has received considerable media attention and been the subject of recurrent moral panics. In contrast, online violence has been given much less public attention in awareness-raising initiatives. Yet, the empathy and distress demonstrated by participants in response to violent online content, compared to less emotional responses to unwanted online contact, suggest that these scenarios may resonate on a deeper level with young people, possibly reflecting their own online experiences. Such a finding is consistent with earlier studies which have found that distressing online content, including violent content, is at the top of children's concerns (Livingstone et al., 2014).

Theme 2: 'Block, delete, ignore': Participants identified potentially risky situations and demonstrated a range of appropriate practical/technical and remedial strategies in response to the issue

Young people and parents articulated a range of practical, technical and remedial strategies for addressing the risks depicted. The most common strategies included: Delete/take down content, block offending user, report content/behaviour, ignore, switch off Auto play (YouTube), cease activity, block channel, change settings, and do something else.

Young people were succinct in articulating a range of strategies for addressing the problem, suggesting a pragmatism that was less evident in their parents' responses and signalling that they have existing strategies for addressing risks, possibly due to encountering similar online risks personally. For example, in response to George encountering a video of a dog being hurt online (scenario 2), children offered the following strategies:

'He would probably stop the video if he was feeling upset. He could report it or just not watch the video. There's also a great app called YouTube kids, which can moderate what is shown'.

'Tell parent. Block YouTube Channel. Stop watching. Find out if the video shows illegal behaviour + report it to police. Dislike it'.

In response to Mandy, who is approached by someone she doesn't know online (Scenario 3), young people similarly demonstrated a range of pragmatic problem-solving strategies.

'Report/ban, ignore, tell a parent, don't reply, tell an adult, block, change privacy settings, say no'.
'Mandy blocks the person that makes her uncomfortable. The end'.

Far from reproducing panic discourses about stranger danger online, these succinct and pragmatic responses provided by young people may be indicative of their own online experiences, whereby risks are proactively dealt with and rarely result in harm. Parents' responses, while similarly eschewing panic discourses, in contrast appeared more empathetic and descriptive:

'Mandy tells her mum and dad about the messages and asks them what she should do. Her mum and dad read the messages and suggest she should turn off or opt out of the messaging function in the game if possible. They also suggest she moves out of that group and joins another one, or perhaps she should try to find a different game altogether where there is no chatting. If the messages are suggesting criminal acts, Mandy's parents could contact the police to report them'.

'The character would be uncomfortable, as suggested in the text. The character might first respond to the person telling them to leave her alone. If the messaging continued the character might first ask her siblings for advice/help. If the advice/help is ineffective, the character may take the issue to her parents or other authority figures'.

The range of strategies and coping responses from young people is consistent with previous studies which show that the problem-solving strategies most commonly adopted by young people are to delete content, block users, and discuss the issue with others.

Theme 3: 'Tell a parent or trusted adult': Participants' responses document discursive/communicative strategies to cope with the incident

As many of the quotes above indicate, most responses from parents and young people alike include discursive/communicative strategies. In fact, discursive strategies were the most common response (see Table 6.2) and were usually utilised in combination with remedial strategies outlined above. Discussion with parents, or another 'trusted adult' such as a teacher was the most frequently mentioned response although some suggested discussing the issue with classmates or an older sibling. Discursive strategies were framed as being effective for two main reasons by both children and parents: to provide emotional support for the child, and to help the child manage the situation and potential future situations. For example, young people's responses to Thanh, aged 11, who experiences bullying online (Scenario 7) included:

'Thanh told his parents and showed them. Then they had a chat to those children and their parents. His parents then decided that it may not be safe and watched Thanh's videos and makes sure there are no rude comments. They talked to the school, and the school decided to make a presentation about cyber safety and everything went well'.

'Thanh then tells his parents. His parents tell him to stop posting videos and to tell his school teacher, so that he can talk to the kids in his class about cyberbullying. The kids are made to say sorry and his parents let him keep posting his videos after talking to the school'.

Young people's responses to Mandy being approached by a stranger online also commonly included discursive strategies:

'Mandy should tell her parents and brother. Show them the messages and report him/ her. Don't play the game. Play private servers with people you know in real life/trust. Ask her big brother what to do and their parents'.

Parents' similarly privileged discursive strategies that also involved collaborative problem solving between parents, teachers and their children:

'Thanh felt very upset that his classmates were making mean comments. He discussed what happened with his parents and also his teacher at school. Together, they came up with a plan. The teacher made sure the other kids took down the links, removed the comments and apologised to Thanh. Thanh and his parents and teacher kept in touch regarding his YouTube and other online activity to make sure nothing like this happened again'.

'She talked to her parents and her friends about the video and how it made her feel, and that made her feel better. She also talked to them about how she might be able to recognise sites that could have things she didn't want to see and which sites she knew she could trust'.

The dominance of discursive strategies in both adolescent and parent responses is not surprising given that discursive/communicative strategies are a commonly cited coping strategy for young people experiencing online risk (Staksrud & Livingstone, 2009; Wisniewski et al., 2016). Additionally, the workshops were promoted as 'facilitating discussion between parents and their children about online risks to reduce family conflict', priming participant expectations about the purpose of the workshop. As well, parents and their children were given the opportunity to discuss their responses as part of the story completion activity. As such, there may be a degree of performativity and 'telling parents what they want to hear' with each party reproducing cyber safety scripts such as telling a trusted adult. Yet, parents and their children may have also used the activity to signal to each other a willingness, or an invitation (especially on the part of parents), to discuss online safety issues when they arise.

What are the implications of these findings?

The story completion activity undertaken as part of the family workshops revealed that there were not significant differences between adolescent and adult responses to online risks, with both groups demonstrating that they are able to identify online risks, foresee potential consequences, and demonstrate appropriate online safety knowledge and skills. The following discussion focuses predominantly on adolescent responses, as it is they who are assumed to be most lacking in knowledge and skills, and as such subjected to greater protection and control.

Consistent with previous studies, adolescents in this study were sanguine about online risks and deployed problem solving/remedial strategies, and discursive/communicative strategies to mitigate online risk (Vissenberg & d'Haenens, 2020; Staksrud & Livingstone, 2009; Wisniewski et al., 2016; Vandoninck & d'Haenens, 2015; Livingstone et al., 2011; Vandoninck et al., 2013). Adolescents thus employ a combination of both problem-solving coping to tackle the problem directly, and emotion-focused coping to minimise the negative emotional consequences (Lazarus & Folkman, 1984, as cited in Vandoninck & d'Haenens, 2015). Adolescents in this study similarly deployed *multiple* coping strategies in response to online risk (Vandoninck & d'Haenens, 2015) and the combination of problem solving/remedial strategies with communicative/discursive behaviours are demonstrative of adolescent resilience (Vissenberg & d'Haenens, 2020). Contrary to findings from Mascheroni et al. (2014); Third et al. (2019), but consistent with Mýlek et al. (2021) there was little evidence of adolescents reproducing panic discourses about online risk, although parents were slightly more ambivalent in this respect, with a small minority documenting worst-case scenarios. In eschewing panic discourses, adolescents instead portrayed the child protagonist as one who is both capable of recognising and addressing online risk, but at the same time emotionally vulnerable to distressing online content and upsetting online situations. It is possible that through their responses, which were shared with their parents during the workshops, adolescents were constructing their own counternarratives in direct response to adult concerns, actively resisting common portrayals of young people as victims (Buckingham & Bragg, 2005). Adolescents did, however, appear to reproduce common online safety narratives in some of their responses, drawing on commonly cited strategies to mitigate risk including telling a 'trusted adult' – terminology which is suggestive of public cyber safety advice, and also in some situations, providing 'overt advice' and 'lessons learned'. This is perhaps not surprising considering that the scenarios depicted in the story stems could be interpreted as reproducing, to some extent, public scripts. Through their responses, adolescents appeared to simultaneously reject sensationalist panic discourses, but embrace some cyber safety discourses, signalling their own experiences and competence to their parents.

The story completion exercise revealed that different scenarios elicit their own nuanced responses demonstrating varying levels of affective intensity. The response of retaliation, for example, while not prominent enough across all scenarios to be explored as a theme, arose in relation to some scenarios and also highlighted an emotional intensity related to friendship and betrayal that was absent in scenarios depicting contact from online strangers.

While this wasn't explored in detail in this study, such a finding may highlight the importance of friendships to young people – particularly girls – and the hurt and distress that betrayal can bring to a young person.[2] It's an important reminder for parents to attempt to understand their child's own online experiences of risk and harm, rather than imposing their own views about what constitutes a serious online risk onto their children.

Conclusion

The story completion exercise shows that children are able to recognise and, in theory at least, mitigate online risk. This is no guarantee, however, that they will enact the various strategies that they described if personally faced with such a risk. Third et al. (2019), drawing on Herring 2018, note that young people navigate a 'dual consciousness' where they attempt to reconcile what they know from online safety education and discourse with their own experiences of navigating online risks. This duality produces 'contradictions between what they know they *should* do and what they want to or can reasonably do' (p. 38). Further, the semi-public nature of the family workshops likely led children to perform online safety knowledge and competence for their parents, as well as myself and colleagues delivering the workshops, drawing on multiple sources including online safety education delivered via schools and parents, as well as public scripts. Children are well aware of the public debate that plays out in relation to their media practices, and this inevitably shapes the responses that they give to parents, researchers, and other authority figures (Buckingham & Bragg, 2005).

Indeed, the possession of particular knowledges and theoretical skills do not necessarily translate to correlative behaviours. Adolescence is characterised by self-discovery, identity-seeking, growing independence, increasing autonomy and risk-taking (Arnett, 2014; Strasburger et al., 2009). Young people, despite comprehensive knowledge of online safety, may still take risks online. But protectionist approaches premised upon an assumed deficit in adolescent knowledge and skills that constrain young people's agency and autonomy thwart their ability to develop the online skills and resilience that are needed to navigate and thrive in the digital world.

Parents nonetheless play a critical role in supporting their children to navigate risky online situations. While this project indicated that young people know more than they are given credit for, the strong affective and empathic responses from young people, particularly in relation to violent online content and cyberbullying, may signal that young people rely on social and emotional support from parents and peers. Parental support – both emotional and practical – availability, and dialogue, as demonstrated through the discursive strategies documented by many child and parent participants, are essential for helping young people to navigate online risk and thrive in online spaces.

These findings provide empirical weight to critiques of deficit and protectionist approaches to online safety by demonstrating that children (and also their parents) are aware of online risks and have a range of tools in their arsenal to navigate risky situations online. And while this awareness can likely be partly attributed to online safety resources and discourses, we cannot say with any certainty that they lead to behaviour change. Nor can we determine from this study the degree to which online safety resources and public narratives contributed to young people's knowledge and skills in this area, compared to other potential sources of knowledge such as their peers, their own online experiences and trial and error. I suggest that young people's (and their parents') knowledge about online safety is multi-faceted, and likely derived from a combination of personal experience, peer and family interaction and discussion, as well as public scripts. Rather than assuming a deficit in young people's – and their parents' – skills and knowledge, online safety resources and programs should acknowledge and build on them. Accordingly, I advocate for an approach which facilitates and encourages parent/child communication, not only about high-profile online risks such as those explored in this study, but also about young people's everyday digital encounters and what bothers them online. Such dialogue facilitates ongoing support for young people, and 'flips the script' to enable young people to be active participants in discussions of online safety. This is discussed in the next chapter.

Parts of this chapter have been published in Page Jeffery, C., Atkinson, S., & Graham, C. (2023). Using the story completion method to explore Australian parent and child responses to online risk. *New Media & Society*, *0*(0). https://doi.org/10.1177/14614448231206458

Notes

1 In addition to the critiques that I have documented throughout this book, I and colleagues have published other commentaries criticising control and exclusion of young people from online spaces. See: https://theconversation.com/is-13-too-young-to-have-a-tiktok-or-instagram-account-199097 https://theconversation.com/age-verification-for-social-media-would-impact-all-of-us-we-asked-parents-and-kids-if-they-actually-want-it-230539 https://theconversation.com/should-parents-be-worried-about-social-media-we-asked-5-experts-238772.
2 For a more detailed account of young people's online friendships, drama and cyberbullying, see Page Jeffery (2022).

References

Arnett, J. J. (2014). *Adolescence and emerging adulthood*. New Jersey: Pearson Boston, MA. Boston, MA: Pearson.

Australian Government. (2023, August). Government response to the roadmap for age verification. Retrieved from https://www.infrastructure.gov.au/sites/default/files/documents/government-response-to-the-roadmap-for-age-verification-august2023.pdf

Bailey, R. (2011). *Letting children be children: Report of an independent review of the commercialisation and sexualisation of childhood* (Vol. 8078). London: The Stationery Office.

Buckingham, D., & Bragg, S. (2005). Opting in to (and out of) childhood: Young people, sex and the media. *Studies in Modern Childhood: Society, Agency, Culture*, 59–77.

Coulter, N. (2020). Child studies meets digital media: Rethinking the paradigms. In L. Green, D. Holloway, K. Stevenson, T. Leaver, & L. Haddon (Eds.), *The Routledge companion to digital media and children* (pp. 19–27). New York and London: Routledge.

d'Haenens, L., Vandoninck, S., & Donoso, V. (2013). How to cope and build online resilience? Short report. EU Kids Online. Available at: https://core.ac.uk/download/pdf/9694255.pdf

Humphry, J., Boichak, O., & Hutchinson, J. (2023). Emerging online safety issues – Co-creating social media with young people – Research report. Retrieved from https://ses.library.usyd.edu.au/handle/2123/31689

Livingstone, S., Haddon, L., Görzig, A., & Ólafsson, K. (2011). Risks and safety on the internet: The perspective of European children: Full findings and policy implications from the EU Kids Online survey of 9–16 year olds and their parents in 25 countries. EU Kids Online, Deliverable D4. EU Kids Online Network, London, UK. https://eprints.lse.ac.uk/33731/1/Risks%20and%20safety%20on%20the%20internet%28lsero%29.pdf

Livingstone, S., Kirwil, L., Ponte, C., & Staksrud, E. (2014). In their own words: What bothers children online? *European Journal of Communication*, *29*(3), 271–288.

Lupton, D. (2020). *The story completion method and more-than-human theory: Finding and using health information*. London: SAGE Publications Ltd.

Mascheroni, G., Jorge, A., & Farrugia, L. (2014). Media representations and children's discourses on online risks: Findings from qualitative research in nine European countries. *Cyberpsychology: Journal of Psychosocial Research on Cyberspace, 8*(2), 2.

Mýlek, V., Dedkova, L., & Smahel, D. (2021). Information sources about face-to-face meetings with people from the Internet: Gendered influence on adolescents' risk perception and behavior. *New Media & Society, 25*(7), 1561–1579.

Nelissen, S., & Van den Bulck, J. (2018). When digital natives instruct digital immigrants: Active guidance of parental media use by children and conflict in the family. *Information, Communication & Society, 21*(3), 375–387.

Page Jeffery, C. (2022). '[Cyber] bullying is too strong a word…': Parental accounts of their children's experiences of online conflict and relational aggression. *Media International Australia, 184*(1), 150–164.

Parris, L., Varjas, K., Meyers, J., & Cutts, H. (2012). High school students' perceptions of coping with cyberbullying. *Youth & society, 44*(2), 284–306.

Savic, M., McCosker, A., & Geldens, P. (2016). Cooperative mentorship: Negotiating social media use within the family. *M/C Journal, 19*(2). https://journal.media-culture.org.au/index.php/mcjournal/article/view/1078

Spišák, S. (2016). 'Everywhere they say that it's harmful but they don't say how, so I'm asking here': Young people, pornography and negotiations with notions of risk and harm. *Sex Education, 16*(2), 130–142.

Staksrud, E., & Livingstone, S. (2009). Children and online risk: Powerless victims or resourceful participants? *Information, Communication & Society, 12*(3), 364–387. doi:10.1080/13691180802635455

Strasburger, V. C., Wilson, B. J., & Jordan, A. B. (2009). *Children, adolescents, and the media*. Thousand Oaks, London, New Delhi: Sage.

Third, A., Bellerose, D., De Oliveira, J. D., Lala, G., & Theakstone, G. (2017). Young and online: Children's perspectives on life in the digital age (the state of the world's children 2017 companion report).

Third, A., Collin, P., Walsh, L., & Black, R. (2019). *Young people in digital society: Control shift*. London, UK: Palgrave Macmillan Nature.

Vandoninck, S., & d'Haenens, L. (2015). Children's online coping strategies: Rethinking coping typologies in a risk-specific approach. *Journal of Adolescence, 45*, 225–236.

Vandoninck, S., d'Haenens, L., & Roe, K. (2013). Online risks: Coping strategies of less resilient children and teenagers across Europe. *Journal of Children and Media, 7*(1), 60–78.

Vissenberg, J., & d'Haenens, L. (2020). Protecting youths' wellbeing online: Studying the associations between opportunities, risks, and resilience. *Media and Communication, 8*(2), 175–184.

Wisniewski, P., Xu, H., Rosson, M. B., Perkins, D. F., & Carroll, J. M. (2016). Dear diary: Teens reflect on their weekly online risk experiences. *Paper presented at the Proceedings of the 2016 CHI Conference on Human Factors in Computing Systems*. New York: Association for Computing Machinery, pp. 3919–3930.

Zhao, J., Wang, G., Dally, C., Slovak, P., Edbrooke-Childs, J., Van Kleek, M., & Shadbolt, N. (2019). I make up a silly name' Understanding Children's Perception of Privacy Risks Online. *Paper presented at the Proceedings of the 2019 CHI Conference on Human Factors in Computing Systems*.

7
PROMOTING PARENT/CHILD UNDERSTANDING ABOUT MEDIA USE THROUGH DIALOGUE

Up to this point, I have suggested that there is a gap between parents and children in relation to knowledges about online practices, and that ongoing dialogue and communication is needed to bridge this gap and facilitate understanding, support young people online, and reduce family conflict. The previous chapter provided evidence for the need to move away – amongst older children at least – from discursive approaches that start from a presumed deficit amongst young people. But two-way communication that is open, non-judgemental and non-hierarchical is not always so easily achieved. This chapter draws on empirical findings to argue that young people and 'experts', parents, and other people in positions of authority often conceptualise and talk about online risks and practices quite differently, which presents discursive barriers to effective parent/child communication. Such non-hierarchical, open dialogue entails not only shared terminology, but critically also entails parents genuinely listening to the perspectives of young people, rather than seeking to address the assumed adolescent knowledge gap by imposing their own adult concerns and perspectives onto young people's practices.

Different generations, different discourses

The variations between how adults and young people identify and conceptualise online risks have been demonstrated by scholars particularly in relation to bullying and sexting/sending nudes. Cyberbullying is one example where scholars have found distinct conceptualisations of the issue between adults and young people (Allen, 2015; Marwick & boyd, 2014). Marwick and boyd's work on cyberbullying found that the term 'bullying' was not used by young people:

> Although adults often refer to [online practices of conflict] with the language of 'bullying', teens are more likely to refer to the resultant skirmishes and their digital traces as 'drama'. Drama is a performative set of actions distinct from bullying, gossip and relational aggression, incorporating elements of them but also operating quite distinctly.
>
> *(Marwick & boyd, 2011, p. 1)*

DOI: 10.4324/9781003346708-8

The difference is more than semantic because it marks distinct discourses that conceive of the issue in quite different ways. This separation:

> allows teens to distance themselves from practices which adults may conceptualise as bullying. As such, they can retain agency – and save face – rather than positioning themselves in a victim narrative.
>
> *(Marwick & boyd, 2011, p. 1)*

The dominant, adult-centred construction of cyberbullying frames its putative prevalence, potentially tragic consequences, its potential anonymity, the speed at which material can spread to large audiences (Juvonen & Gross, 2008), as well as its constant, 24/7 nature and encroachment into the safe space of the home, hence denying victims any reprieve from the abuse. Bullying panics also suggest that new media technologies are responsible for bringing about a serious *new* problem which requires action, and thus that social media radically increases bullying (boyd, 2014). This conceptualisation does not match the experience (thankfully) of the majority of young people, who are far more likely to conceptualise their negative online social interaction experiences in terms of 'bitchiness', 'drama', and 'exclusion', and as an extension of regular 'offline' drama (rather than a new phenomenon) (boyd, 2014; Page Jeffery, 2022).

Similarly, when researchers speak to young people about digitally distributed, sexually explicit material they find a disjunction between the dominant discourse about this material used by adult stakeholders – parents, policy makers, medical experts, teachers and journalists – and the young people's experiences. Debates about 'sexting' do not match the language that is used by young people in making sense of the practices. For example, a study based on interviews with groups of 16–17-year-olds undertaken by Albury reported that participants 'rejected the imprecision of the term sexting' (Albury, 2015, p. 1734) and instead used a typology of 'pictures' that included private selfies, public selfies, and inoffensive sexual pictures. Albury notes that the young people 'called attention to the ways that the term 'sexting' was misapplied to young people's digital practices' (Albury, 2015, p. 1738), with particular reference to the sub-genre of 'joke images' which typically consist of humorous nude and semi-nude images that are frequently misread by adults. Albury argues that the sophistication of young people's typology of sexual self-representation compared to the blanket term 'sexting' used by adults illustrates the 'gaps in adult understandings of selfie practices' (Albury, 2015, p. 1735).

As argued in Chapter 1, parental understanding of online risks and digital practices is often (but not always) shaped more by discourses of risk and online safety than an intimate knowledge of their children's online practices and preferences. Broader discourses of risk, often manifested through media panics and online safety discourse, rarely align with the diversity of young people's actual experiences. Parental attempts at mediation and restriction in response to dominant discourses of online risk are often met with resistance from young people who feel as though their parents don't understand or appreciate the value of media in their lives or their existing skills and knowledge. Many parents appeared to have little knowledge or understanding about their children's online practices or concerns. When asked in focus groups and interviews about their children's online practices, many parents responded with, 'I don't know!' or, 'I thought you might ask me this and I should have checked!' One mother said, 'Who knows what they see [online]?'

Parents indicated that one of their main strategies for addressing their concerns about online risks was through 'dialogue' and 'open communication' with their children, however the degree to which this occurs is highly varied, and in part appears to depend on the topic. Amongst participants in my study, parents indicated a greater level of knowledge about their children's online 'dramas'. In contrast, parents demonstrated very little knowledge about their children's encounters with online pornography, and as such, this was one area where parents reproduced public scripts about the damaging effects of pornography, and the ways in which it 'distorts' what is 'normal'.

Parental knowledges about their children's experiences of negative social interactions online resulted in a greater alignment between parent/child understandings of online bullying. Parents in my study recounted numerous incidents of negative online interaction and exclusion experienced by their (almost always) daughters. In narrating their experiences, parents took care to distance the described behaviours and incidents from the dominant discursive construction of cyberbullying, referring instead to these instances as general 'nastiness', 'bitchiness' and 'exclusion' – like the young people in Marwick and boyd's study. As argued in Chapter 4, parents thus implicitly delineated between what they considered to be the common, overt, bitchy behaviours that they believed to be an inevitable feature of childhood and adolescence, and what they considered to be the more serious, harmful, targeted and overt practice of cyberbullying. While only one participant explicitly used the term 'drama' to describe her daughters' online and offline interpersonal relations, several other participants alluded to incidents which appeared to fit the description outlined by Marwick and boyd (2014). One mother of two daughters aged 16 and 19, explicitly rejected the term cyberbullying, preferring instead to refer to her daughters' online conflict as drama. She explained that one daughter:

> signed up to Facebook aged 13 but deleted her account one week later because, 'She just thinks "Facebook's ridiculous and it's bitchy and all her friends are on it and they talk about crap," and she's just not interested.

When prompted further about the kinds of bitchiness her daughter was describing, the mother said:

> I think she saw Facebook as an extension of what was happening at school, which wasn't something that she necessarily wanted to engage in. She had a good bunch of friends, but in her group they all have a love/hate relationship with each other. So frequently throughout primary school, one day she would be best friends with somebody and then the next day she wouldn't be, and so I think she saw Facebook as just replicating all of that drama and angst.

One father to a 14-year-old girl shared another experience that his daughter had shared with him.

> There was a bit of a falling out between my daughter and her friend. My daughter was telling me about her friend, saying 'She's just not really very nice to people, I just don't want to be around her,' so she just distanced herself. And I don't think she was nasty about that...But then there was a Snapchat exchange where my daughter said

something which was a Snapchat broadcast to all of the people following her on Snapchat. This one girl took offence at it and that led to my daughter posting a photograph ... that was completely unnecessary and unwise and it all just exploded. And it happened in the blink of an eye.

Another mother to a teen daughter shared another story about online exclusion:

They set up some sort of messaging group between their school group, where they would talk about, 'Let's go hang out together, or let's talk about this assignment, or whatever'. And they didn't add [my daughter] to it, and I know that she found that to be quite painful at the time.

The detail provided in the accounts above – where parents share specific things that their children have told them – demonstrates that parent/child dialogue about these issues has taken place. Importantly, these accounts provide evidence of parents actively listening to their children, rather than simply imparting messages that parents want their children to heed. Perhaps not surprisingly, the parents demonstrating knowledges and insights into their children's experiences were more likely to be critical of sensationalised accounts of cyberbullying. Recall the 60-year-old father of a 14-year-old girl who said:

There's a great tendency to overreact because there's so much out in the media, things like the 11-year-old boy committing suicide because he was being bullied. And god, we're all going to commit suicide. Well no, we're not.

The situation is quite different, however, in relation to the issue of online pornography and sexting. Here, there is little evidence to indicate that parents are engaging in dialogue with their children, or listening to them to understand their practices, their concerns and their perspectives. Despite parental claims that they talked to their children about the issue, this did not appear to involve dialogue or listening. Indeed, the conversations parents indicated they were engaging in appeared to be more about 'educating' their children about online dangers in ways which reflect dominant risk discourse, and imparting key messages – or 'preaching' to their children (Buckingham & Bragg, 2003), rather than talking to their children to understand their perspectives and practices. Some examples from participants:

'We've had lots of conversations with our son over the years about things like respecting women and .... about pornography too, and how it's not real... It's all make believe.'

'I've talked to him about that there's no limit to what's on the internet, but you need to restrain yourself and you should wait until you're an adult.'

'We talk about it a lot and ... I've done what I can to teach them what's right and wrong'.

'You've got to have that discussion... And sometimes it gets down to 'because I'm the mum' but usually we get there.

"I guess one of things that he's [husband] always said to the kids is 'I can always go and check the internet history of anyone who's using a computer in this house, so if you want to go and look at stuff that's inappropriate I can always find it'. So he's always made it really clear that you never do anything anonymously online, that there's always a record of it, and once you've done it it's there forever, it will always be there. That sort of education has been really important for the kids I think, to at least think about what they're doing.'

'We do try to talk to them about the fact that if you put something out there, it's out there for everyone, and you shouldn't put anything on there that you don't want your grandmother to read.'

Parents' apparent lack of knowledge about their children's experiences with online pornography meant that they were much more likely to reproduce dominant discourses about online pornography and sexting. The following quotes from parents demonstrate this, as well as an apparent lack of knowledge of their children's perspectives or experiences:

'What I'm worried about for our kids is that normal will become different. That the normal is going to be skewed.'

'I think I am concerned about the messaging about love and intimacy that teenagers get from what they see, that, you know I'm a nurse, but there's a lot of people out there that think body hair is abnormal, because of what they see. And what respectful relationships, or even what sex is, because of what they see. They've been seeing a lot of porn, a lot of violent sex in some ways as well, so that's concerning, this distorted message of what that is.

'Whenever we go and socialise with friends and neighbours, the kids inevitably end up in a room all YouTubing, showing each other their favourite YouTube clips. I worry horrendously, I really worry about them finding pornographic material or other dangerous material that I don't wish them to see. We've got parental locks at home, I don't know where the parental locks are when we go out, but I work on the assumption that my children are not going to seek out that content because we have very open discussions around the table about things.'

This final quote from one mother highlights what was quite common across discussions about pornography and sexting. Parents said that they were discussing it with their children, yet it was evident that they were still speaking from assumptions about what their children were doing rather than actual knowledge acquired through dialogue and listening.

Some parents admitted that they had not openly discussed pornography with their children. For example, when asked about whether she talked to her sons about pornography a mother of three boys aged 12, 15 and 17 said she had only broached the issue with the 17-year-old because 'he's very open and likes to discuss things.' Yet, when asked if she had discussed it with one of her younger sons she said:

I have a little, and he doesn't know anything and doesn't want to talk about it. He's like, 'Mum, why are you so embarrassing? This is why I don't talk to you because you just say these ridiculous things!'

Another mother of a 13-year-old boy was adamant that her son was not interested in looking at pornography. When asked if she would have pre-emptive discussions about pornography with her 13-year-old son, she stated:

> I think if it becomes an issue we'll talk to him about it. But I've always thought that if it's not broke, don't fix it. So if it emerges as an issue then we'll deal with it, but to bring it up might just invite him to think about stuff that he hasn't thought about and right now he just doesn't care.

There is a stark difference here in the way that parents talk about online exclusion and drama, and the way that they discuss pornography. Where parents demonstrated knowledge – acquired through dialogue with and listening to their children – the way parents talked about and conceptualised that particular issue appeared much more aligned with young people's actual experiences and accounts. Parents appeared to be much more open to listening to their children talk about their friendships and the various dramas that occurred from time to time. Open discussions about sex and pornography which provide young people the opportunity to share their perspectives and experiences, however, appeared less common-place.

This is perhaps not that surprising. Open discussion about sex and pornography is still awkward or embarrassing for families. Parental accounts suggest that parents also drew on dominant discourses of childhood 'innocence', long after their children had passed puberty. It has long been recognised that parents often want to keep their children ignorant about sex for as long as possible, under the rubric of 'innocence' (Angelides, 2019). This can result in parents wanting to hold back sex education until it's too late for young people, who have already had to work things out for themselves (McKee et al., 2018). This approach again refuses to listen to young people about their needs, but rather constructs them as objects of concern to be managed.

Closing the knowledge gap

The family workshops that were conducted three years after the first round of interviews and focus groups with parents (Project 1) were designed as a first step towards overcoming the general knowledge gap by providing the opportunity for children (and their parents) to share their perspectives, practices, preferences, and what they value about digital media in a supportive environment. Through these workshops we wanted to help address parents' perceived lack of knowledge about their children's digital activities by giving them some insight into their children's online practices. We wanted to provide young people with the opportunity to share what they value about digital technologies; demonstrate their existing digital skills and competencies including the ability to identify and respond to risk (and concomitantly alleviate parental anxiety about their children's vulnerability to online harm); and importantly to provide their own input to family decision making about digital media. Most importantly, we wanted to help establish the conditions for ongoing sharing, dialogue and mutual interest between parents and their children about digital media use. The digital conflict experienced within families stemming from parental anxieties and child reactance cannot be easily solved in a two-hour workshop. It requires ongoing dialogue and between parents and their children.

What do parents and their children want each other to know?

One knowledge-sharing activity that we conducted during the workshops included parents and their children separately sharing one thing that they wanted the other to know. These responses were then shared as a group and highlighted some common themes amongst parents and children.

'Technology is a tool, not a religion!' Parental advice

While digital media was clearly central to the lives of the adolescent participants, parents' responses indicated that while technology had an important role to play, it must be used in a particular way to be beneficial, it was not the 'be all and end all', and was no replacement for the 'real world'. In response to the prompt to share one piece of advice that they wanted their children to know, parents' responses aligned with five dominant but overlapping messages.

Technology is good, but only if we use it in a balanced way. The 'tech is good, but only if we use it in a balanced/careful/appropriate way' was a recurrent theme across all workshops, confirming parents' main concern about what they perceived to be their children's excessive device use. This advice was imparted in a range of ways which implied that their children's use was not balanced, that children lacked agency and control over their technology use (many parents drew on a 'master/slave' analogy to denote this), and that this diminished the benefits flowing from media use. Responses, for example, included:

> 'It's great to have but we need to use it in a balanced way'; 'it can be fantastic but don't become a slave to it'; 'blessing if we use it in a good way', 'used the right way technology has great benefits, but it has to be used correctly or it can be an unsafe place'; 'Tech is necessary and great when used well + with awareness'; 'use it to facilitate your life, not rule it'; 'learn how to use it, not let it use you'; 'enrich, not take over'; 'make sure *you* choose how to use your time, not the technology'; 'master it but don't let it master you!'; don't be a slave to it'; and various variations on the theme 'technology is a good servant but a terrible master'.

It's just a tool. Relatedly, the declaration that technology was 'just' a tool was a recurrent one amongst parents. This advice similarly emphasised that technology had to be used 'wisely' or 'appropriately' (whatever that might entail) to be beneficial:

> 'Tech is a tool – use it wisely'; 'it's only one tool to use'; 'technology is an enabler – it's just a tool, use it wisely'; 'technology is a tool – use it correctly to produce effective results'; 'Be careful! Be aware tech is a tool – can be – or +'; 'technology is just an enabler, it does not control you'; and 'technology is a tool, not a religion!'

There's more to life than technology. Parents' repeated pleas that 'there was more to life than technology' again revealed their concerns about the extent of their children's media use, and the perceived importance that their children placed on technology and their digital practices. This particular concern also ties in with the final theme in which parents implicitly make a distinction between the online world and the offline 'real' world, which indicates that parents do not acknowledge that increasingly their children live parts of their 'real' lives online. Once again, this advice recurred time and again across all workshops, with little variation:

> 'More to life than tech'; there is so much more to life!'; 'there's a big wide world to live in so don't just live in front of your screen'; 'there is more to life than looking at a screen', 'you can live life without it', don't forget about life outside of technology'; 'there's more to life than sticking your head in a device'; 'it's not entirely necessary. You can live without it!'; 'don't let technology take over your life'; 'don't look for personal satisfaction in technology'.

Be critical/be safe online. Many parents took the opportunity to provide general advice to their children about being safe online. For example: 'use safely and wisely', 'be careful', 'moderation'. Others provided more specific advice: For example:

> 'Don't believe everything you see or hear; people online are not always who they say they are'; 'everything you do is recorded'; 'your digital footprint lasts forever'; 'don't share personal information'; 'don't believe everything you see on a screen'; 'not all apps or websites are created just to help or entertain you (e.g. their aim might be to make money')'; 'don't trust Google, Wikipedia, YouTube etc'.

Technology as distinct from the 'real' world. Parents frequently invoked a distinction between the online world and the 'real' world when discussing their concerns and sharing their key message. When invoking this distinction, parents implied that the 'real' world was more authentic and more meaningful than the online world. Common responses from parents included:

> 'The digital world is not the real world'; 'technology is so useful but not a replacement for the real world'; 'there is a world outside of devices and gaming'; 'it will never replace a human touch!'; 'It's not really human!' 'You won't remember your device time but you will remember experiences'.

These five parental messages were quite consistently repeated across all workshops and parents often employed the same terminology and rhetoric to impart what presumably most believed to be excellent advice that would serve their children well. Parental responses clearly indicate that they see value in technology. Of course, digital technologies and social media are not the domain solely of adolescents and are widely used, relied upon and valued by people across all generations. However, parental framings suggested that there was a 'right' way to use technology (in a way which is balanced, or to enhance/enable other activities), and that the value of technology is limited ('it's *just* a tool') – perspectives which do not appear to align with young people's views. Further, parental framing of digital technologies as separate from and secondary to our lived, 'offline' experiences, points towards a lack of understanding about children's digital lives; the ways in which their online and offline lives converge, and how online spaces provide a separate (and powerful) space of autonomy away from the parental gaze.

'Trust us – we know what we are doing!' Adolescent perspectives

Adolescents were separately given the opportunity to share the various ways that they used digital technologies and the value that they derive from their online activities. They shared and discussed a range of popular activities and practices including gaming, messaging, 'FaceTiming' or texting friends; watching content (Netflix, YouTube); using social media (e.g. YouTube, TikTok, Instagram, Snapchat); communicating with others (including family); playing music; doing research and completing homework. When asked about why they enjoyed these activities, several recurring major themes emerged. Most commonly, adolescents said that their digital practices were fun and entertaining and a way to stave off boredom. They also said that it provided a form of escape, or a welcome distraction, to experience different things and do 'cool' things that you couldn't do in 'real' life (e.g. fantasy games). Relatedly, many said that it took their mind off things and helped keep them calm and relaxed. The social connection afforded by digital technologies also made adolescents feel happy and connected with people they cared about. Adolescents also talked about playing 'cool' games, creating or building 'cool' things and learning new things.

Adolescent participants were also asked to share one thing that they wanted their parents to know, which was then fed back to parents collectively. The responses indicated that adolescents clearly want their parents to understand the important role that media plays in their lives, and that they deserve more trust. Adolescent responses were categorised according to three main interrelated themes, set out below.

We value digital technologies. Adolescents took the opportunity to convey the ways in which technology enhances their lives. Such assertions might be interpreted as a direct response to risk-focused parent narratives and advice, as well as parents' well-documented concern that media use is a waste of time and is 'just a tool'. Responses included:

'There are so many good things you can use technology for – it's not all a waste of time'; 'We can learn so much using technology – using technology in the class room, teaching materials,' 'the internet is very useful', 'it calms me down', 'it's educational', 'I am learning new and creative skills', 'I'm communicating with friends'; 'When I am unwell, it helps me', 'it's good for winding down'.

Don't worry, it's not all bad. Adolescents also pointed out to their parents that they shouldn't worry so much, because not everything online is bad. Such responses are an implicit response to media panics and discourses of risk and harm which frame and often pathologise young people's media use, including gaming practices. Responses included: 'Don't worry so much', 'I'm only playing with my friends, not strangers'; 'it's not all bad', 'the internet is a lot more than you think', 'the internet can be a good thing', 'the internet is not all p*rn hub', 'not all the games I download are bad'.

We have more knowledge/self-control/competence than you think. Adolescents wanted their parents to know that they had more skills, knowledge and self-control than they were given credit for. This theme highlights the prevalence of the deficit model which assumes that young people do not possess the required competencies to conduct themselves appropriately online. Responses included:

'We are not helpless', 'we know what we are doing', 'I'm not actually as addicted to social media as you think. Generalising all teens as social-media addicts doesn't actually fit'; 'that we don't do anything wrong', 'we don't do anything bad on our devices'; 'we do everything right and safe', we are 'old enough to look after ourselves', and 'we know stuff about technology'.

Adolescents demonstrated an impressive self-awareness about their own practices and behaviours, and also the effects that they had on their parents. But adolescents also had a keen sense of the injustice of some of the digital rules at home, using the workshops to convey these concerns and to express their media-related needs. They expressed frustration that their parents 'blame the phone for everything', and that there were often different rules for parents. Adolescents also said that their parents sometimes took their devices away 'for no reason' and that digital devices had come to be used by parents as leverage or punishment in relation to other non-media related issues and transgressions, which adolescents perceived to be deeply unfair. Several adolescents pleaded for more time 'to socialise and call people after school and other important things', and for 'more flexibility'. Others indicated that they 'would like to have a say', and that 'it would be great to negotiate rules'.

Conclusion

There is some evidence that parents rely in part on the frameworks of public discussion and discourses of risk in order to make sense of their children's digital practices and online engagements. This is especially the case where parents have limited understanding of their children's practices, experiences and perspectives due in part to an absence of open parent/child discussion. It is evident that young people have more complex and nuanced understandings of online risks than is framed in dominant discourses, and use digital media in a range of ways which they find both enjoyable and valuable. Open, continuous dialogue between parents and their children is necessary to help bridge this divide. This entails more than simply 'talking to' young people about online risks and the perceived harms presented by networked technologies which many parents in these studies purported to do. Rather, it involves *dialogue* which invites young people to share their perceptions, questions and experiences – both positive and negative – and requires parents to actively listen to these accounts. How can we help parents and their children engage in ongoing open dialogue with a view to helping young people to safely navigate online spaces, while minimising family conflict and helping young people realise the many benefits that digital media afford? This is the focus of the final chapter.

Parts of this chapter have been published in the following three journal articles:

Page Jeffery, C. (2024). 'Trust us! we know what we are doing!' Parent-adolescent digital conflict in Australian families. *Journal of Children and Media*, 1–17.

Page Jeffery, C. (2022). '[Cyber] bullying is too strong a word…': Parental accounts of their children's experiences of online conflict and relational aggression. *Media International Australia, 184*(1), 150–164.

Page Jeffery, C; McKee A., Lumby, C (2024): Young people and sexually explicit content online: Exploring Australian parents' concerns. *New Media and Society*. (Accepted for publication).

References

Albury, K. (2015). Selfies, sexts and sneaky hats: Young people's understandings of the gendered practices of self-representation. *International Journal of Communication, 9*, 1734–1745.

Allen, K. P. (2015). "We Don't Have Bullying, But We Have Drama": Understandings of Bullying and Related Constructs Within the Social Milieu of a US High School. *Journal of Human Behavior in the Social Environment, 25*(3), 159–181.

Angelides, S. (2019). *The fear of child sexuality: Young people, sex and agency.* Chicago: The University of Chicago Press.

boyd, d. (2014). *It's complicated: The social lives of networked teens.* London, New York: Yale University Press.

Buckingham, D., & Bragg, S. (2003). *Young people, sex and the media: The facts of life?.* Basingstoke and New York: Palgrave Macmillan.

Juvonen, J., & Gross, E. F. (2008). Extending the school grounds? – Bullying experiences in cyberspace. *Journal of School health, 78*(9), 496–505.

Marwick, A., & boyd, d. (2011). I tweet honestly, I tweet passionately: Twitter users, context collapse, and the imagined audience. *New Media & Society, 13*(1), 114–133.

Marwick, A., & boyd, d. (2014). 'It's just drama': Teen perspectives on conflict and aggression in a networked era. *Journal of Youth Studies, 17*(9), 1187–1204.

McKee, A., Albury, K., Burgess, J., Light, B., Osman, K., & Walsh, A. (2018). Locked down apps versus the social media ecology: Why do young people and educators disagree on the. best delivery platform for digital sexual health entertainment education? *New Media & Society, 20*(12), 4751–4789.

Page Jeffery, C. (2022). '[Cyber] bullying is too strong a word...': Parental accounts of their children's experiences of online conflict and relational aggression. *Media International Australia, 184*(1), 150–164.

8

TOWARDS A NEW THEORY OF PARENTAL MEDIATION

This book has explored the ways in which parents understand, make sense of, and attempt to address their concerns about their children's digital media use, against a backdrop of media panics and discourses of risk, and adolescent resistance and family conflict. In the years since the first data were collected as part of Project One, there have been some notable shifts in this space, including in legislation and policy, media discourse, and specific issues of concern, some of which I have already documented. Many of these developments are encouraging. While parents are still ultimately responsibilised for ensuring their children's safety and wellbeing, there is increased acknowledgement that online safety is a shared responsibility, with growing pressure on platforms and services to do more to protect young people. And social media platforms may be beginning to respond to this pressure. In September 2024 Instagram introduced a new 'teen' version of the app which embeds more safety features and enables greater parental oversight (Taylor, 2024). It's a small step, but an encouraging one which may signal more willingness on the part of platforms to respond to mounting political pressure and consumer backlash.

There have also been encouraging developments in some online safety resources. There has been a clear shift amongst some providers (but not others) away from a primary focus on risk and danger (such as the arguably 'scaremongering' Cyber Safety Detectives activity outlined in Chapter 1 from several years ago) and implicit victim blaming (e.g. the anti-sexting 'Megan's Story' campaign). Instead, we've seen an encouraging move towards resources that acknowledge the importance of digital technologies and help develop young people's growing agency and skills to help them thrive in online spaces.[1]

Still, media panics remain a familiar feature within the Australian news cycle. Concerns about screentime, youth mental health, and the effect of online pornography (for example, that it is leading to degrading treatment of women and normalising dangerous practices such as choking), continue to occupy media headlines. Many of these concerns about online risks coalesce around social media, resulting in knee-jerk political responses. As I write this concluding chapter, debate still rages about banning young people from social media, with politicians, including the Prime Minister, Anthony Albanese, using rhetorical

DOI: 10.4324/9781003346708-9

and emotive language to try to 'get kids off phones and back on the footy field' (Long, 2024). And while a substantial proportion of experts have publicly criticised this approach highlighting compelling evidence for why a ban is not the right approach – myself included – politicians do not appear open to expert input that challenges their position. Indeed, while both the South Australian and the NSW Governments announced respective 'social media summits' to 'bring together a range of voices to explore the profound impact of social media on young people to inform the development of policies that support online safety and wellbeing for all members of the community',[2] the prospective social media bans were announced before these summits even took place, raising questions about the degree to which governments are actually willing to listen to experts and respond to the evidence. Greater platform regulation and accountability is the desirable response to these panics, but these regulations and policies must be carefully considered. Good policy is rarely, if ever, an outcome of media panics. One thing is certain, increased restriction and attempted control of young people's online presence are not desirable outcomes.

As I argued in Chapter 1 there is a long history to media panics about young people and media. On a broad level, media panics are underscored by concern about the ways in which media disrupt social norms. While concerns about contemporary digital media draw on longstanding anxieties that emerged in response to media modes that went before it, I have argued that digital media elicits its own set of unique anxieties through its interactive affordances and capacity to subvert traditional family power relations. This reconfiguration has resulted in young people having more agency and autonomy via digital media, which not everyone is comfortable with.

Dominant discourses, including media panics and discourses of opportunity and benefit, appear to shape, to some degree, parental concerns and perspectives. Parents often drew on dominant discourses when nominating certain risks, especially those related to pornography and sexting, where parent/child dialogue appeared less likely to have occurred. However, it was evident that parents also drew on their own knowledges and lived experiences with their children when sharing their concerns and perspectives. They expressed the greatest enthusiasm, and often frustration, when sharing their own personal anecdotes involving their children's use of digital media, and the challenges of negotiating digital media use in the home. It is these anecdotes and experiences so generously shared by participants that provided the greatest insight into what really was concerning parents. Participants who had evidently listened to their children about their experiences (for example, of drama and exclusion as discussed in Chapter 7) were less likely to buy into the media panics and instead help their children navigate these tricky situations. Evidently, there is a need to extend these discussions to include all aspects of media use, including sexual representations and online pornography.

The concerns and challenges of mediation expressed by parents throughout this book also lend additional support to critiques of the media effects research tradition, and further highlight the inadequacy of concrete screen time guidelines which fail to take into account the various purposes for which digital media are used by young people, including for the completion of homework. While some concern about media effects was documented by parents, primarily in relation to pornography, these were largely mobilised by the dominant risk discourses about the effects of pornography consumption (in other words, it is the media panics which are the main cause of parental anxiety). On the whole, parents' major concerns pertained not to the *effects* of media, but to their children's broader *engagement* with media and the ways in which this might compromise 'balance' in their lives or their 'normal' development. Parents thus demonstrated a more sophisticated understanding about the ways in which media impacted their children's lives, acknowledging their children's own (albeit sometimes limited) media literacy, and implicitly eschewing the hypodermic media effects model.[3]

The research presented in this book suggests that while concerned, parents aren't panicking. I am aware that parental concerns and anxieties have dominated much of this book and as such have overshadowed some of the benefits that parents acknowledged about digital media. For the majority of parents (although not all) their concerns and frustrations were front and centre in their minds, and thus were the subject of much enthusiastic discussions in the focus groups, interviews and family workshops. Instead, parents are ambivalent about their children's media use. Discourses of risk exist alongside discourses of opportunity, but rarely do the two discourses coalesce. Discourses of risk, which often manifest in moral panics, frame the potential harms posed by digital media to young people and for which parents are responsibilised for mitigating. At the same time, discourses of opportunity and benefit frame digital media as essential to young people's future success. It is a discourse that appeals to middle-class parenting subjectivities which are characterised by an approach to parenting that is not merely about mitigating risk but ensuring that children are afforded the opportunities to enable them to succeed in a future global marketplace characterised by uncertainty. I have suggested that in many ways discourses of benefit and opportunity, rather than alleviating parental concerns, have served to amplify them in the sense that they complicate parental attempts to mediate their children's media use and compound one of the key concerns expressed by parents in these studies – the amount of time that their children spend using devices.

Parents did, however, recognise various benefits of digital media that represented a departure from the dominant discourses of benefit and opportunity which have typically focused on the educational benefits of digital media. In the same way that parents' lived experiences and knowledges in relation to their children shaped their anxieties and concerns, they also shaped some of the more positive aspects of technology acknowledged by parents. For example, a couple of parents acknowledged the benefits of social media for their daughters who were socially awkward or had difficulty socialising face-to-face. In these instances, parents encouraged their daughters' use of social media as it afforded them the social support and connection that they often struggled to achieve in unmediated settings. Additionally, YouTube was hailed by many parents as a fantastic learning, socialising and bonding tool. From mothers' respective claims that they enjoyed singing along to YouTube videos or watching funny animal videos together as a family, to respective fathers' acknowledgement that YouTube provided answers and solutions for their children on demand, for many (but not all) parents, the 'world was a better place' because of YouTube.

Despite the continued recurrence of media panics around young people and digital media, the majority of parents were more measured and pragmatic in their responses to their children's media use. Some parents indicated that they had, in the heat of the moment, instigated bans or required their children to delete a certain social media account, but these parents acknowledged that this was not a long-term solution to their concerns. Many parents indicated after the family workshops that they were able to see the value of digital media in the lives of their children, and as a result, relaxed some of the previously enforced rules and restrictions. And while many parents evidently drew on some panic discourses when discussing their concerns, especially in relation to pornography, many parents simply refused to 'buy-in' to the panic. A number of participants explicitly rejected 'sensational-ised' media accounts, others took them 'with a grain of salt', demonstrating a critical liter-acy approach – despite their concerns.

I suggest therefore that parental anxieties and concerns, documented throughout this book, represent less a panic, and instead an underlying anxiety that more accurately reflects a parental 'risk consciousness' rather than a 'panic' as defined by Cohen (2002). Parental 'risk consciousness' emerges in response to parental desire to be a 'good' parent, and involves a parental awareness of the *possibility* of risks occurring, rather than the *probability* that such risks would lead to harm (Faircloth & Murray, 2015). Parents in both studies demonstrated an awareness of the many risks posed by digital media, and many attended focus groups and family workshops specifically to increase their knowledge about the var-ious risks. I argue that the parental awareness of the multitude of risks collectively contrib-ute to a latent, somewhat permanent low-level anxiety or concern that appears to more accurately reflect the contemporary context than panics which appear suddenly and dissi-pate shortly after running their ideological course.

In 2024 social and digital media are ubiquitous and are imbricated within many facets of contemporary life. Following the Covid-19 pandemic, wherein digital media helped us to maintain some semblance of our pre-pandemic lives, we might have anticipated more acceptance of them. At best, this may have been some gratitude for what they afforded us during these isolating times. At worst, perhaps a resignation that they are here to stay. These technologies are no longer new, so we might reasonably have expected the panic to have died down, giving rise to some other object of concern threatening the 'innocence' of our youth. Yet, on the contrary, the panic is as intense and protracted as ever. It seems that it is precisely their ubiquity and embeddedness, along with their lack of transparency (particularly in the eyes of adults), and their valorisation by young people, which have turbo-charged the panic. We seem to be moving further away from rational, critical debate about digital media and young people, and are instead left with politicians, moral entrepre-neurs, and other alarm raisers dominating the discourse with emotive, nostalgic rhetoric that does little to either engage with advice to the contrary, or consult with young people to try to understand their experiences. I am left wondering where this will all end up. Perhaps the panic, like ones before it, dissipate as these technologies are – if not embraced – at least accepted as here to stay (perhaps in the way that the internet has been). I suspect that if and when this does occur (and history tells us that this is the likely outcome), new technologies 'the likes of which we haven't see before' will emerge shifting the locus of concern away from social media and onto something else that once again raises familiar concerns about the corruption of youth. Indeed, we are already seeing growing anxiety in relation to generative artificial intelligence (particularly in the generation of sexually explicit material) and immersive technologies.

Many parents in this study drew on their own adolescent experiences to attempt to make sense of their children's practices and despite the significant changes brought about by digital media, parents attempted to find various 'points of resonance' between their children's digitally mediated experiences, and their own unmediated, or differently medi-ated, experiences growing up. In doing so, parents implied that digital media are not necessarily producing entirely new behaviours, but instead are changing the *character* of behaviours and practices. Parents attempted to find these points of resonance as a way of making sense of their children's experiences, bridging the perceived knowledge gap and boosting their confidence in helping their children navigate some of the difficulties of digital media. With this in mind, and taking into account the fact that an increasing number of parents are themselves being born into the digital age, might we hope for a future in which parents' own adolescent experiences more closely resemble those of their children, resulting in fewer parental anxieties about the 'unknowns' of their children's digital practices? We can only hope. However, I suspect that adolescents will always endeavour to engage in activities and practices that are different to those of their parents. This is particularly the case within a context of rapid technological change.

In any case, despite the parent/child knowledge gap, it appears that there remain more continuities than differences. While most parents acknowledged the various ways in which digital media had indeed changed the nature of a range of developmental experiences and milestones in a way which was problematic, some suggested that the experiences remained fundamentally the same. This was particularly evident in parental accounts about drama and online bullying and exclusion, where most parents acknowledged that peer drama had always been part and parcel of adolescence. It is in these continuities that parents appeared more comfortable helping their children. As technology continues to change, and new apps and technologies appear which elicit collective concern and anxiety, perhaps we need to focus more on the continuities rather than the differences. Researching digital media is a moving target after all. By the time this book is published, things will have already changed. As such, we should focus on helping parents and children acquire the knowledge and develop the skills needed to safely navigate online spaces more broadly.

A way forward? Moving beyond risk vs opportunity and parental mediation theory towards democratic parenting and incorporating young people's perspectives

Even amongst online safety advocates and scholars who oppose overly protectionist approaches to online safety, managing online risk has typically been framed in terms of a risk vs opportunity dichotomy whereby a range of risks (e.g. cyberbullying, online pornography, grooming) and opportunities (e.g. social connection, online learning, civic engagement) are identified and conceptualised as distinct and clearly-defined, with advice and resources aimed at minimising the distinct risks, while maximising the distinct benefits. As previously mentioned, minimising risk while maximising opportunity has been referred to as the 'holy grail' of digital parenting (Livingstone, 2017). Research that focuses on parents has been dominated by parental mediation theory (Clark, 2011; Livingstone & Helsper, 2008; Symons et al., 2017) which has sought to understand how parents mediate their children's media use within this conceptual framework of risk and opportunity (Livingstone et al., 2017). Yet, as the parental accounts documented in this text highlight, the main challenges for parents and carers lie in supporting their children in their online activities, and negotiating what they consider to be healthy, or beneficial use, while managing the conflict that typically ensues. This is where parental mediation theory and the categories of risk and opportunity fall short, as the online activities that concern parents, and parents' responses to them, belie convenient categorisation. In reality, risks and benefits are overlapping, context-dependent and not easily delineated.

Many scholars and commentators have also emphasised that risk does not equate with harm, and that navigating risk is an important part of adolescent development (see, for example, Third et al., 2019). Attempting to eliminate risk – either through excluding young people from online spaces altogether, or through imposing rigid restrictions on use – denies young people the opportunity to cultivate the necessary skills for effectively navigating risk and building resilience; skills which they will need as they become adults. This nuance has been notably absent from politicians in their discussion of social media bans, yet as demonstrated in Chapter 4, this has not escaped the attention of parents who identified that there were no clear boundaries between opportunities and risks. For example, parents expressed concern about the amount of time their children spend on devices. There is no consensus on how much screen time constitutes a risk, and what might be considered a beneficial amount, particularly when not all screen time is equal (Blum-Ross & Livingstone, 2018). Parents also harbour some concern about online bullying and want to help their children manage the complexities of peer sociality online. At what point does peer 'drama' become cyberbullying, and therefore constitute a risk? Or, as some parents pointed out, a certain degree of negative online sociality provides an *opportunity* for adolescents to develop valuable skills for managing peer relationships, with assistance from their parents. Parents also wonder to what extent they should leave their children to manage online risk themselves, as granting autonomy in this way provides an *opportunity* to develop resilience and digital skills, but obviously entails exposure to risks and potential harms. In short, as parents in this study noted, potential harms exist on a continuum, and only when the issue has the potential to disrupt their child's development rather than enhance it, does it become a source of parental anxiety.

There is also a need to move beyond parental mediation theory which focuses on the practices of parents, towards a greater consideration of the relational aspects of family life in the digital age. While parental mediation theory does of course acknowledge parent/child discussion about digital media – known as 'enabling' or 'active' mediation – parents are still implicitly positioned in this relationship as the authority. However, the role of parent as 'expert' has been subverted in many ways by digital technologies. Rather than attempting to resist these shifting power dynamics, we need to reconceptualise the role of the parent as one who supports and guides their child, rather than as an authoritarian rule-maker. Such a shift accords with notions of democratic parenting which is egalitarian, child-centred and 'empowering' and which privileges negotiation, agreement and trust. The notion of democratic parenting is not new. As Livingstone and Bober (2006) pointed out almost 20 years ago, prominent sociologists Giddens and Beck had already been arguing since the 1990s that a shift in power relations had taken place within families, away from authoritarian models towards more democratic ones.

My workshops with families demonstrated (along with Humphry et al., 2023; Third et al., 2019) that young people want a say in decisions which affect them, and indeed through these workshops we provided a template for these sorts of parent/child negotiations which provided young people the opportunity to have a say within the home. The result was greater buy-in from young people, increased trust between parents and children, and reduced family digital conflict (Page Jeffery et al., 2022). A democratic parent/child relationship in which traditional hierarchies are bracketed in discussions about digital media use, entails parents not just 'talking to' their children about their media use, but must involve parents actively listening to their children. Many parents in my study stated that trust and dialogue were their primary approaches for addressing online risks, but when parents talked about how this was enacted in the home, it became clear that many parents were simply imparting key messages about online safety to their children. Parents indicated that they used real events that may have occurred in their child's school or which appeared in the media as 'teachable moments' to talk to their children about online risks. Rarely did parents indicate that they asked their children about what they liked to do online or about their digital practices. For example, it was clear that parents rarely asked their children if, they had encountered pornography and what they felt and thought about it. As such, parents drew on the dominant risk discourses about pornography to fill the gap in their knowledge. It was clear, however, that children and parents were engaging in dialogue about online drama and friendships. Here parents demonstrated much more knowledge about their children's experiences, and demonstrated a greater resistance to the dominant risk discourses that most young people were also rejecting.

If we are to successfully bridge the digital generational divide, discussions about digital practices and online safety must be two-way and extend to all aspects of young people's digital practices. Young people should feel that their parents are interested in their online practices and understand the value they have in their lives. Parents need to listen without judgement. Young people need to feel that they can come to their parents without fear if they encounter something upsetting online. Starting these discussions early, and having them often, is absolutely critical for establishing the parent/child trust needed to help young people thrive online. Such discussions will also facilitate a shared vocabulary between young people and adults about digital technology, helping to break down the discursive barriers that currently exist between how young people and adults talk about and conceptualise digital media use.

Beyond prioritising more democratic parent/child relationships in the home, there is also a pressing need to involve young people in political decision making about their use of technologies. Young people are increasingly indicating that they want a seat at the table in discussions which primarily affect them (Page Jeffery, 2022), but we are yet to see much evidence of this at the national policy level. Politicians and experts continue to assume presume to know what is best for young people, without asking them what they want or think. This is despite an increasing focus on young people's rights globally. In 2021 the United Nations Committee on the Rights of the Child (UNCRC, 2021) released General Comment number 25 which acknowledges the vital importance of digital technologies in the lives of young people, particularly for supporting children to 'realise the full range of their civil, political, cultural, economic and social rights' (UNICEF, 2021). The general comment sets out that 'the rights of every child must be respected, protected and fulfilled in the digital environment' (UNICEF, 2021).

We have, however, seen some progress in including young people at the policy level. The Office of the eSafety Commissioner, for example, formed a Youth Advisory Council in 2022 to 'provide young people a voice about online safety policy' (eSafety Commissioner, 2023b). This is an encouraging development, but we are nonetheless left wondering how much these young people's views are actually filtering through to decision makers. Indeed, in recent years the Office of the eSafety Commissioner has produced many excellent research reports which highlight the nuances and complexities of young people's digital media use (see for example, their report into young people's pornography use which highlights that young people want more agency over how and when they see pornography, and that pornography can be pleasurable, eSafety Commissioner, 2023a). Yet there is no evidence that the views put forward in this research has been factored into policy or decision making.

Parents' knowledges, experiences and concerns also need to be taken into account in the development of policy and online safety resources. Parents in my studies indicated that they rarely consulted online safety tools or resources. Other research supports this finding, revealing that only 2 per cent of respondents would turn to the eSafety commissioner for help (Rowland, 2024). The parental accounts set out in this book reveal that parental concerns do not neatly map onto the major issues which have been the focus of media panics and much of the cyber safety resources and literature. If cyber safety resources and advice created specifically for parents fail to reflect and resonate with parents' actual anxieties, concerns, knowledges and lived experiences, it is unlikely that parents will make much use of them, which is a problem given the substantial money and resources that have been allocated to the Office of the eSafety Commissioner in recent years. Further, as parents in this study revealed, parental attempts to restrict their children's media use typically resulted in adolescent resistance and parent/child conflict. Family dynamics also need to be considered within the context of a broader shift towards more democratic and egalitarian models of parenting throughout the developed world and increasing focus on children's rights to digital participation. The conflict and intra-familial tension that result from negotiation of digital media use need to be addressed within a broader context of family cohesion and wellbeing. New approaches to online safety are needed that avoid the top-down, deficit, and restrictive approaches that have been the norm, and instead bring families on board in the development of materials and resources.

A wish list

Here I draw on the findings presented throughout this book to summarise several recommendations for online safety policy in Australia. However, given Australian governments' apparent resistance to views that do not support their proposed, protectionist position, and the likelihood that media outlets will continue raise alarm about the dangers of technology, it seems more appropriate to label this section as a 'wish list' instead.

- To fully realise the potential for digital media to support children's rights, participation and wellbeing, **there is a pressing need to move beyond a primary focus on risk, harm, protection and prohibition towards more detailed considerations of provision, support and participation**. This can only be achieved through acknowledging the messy realities of contemporary family life which has become 'digital by default', and that there are no silver bullets – such as social media bans – in relation to online safety. Policy in this area must be based on empirical evidence, not media panics.
- **Online safety is a shared responsibility**. Governments, parents, schools, educators, young people, social media services and regulators all have an important role to play. Social media companies need to do more to embed safety into their platforms. Regulators and governments need to hold social media companies to account to ensure that they meet their safety obligations. Schools not only need to provide high quality online safety programs, but also critical media literacy skills, comprehensive sex education, and the essentials of what it means to be a good digital citizen. Parents have a responsibility to help guide their children in online spaces, supporting them to make good decisions, navigate tricky situations, and talk to them if they encounter anything upsetting online.

- **Programs and resources should help facilitate ongoing, open discussion between young people and their parents about the online world and young people's digital practices**. Parents should actively listen to their child without judgement. There is still work to be done to break down barriers to open discussions about sex, sexuality and pornography.
- **The development of cyber safety materials aimed at parents and young people should seek to involve them in the process to ensure that their knowledges and concerns are taken into account**. This could be accommodated in various ways, but a living lab involving policy makers, scholars, young people and parents to co-design materials would be an ideal way of achieving these objectives. A living lab would foster dialogue amongst various participants from different backgrounds, enabling them to share experiences, knowledges and views, bridge any knowledge gaps, and would enable various perspectives to be taken into account without defaulting to the assumptions that circulate throughout popular media and cyber safety materials.
- We must acknowledge that **young people are not one homogenous group, but rather are incredibly diverse, with different concerns, needs and experiences, which must be accounted for**. This includes not only children of different ages (there is, for example, a massive difference between the knowledges, practices and experiences of 7-year-olds compared to 17-year-olds), but also LGBTQIA+ youth, neurodiverse youth, and those with a physical or intellectual disability.
- **Resources and programs designed to help parents and children safely navigate the digital world must also privilege the practices and perspectives of adolescents as much as their parents,** and acknowledge that top-down authoritarian digital parenting styles are likely to elicit adolescent resistance and media related conflict. Programs and resources that enable and facilitate discussion between parents and children about online risk, rather than providing top-down information, help to strengthen the foundations upon which parents and their children can navigate the online world together, through open dialogue, mutual availability, support, and empathy.
- **We need to abandon the notion of 'screen time' as a parenting guideline**. It does not take into account the full range of activities of varying qualities that young people undertake on screens and only serves to fuel parental anxieties. The findings documented in this book support existing critiques of 'screen time' rules (see for example Blum-Ross & Livingstone, 2016; 2018), and while most resources have abandoned the long-standing 2 × 2 rule[4] for screen time recommended (but also since abandoned) by the American Academy of Paediatrics, the idea of 'screen time' is still very much forefront in parents' minds as they struggle to balance their children's media use. Rather than focusing on time, parents instead should consider the content and activities that occupy young people's time online. Parents should acknowledge that young people engage in a variety of activities – some of which may be considered more legitimate than others (e.g. homework vs TikTok), but keeping in mind that young people enjoy socialising online and entertainment, and have a right to both. Parents instead might talk to their young person about effectively balancing these online activities along with their offline ones, to ensure a healthy balance in their children's lives.

It should be acknowledged that these recommendations are premised upon an assumption that parents are concerned about their children's digital media use and are invested in safeguarding their children's wellbeing. Sadly, we know that that is not always the case.

Many adolescents do not have the privilege of loving and involved parents who have their best interests at heart. Where this is the case, comprehensive school-based education to develop and foster critical digital media literacies and provide support for young people, along with proper regulatory safeguards and more accountable online platforms, are critical. Online safety is a shared responsibility after all.

Conclusion

In the current context where debates continue to rage about the potential harms of digital media for young people, moving beyond protection and control towards children's rights, autonomy and agency seems like an ambitious leap. I do not deny that the internet and other networked technologies present risks to young people. I do suggest, however, that the prohibitions, restrictions and proposed bans that are typically adopted in response to assumptions about young people's vulnerability, corruptibility, and lack of skills and knowledge, may do more harm than good, as they limit young people's online opportunities and their capacity for developing critical online skills and resilience.

Adolescents will likely continue to take risks – online and off – that belie many of the rational responses articulated by adolescents in the family workshops and documented in Chapter 6. However, helping parents to support their children online including providing them the opportunity to discuss digital technologies with their parents and other authority figures, and share their experiences, knowledge and understanding of online risks, provides an important pathway towards recognition of young people's knowledges and perspectives, and thus a step towards children's agency, rights, and meaningful participation in the digital world.

It is not my aim to criticise or shame the Australian parents who participated in this study, who evidently have their children's best interests at heart. Indeed, the vast majority of parents in this study appeared deeply invested in their children's wellbeing and committed to talking with and educating their children to help them navigate online spaces. However, it is clear that parents need help in having these open discussions with their children, particularly in relation to online pornography, sexual self-representation, or other topics which may be considered 'sensitive'. Indeed, young people themselves have expressed a desire for more of these conversations with their parents, but noted that their parents are ill-equipped to deal with such concerns (eSafety Commissioner, 2023a).

It was clear that underlying parents' concerns was a fundamental parental desire to care for and protect their children. And while many parents appeared to relish the opportunity to vent their concerns and frustrations in the focus groups, interviews and workshops, it was evident that most were there in the hope of working through the issues and acquiring help, tips or guidance about how they might be able to be a better parent.

Almost all parents spoke about their children with a demonstrable sense of pride and love. One mother proudly talked about her children's mastery of Minecraft. Another mother claimed that her son's gaming prowess was so good that people tuned in around the world to watch him play. We heard about one teenage girl who had produced a 'brilliant' video of herself singing along to TikTok which was copied by her friends and spread further because it was so 'fabulous'. Two fathers described how their sons had built furniture themselves with nothing other than an instructional YouTube video. We heard about young people's beautifully curated Instagram feeds, full of 'amazing' photos demonstrating their talent.

Finally, despite parents' concerns and frustrations, it was also clear that digital media provided additional opportunities to bring parents and their children together. Most participants described a domestic environment characterised by two working parents, various extra-curricular activities, and busy social lives in which family members were increasingly apart as they went about their own activities and social commitments. The existence of digital media such as messaging apps, family Facebook groups, and mobile phones meant that parents could call their children while they were apart to say 'Hi,' and have a chat, text their children after school to ask them how their day was, or simply send a smiley or heart emoji to tell their children that they love them and are thinking about them.

Notes

1 A notable example of this shift can be seen when comparing the online safety campaign called 'Megan's Story' that implicitly blames a victim for sharing nude images (Albury & Crawford, 2012), with 2024 resources about nude images, which state 'if someone shares a nude image or video of you online without your consent, that's image-based abuse (or 'revenge porn') and it's illegal. You can report it to eSafety straight away and we will help remove it.' (eSafety Commissioner, 2024).

2 This text came from the official invitation that I received to attend the summit – as an attendee, not as a speaker.

3 The hypodermic media effects model is based on the assumption that audiences passively receive media messages the way they were intended by the communicator, rather than accounting for the different ways that audiences decode and interpret media messages.

4 The 2 × 2 rule recommended no screens under 2 years, and no more than 2 hours per day thereafter.

References

Albury, K., & Crawford, K. (2012). Sexting, consent and young people's ethics: Beyond Megan's Story. *Continuum*, 26(3), 463–473.

Blum-Ross, A., & Livingstone, S. (2016). *Families and screen time: Current advice and emerging research.* Retrieved from http://eprints.lse.ac.uk/66927/1/Policy%20Brief%2017-%20Families%20%20Screen%20Time.pdf

Blum-Ross, A., & Livingstone, S. (2018). The trouble with "screen time" rules. In G. Mascheroni, C. Ponte, & A. Jorge (Eds.), *Digital parenting: The challenges for families in the digital age* (pp. 179–187). Gothenburg: Nordicom.

Clark, L. S. (2011). Parental mediation theory for the digital age. *Communication Theory*, 21(4), 323–343.

Cohen, S. (2002). *Folk devils and moral panics: The creation of the mods and rockers* (3rd ed.). New York: Routledge.

eSafety Commissioner. (2023a). *Accidental, unsolicited and in your face. Young people's encounters with online pornography: A matter of platform responsibility, education and choice.* Retrieved from Canberra: Australian Government. https://www.esafety.gov.au/sites/default/files/2023-08/Accidental-unsolicited-and-in-your-face.pdf

eSafety Commissioner. (2023b, 15 October). *The online safety youth advisory council.* Retrieved from https://www.esafety.gov.au/about-us/consultation-cooperation/online-safety-youth-advisory-council

eSafety Commissioner. (2024, 29 May). *My nudes have been shared.* Retrieved from https://www.esafety.gov.au/young-people/my-nudes-have-been-shared

Faircloth, C., & Murray, M. (2015). Parenting: Kinship, expertise, and anxiety. *Journal of Family Issues*, 36(9), 1115–1129.

Humphry, J., Boichak, O., & Hutchinson, J. (2023). *Emerging online safety issues – Co-creating social media with young people – Research report.* Retrieved from https://ses.library.usyd.edu.au/handle/2123/31689

Livingstone, S. (2017). Digital skills matter in the quest for the 'holy grail'. *Parenting for a digital future*. 7 February. https://blogs.lse.ac.uk/parenting4digitalfuture/2017/02/07/digital-skills-matter-in-the-quest-for-the-holy-grail/

Livingstone, S., & Bober, M. (2006). Regulating the internet at home: Contrasting the perspectives of children and parents. In D. Buckingham & R. Willett (Eds.), *Digital generations: Children, young people, and new media* (pp. 93–113). Mahwah, New Jersey, London: Lawrence Erlbaum Associates Inc.

Livingstone, S., & Helsper, E. J. (2008). Parental mediation of children's internet use. *Journal of Broadcasting & Electronic Media, 52*(4), 581–599.

Livingstone, S., Ólafsson, K., Helsper, E. J., Lupiáñez-Villanueva, F., Veltri, G. A., & Folkvord, F. (2017). Maximizing opportunities and minimizing risks for children online: The role of digital skills in emerging strategies of parental mediation. *Journal of Communication, 67*(1), 82–105.

Long, C. (2024, 9 September). Social media ban for children to be introduced this year, but age limit undetermined. Retrieved from https://www.abc.net.au/news/2024-09-09/government-plans-social-media-porn-site-age-limit/104329920

Page Jeffery, C. (2022). '[Cyber] bullying is too strong a word...': Parental accounts of their children's experiences of online conflict and relational aggression. *Media International Australia, 184*(1), 150–164. doi:10.1177/1329878X211048512

Page Jeffery, C., Atkinson, S., & McCallum, K. (2022). The Safe Online Together Project: A participatory approach to resolving inter-generational technology conflict in families. *Communication Research and Practice*, 1–16. doi:10.1080/22041451.2022.2056426

Rowland, M. (2024). Ensuring our online safety laws keep Australians safe [Press release]. Retrieved from https://minister.infrastructure.gov.au/rowland/media-release/ensuring-our-online-safety-laws-keep-australians-safe

Symons, K., Ponnet, K., Walrave, M., & Heirman, W. (2017). A qualitative study into parental mediation of adolescents' internet use. *Computers in Human Behavior, 73*, 423–432.

Taylor, M. (2024, 18 September). Meta to put under-17 Instagram users into new 'teen accounts'. Retrieved from https://www.theguardian.com/technology/2024/sep/17/meta-instagram-facebook-teen-accounts-social-media-ban-australia

Third, A., Collin, P., Walsh, L., & Black, R. (2019). *Young people in digital society: Control shift*. London: UK: Palgrave Macmillan Nature.

UNCRC. (2021, 2 March). United Nations Committee on the Rights of the Child General Comment 25. Retrieved from https://www.ohchr.org/en/instruments-mechanisms/instruments/convention-rights-child

UNICEF. (2021, 2 March). Convention of the Rights of the Child. General comment No. 25 (2021) on children's rights in relation to the digital environment. Retrieved from https://www.unicef.org/bulgaria/en/media/10596/file

APPENDIX A

Project methods

Project One: Interviews and focus groups with 40 Australian parents

The first study sought to gain an in-depth and rich insight into the perspectives, concerns, practices, feelings, and experiences of parents in relation to their teenage children's use of digital and mobile technologies, rather than merely surveying previously identified concerns and practices informed by existing discursive constructs about children and digital media. To do this, a qualitative research design was adopted. Focus groups and interviews with 40 parents of at least one teenager aged 12–16 were held in the Australian Capital Territory region during 2016–2017. This age group was selected because this period of adolescence is known for being turbulent, and is also a time when young people are often acquiring their own devices and developing greater independence, self-determination, and autonomy from parental control, which often leads to family conflict (Eccles et al., 1993).

A call for participants was disseminated via existing social, personal, professional, and community networks, and participants were recruited via a combination of purposive and snowballing methods. Five focus groups of between 4–6 participants were held with 27 participants. Participants were first asked to discuss what devices and apps their children used. I then followed up with a question about whether or not they had any rules to manage their children's use of mobile and digital technologies at home. These more general questions were asked initially instead of directly asking parents about their technology related concerns. This reflected my overall approach which involved willingly relinquishing some control within the focus groups to enable parents' concerns to surface independently and be discussed amongst participants with as little intervention and probing on my part as possible, Bryman (2015). Similarly, I enabled discussion to go off 'on a number of tangents' to see what they revealed about parental perspectives, concerns, and practices, bringing the discussion back on topic only when these digressions did not sufficiently relate to my key topics of interest.

The focus groups revealed a number of prominent themes – which included widely held concerns and experiences and common strategies for managing technology use in the home. These initial themes provided a provisional theoretical basis for more in-depth exploration of the issues via both subsequent focus groups as well as one-on-one interviews. Focus groups also provided something in return to participants who had generously given up their time to participate in my research. My call for participants highlighted that parents would hear from other parents about this issue, and many participants indicated a willingness to attend for this reason. Many parents arrived armed with a pen and paper, and diligently jotted down tips and strategies revealed by other participants for negotiating technology use in the home, and risks about which they had previously been unaware.

Focus group participants selected for in-depth interviews were chosen based on particular experiences they had revealed which I wanted to explore further because they were not fully borne out and explored in the focus group discussions, either due to a lack of 'shared experience' or consensus in relation to the issue, and time constraints. This approach of combining focus groups with follow-up interviews enabled a more detailed exploration of the themes that emerged through these discussions. Conducting one-on-one interviews also provided the opportunity to engage with more fathers and gain a deeper understanding into their practices and how these might differ from mothers, as female participants were over-represented in the focus groups (of the focus group participants, 25 out of 27 were women).[1] Seven participants were asked to participate in follow-up interviews based on issues they had raised in the focus groups. A further 13 participants participated in interviews only.

One-on-one interviews lasted between 45 and 90 minutes with the average being one hour. The precise format of the interviews depended to some extent on the responses and personality of the interviewees themselves. Interviews with less talkative interviewees followed a more structured format because I relied more on an interview guide to elicit responses. The majority of the interviews, however, were less structured in their format, and were broadly guided by a few initial open-ended questions, or an *aide-memoire* (Bryman, 2015) consisting of a brief set of prompts to ensure that I covered the range of desired topics, related to the technology use of their children and the practices of parents in managing their children's technology use. Many of these more unstructured interviews more closely resembled conversations than interviews.

Of the 40 participants, 29 participants were mothers, 10 were fathers, and one was a grandmother who was the primary carer of two boys. Most participants were aged in their mid-40s, with a median age of 46. Participants had 90 children in total: 49 of those were aged between 12 and 16 – the target age range of study. Of these 49 children, 30 were female and 19 were male. The vast majority of participants were married (heterosexual), white, highly educated (60 per cent held postgraduate qualifications), and relatively wealthy (42 per cent had household incomes almost double the median household income for the area). Almost all participants were working professionals, representing mostly middle-class occupations such as academics, psychologists, public servants, and other professionals. Only one participant was a stay-at-home parent. Two participants explicitly identified as being from a different religious or ethnic background, and for one of these participants it was clear that his background shaped his values and beliefs, and thus his concerns about digital media. On the whole, however, the cohort of participants was relatively homogenous, and participants from different religious, ethnic or socioeconomic backgrounds may have revealed different practices or concerns. Existing research strongly suggests that this is indeed the case (see for example, Clark, 2013).

Project Two: Family workshops

The family workshops described in this book formed part of a broader project called Safe Online Together which was designed to explore and address identified gaps in public policy approaches to adolescent online safety. The project was funded by the Australian Government under the first round of the Online Safety Grants program, which supports the delivery of online safety education and training.

The aims of the project were based on the findings of Project One, which identified digital media as a significant source of conflict within Australian families. The project adopted a participatory action research approach (Hearn et al., 2009; McIntyre, 2007) and aimed to facilitate understanding between parents and their children to reduce family conflict and assist families to navigate the risks and opportunities associated with digital media. The overarching aims of the project were to: a) promote intergenerational knowledge and understanding; b) facilitate discussion about managing online risks; and c) help families negotiate and develop their own mutually agreed protocols for media use.

In contrast to typical online safety approaches which are based on assumed deficit in understanding and competencies related to digital media, we adopted a human-centred design that focused on learning from participants' own knowledges, practices and understanding. Our goal was to improve mutual understanding between parents and their children about digital media. This approach adopted a more democratic approach to parenting that encouraged dialogue and more enabling forms of parental mediation which we anticipated would have greater 'buy-in' from adolescents. The overarching goal was to reduce family digital conflict, an issue which did not appear to be addressed in any of the existing online safety materials which frequently adopt a top-down deficit approach to educating both parents and children about online risks.

13 workshops were held from June-December 2021 in the Australian Capital Territory region of Australian. In total there were 225 participants (115 participants and 110 children) with workshops ranging in size from five to 40 participants, with an average of between 15–20. Workshops were held at schools and community centres across the region, including at both private (fee paying) schools and public (Government, non-fee) schools. Workshops were offered in different geographical areas of the region, including affluent areas and less advantaged communities. We sought to bring families together in a space where parents and children aged 10–16 could share their knowledge, practices and experiences with not only us as researchers but with each other. As young people's technology use is experienced in the hybrid environments of home, school and public arenas, family workshops were held in community centres and schools to provide a space in which the parent-child hierarchy of expertise and power is necessarily disrupted, and where family conflict may be reduced.

There were four main phases to the project, of which Phase 3 – the family workshops phase – was the main component, the data from which has been explored in this book. The first two phases of the project consisted of planning and designing the project and entailed working with the project partners to identify and engage seven schools across the ACT, including a mix of public and private, primary and secondary, and geographically diverse schools. In line with our human-centred design approach, multiple stakeholders were consulted as part of the project planning process, including teachers and school leadership teams, young people, and our community services partners. The final phase of the project involved a comprehensive evaluation of the project.

Phase two of the project entailed the delivery of a series of school presentations to upper primary and lower secondary school students. The presentations focused on key elements of digital citizenship, rather than focusing on online risks. Data was not collated during this phase, but the family workshops were promoted to the students as part of the presentations, with letters sent home with families inviting them to participate in forthcoming workshops. There was a strong response to our call for workshop participants through our initial set of schools, with more than 380 participants expressing an interest in attending a workshop. Workshops were also promoted through school newsletters, our community services partners, as well as through social media and local media.

Workshops were not recorded to avoid researcher intrusiveness that may influence the behaviour and responses of the participants. Instead, workshop activities were designed to utilise innovative social research methods that generate various data which researchers take away for collation and analysis. The project goals were achieved through four activities in the family workshops which are outlined below.

Workshop format

Online quiz (icebreaker activity)

The first activity consisted of an interactive online quiz covering various aspects of technology use. The quiz highlighted different generational knowledges and practices and identified any areas of synergy. These knowledge-sharing activities initiated discussion about parents' and children's different assumptions and skills while creating a relaxed and collaborative environment.

Issues and values identification

The second activity facilitated understanding between parents and their children about their attitudes to digital media and demystified aspects of children's media use for their parents. The task gave parents insight into the value and benefits afforded by media to their children, while identifying and exploring parental concerns in a way that helped children understand why their parents respond in particular ways to their media use.

To facilitate this mutual understanding, young people and their parents were guided through separate discussions. Young people shared the different ways they used their devices and why technology is important to them with the project co-facilitator, Susan Atkinson, and what they believe to be their parents' media-related concerns. Parents wrote down their main concerns about their children's technology use and how they address those concerns (their mediation strategies), as well as one thing they wished their children understood about digital technologies. As the facilitator I then discussed these responses with the parents within the context of parental mediation theory and research. A consolidated list and heatmap was generated for both the parent and child groups which formed the basis for a whole group discussion. This method of group presentation de-personalised individual responses and minimised the risk of defensive feelings that might exacerbate intra-family conflict. The activity also generated written data which was qualitatively analysed by the project team.

Story completion activity

The story completion method is a form of narrative enquiry that asks participants to complete a narrative from a supplied story opening or 'stem' (Lupton, 2020). Narrative enquiry is an approach to socio-cultural research that privileges the role of the story in helping people to make sense of and articulate their lived experiences (Clandinin, 2006, cited in Lupton, 2020) 'in a way that does not directly question people about their own feelings or practices' (Lupton, 2020, p. 3). In the workshop, participants were asked to create a story about fictional people related to a potential online risk that responds to a story stem provided by the facilitators. Story scenarios were adapted from resources provided by the Office of the eSafety Commissioner and addressed issues such as respectful online behaviours and relationships, unwanted contact, online bullying, privacy and sending nude images. Young people and their parents completed this activity separately before discussing their approaches as a family group.

This activity explored how young people identify and respond to online risks, and provided an opportunity for young people to demonstrate to their parents their awareness of and strategies for addressing these risks. In turn, they revealed to their parents their approaches and appetite for these risks. The activity was designed to start (or continue) the conversation about online risks between parents and their children. Importantly, it afforded young participants the opportunity to demonstrate that they are worthy of parental trust by sharing their knowledge and strategies for addressing online risk, and thus more enabling and less restrictive forms of mediation.

Conflict issue mapping and discussion

In the final activity parents and children in separate groups discussed the main causes of technology-related conflict at home, such as conflict around screen time (including gaming), use of technology at inappropriate times, or young people's preferred social media activities. The children, facilitated by Susan, discussed the different technology rules they have in their homes and whether they feel they are fair or reasonable. The parents, facilitated by me, shared possible future strategies for managing conflict, drawing on previous discussions and activities which highlight the value of more enabling forms of parental mediation, while acknowledging the value and importance of media in their children's lives as well as their children's own knowledges and practices. The groups then reassembled to discuss the issue collectively, providing another opportunity for both parents and their children to gain a better understanding and appreciation of each other's perspectives. This discussion then provided the basis for the introduction of a family technology agreement through which families can negotiate family protocols around media use in a way which is democratic, recognises the importance of media in the lives of young people, and which places obligations on parents as well as children.

Community partnerships

Integral to the success of the project was the partnership between the University researchers and local community services organisations, Community Services #1 and Capital Region Community Services. These organisations have deep knowledge and understanding of the communities they serve and provided a pipeline for access to families and schools within the region. Their experience and knowledge about the needs of local families complemented the research expertise to support the goal of developing a program which is not only empirically grounded, but which meets the needs of the community.

Data analysis across both projects

Transcripts from all focus groups and interviews, which totalled several hundred thousand words, were analysed according to qualitative thematic analysis (Braun & Clarke, 2006) whereby a number of key themes were identified and refined from parents' responses. Throughout this book, I have tried to allow the participants to tell their own stories as much as possible by including direct quotes, which were lightly edited for brevity and clarity. Ellipses have been used to indicate that parts of what the participant said have been omitted. All data has been anonymised, and identifiable details have been omitted to protect the anonymity of participants and their children. The quotes that have been used throughout have generally been selected for their ability to support and 'give voice to' the various themes presented throughout, and because they communicated sentiments, concerns, views or experiences that were shared by a number of participants and often communicated by them in an interesting or evocative way (Green, 2013). I endeavoured to include quotes from as many participants as possible, however, as might be expected, the Pareto principle was evident as a smaller percentage of participants provided a large percentage of quotable quotes (Green, 2013).

Qualitative thematic analysis

Once all focus groups and interviews had been conducted and transcribed and subjected to the initial analysis detailed above, the entire data corpus was analysed using qualitative thematic analysis (Braun & Clarke, 2006). Qualitative thematic analysis (TA) is a method for systematically identifying, organising and offering insight into patterns of meanings across a dataset, and is rapidly becoming recognised as a unique and valuable research method in its own right (Braun et al., 2019). It provides a flexible and useful research tool, and can provide a rich and detailed, yet complex account of qualitative data (Braun & Clarke, 2006). Braun et al., 2019, p. 57 describe the benefits of TA as follows:

> Through focusing on meaning *across* a data set, TA allows the researcher to see and make sense of collective or shared meanings and experiences… This method, then, is a way of identifying what is common to the way a topic is talked or written about and of making sense of these commonalities.

Consistent with a grounded theory approach and my research objective of privileging and exploring the meanings, experiences and sense-making practices of parents and young people themselves, I adopted an inductive form of TA, meaning that various codes and themes were derived from the data and evolved during the data analysis process. It should be noted, however, that analysis is rarely *purely* inductive, as researchers invariably bring preconceived ideas and constructs to their analysis (Braun et al., 2019).

Both projects were approved by the University's Human Research Ethics Committee, and the names and identifying details of all participants have been changed to maintain their anonymity and protect their privacy.

Study limitations

As foreshadowed, highly educated, white women from privileged socio-economic backgrounds were well-represented amongst the parents in both of my studies, which limits the generalisability of my findings. This is a significant limitation, as many scholars have demonstrated the various ways in which class and cultural background shape attitudes towards digital media, mediation practices and parenting more generally (boyd & Hargittai, 2013; Clark, 2013; Livingstone et al., 2015). In particular, one of my key findings, that parents are very concerned about the amount of time that their children spent online, has been found to be more marked amongst middle-class families who have greater educational and career aspirations for their children which did not accord with device use (Clark, 2013). I acknowledge that had my participants been more diverse in their backgrounds and ethnicity, the key findings may indeed have been different.

Additionally, my call for participants for Project One did specifically foreground parental worries and concerns, meaning that it is likely that it attracted parents who already harboured particular concerns about their children's digital media use, rather than representing the concerns and attitudes of the general population. The call for participants for Project Two specifically targeted families that were experiencing media-related conflict.

Similarly, my findings also suggested differences in the concerns, perspectives and practices between mothers and fathers, with mothers generally expressing greater concern and knowledge about their children's digital media habits. I have speculated that this is likely a product of mothers still bearing the brunt of child care and parenting responsibilities. Further analysis of this observation was lies beyond the scope of this book, and would necessitate engaging with the gendered dimensions of parenting more generally. Nonetheless, further research that examines the differences between mothers and fathers in their approaches to their children's use of digital media, beyond parental mediation is needed.

Note

1 Discussions with other parenting researchers reveals that this is a common problem – women/mothers are typically over-represented in parenting studies, as they are more likely to volunteer for studies about parenting.

References

boyd, d., & Hargittai, E. (2013). Connected and concerned: Variation in parents' online safety concerns. *Policy & Internet*, 5(3), 245–269.

Braun, V., & Clarke, V. (2006). Using thematic analysis in psychology. *Qualitative Research in Psychology*, 3(2), 77–101.

Braun, V., Clarke, V., Hayfield, N., & Terry, G. (2019). Thematic analysis. In P. Liamputtong (Ed.), *Handbook of research methods in health social sciences* (pp. 843–860). Singapore: Springer.

Bryman, A. (2015). *Social research methods*. Oxford: Oxford University Press.

Clark, L. S. (2013). *The parent app: Understanding families in the digital age*. New York: Oxford University Press.

Eccles, J. S., Midgley, C., Wigfield, A., Buchanan, C. M., Reuman, D., Flanagan, C., & Mac Iver, D. (1993). Development during adolescence: The impact of stage-environment fit on young adolescents' experiences in schools and in families. *American Psychologist, 48*(2), 90.

Green, L. (2013). In their own words: Using interview materials when writing up qualitative research. *Australian Journal of Communication, 40*(3), 105.

Hearn, G., Tacchi, J. A., Foth, M., & Lennie, J. (2009). *Action research and new media: Concepts, methods and cases.* Cresskill, NJ: Hampton Press.

Livingstone, S., Mascheroni, G., Dreier, M., Chaudron, S., & Lagae, K. (2015). *How parents of young children manage digital devices at home: The role of income, education and parental style.* London: EU Kids Online, LSE.

Lupton, D. (2020). *The story completion method and more-than-human theory: Finding and using health information.* London: SAGE.

McIntyre, A. (2007). *Participatory action research.* Thousand Oaks, California: Sage Publications.

INDEX

Pages in **bold** refer to tables and pages followed by "n" refer to notes.

For Product Safety Concerns and Information please contact our EU
representative GPSR@taylorandfrancis.com
Taylor & Francis Verlag GmbH, Kaufingerstraße 24, 80331 München, Germany

www.ingramcontent.com/pod-product-compliance
Lightning Source LLC
Chambersburg PA
CBHW080535060326
40690CB00022B/5132